PROBLEMS OF THE PHILOSOPHY OF RELIGION

CHANDLER PUBLICATIONS IN PHILOSOPHY
Ian Philip McGreal, Editor

Problems of the Philosophy of Religion

John K. Roth

Claremont Men's College

CHANDLER PUBLISHING COMPANY
An Intext Publisher • Scranton / London / Toronto

For My Parents,
Doris King Roth and Josiah V. Roth

CONTENTS

PREFACE

This book has been written to fulfill two major objectives. First, it seeks to introduce students to important figures in the history of philosophy and theology by drawing attention to their views on questions concerning the existence and nature of God and some possible relations between God and our experiences of freedom and evil. Second, the book tries to encourage people to become metaphysicians and theologians. The present and the future are not the same as the past. Thus, although our philosophical and theological accomplishments will be slight if they are not grounded in knowledge of what others have done, it is also the case that every age is forced to make new constructive efforts if its life is to be intelligible. The mood of rebellion and discontent that characterizes much contemporary life suggests an urgent need for clear thinking about the nature of our existence and its moral and religious values. Previous thinkers can provide a useful context for our thought, but ultimately we must solve our own problems. Perhaps this book will help people to achieve the background and the confidence needed to build philosophical and theological foundations that can structure our lives and produce hope.

If this book succeeds at all in fulfilling these objectives, credit and thanks must go to many people and institutions. Claremont Men's College provided the summer-study fellowship that enabled me to complete the manuscript. My students have helped to clarify my thinking in more ways than they can imagine. My friend and colleague Frederick Sontag gave me needed encouragement and fresh insights. Any new perspectives that this book contains are largely due to the illuminating comments he made in our daily discussions during the summer days when I was writing. Professor Ian P. McGreal first asked me to write the book for the Chandler series of introductory texts on problems of philosophy, and then he provided the sound editorial advice that improved my book. I am grateful to all these people for making this book possible, but my greatest debts are to my parents, who first taught me to think

about God, and to my wife Lynn and my son Andy, whose love
motivates me best of all.

J.K.R.

Claremont Men's College
Claremont, California

PROBLEMS OF THE PHILOSOPHY OF RELIGION

I

PHILOSOPHY, RELIGION, AND CONTEMPORARY LIFE

We live in an age that is deeply philosophical. Moreover, our present difficulties indicate that our continued existence and well-being depend largely on our ability to be good philosophers. Such claims may seem strange in a time that is characterized more by social activism, rebellion, and violence than by the traditional philosophical virtues of meditation, critical reflection, and dispassionate argument. Some elaboration, however, can clarify both the meaning and the significance of these ideas.

If it is true that man is the only animal who can ask questions, it is also true that contemporary man is using his question-asking capacities to raise fundamental issues concerning the nature and quality of our current political, economic, academic, and religious life. We are presently experiencing an increasing tendency to refuse to take once-accepted beliefs and institutions for granted. The result is that ideas and organizations that unified us at an earlier time in our history are in many instances losing their power to do so.

What is there in this state of affairs that makes our era philosophical and that points toward an increasing need for sound philosophical reflection? One crucial point is this: Philosophy thrives on asking questions about beliefs and styles of life. It seeks to uncover, analyze, clarify, and evaluate the "first principles" of

1

our ways of living. Thus, although our contemporary questioning often takes the forms of cries of frustration and emotionally charged action, it is genuinely philosophical to the extent that it probes deeply, uncovers hypocrisy, and shakes us from a stifling complacency. In this sense a philosophical stance toward life has moved from academic offices and classrooms and has entered the streets and marketplaces of our world.

At the same time, the fact that we live in a period that is philosophical in the sense described pushes toward the conclusion that our continued existence and well-being will rest largely on our ability to be good philosophers. The same questioning that raises criticisms and objections about the validity and value of current beliefs and institutions also contains the potential to leave us hopelessly divided and fragmented and perhaps even to lead to our violent destruction. Questioning, even when it is profoundly philosophical, can lead in the direction of merely tearing down what exists. If this is all that questioning does, we are left with a situation that is essentially negative. Something more than devastating critiques or penetrating questions is needed; namely, the effort and the ability to construct new styles of thought and action or to transform old ones so that they give life instead of thwarting it. The best philosophers are always skilled at both criticism and construction, and it is probably the latter that is now the greatest of our needs. Without efforts that move beyond critical questioning to the construction of a new basis for unity, life will continue to fragment, suffering is sure to increase, and human fulfillment will be threatened.

How does this book fit into the broad and perhaps terrifying picture that we have sketched? I think that there are two main ways in which it does so. First, more than we may realize, contemporary questioning and criticizing reveal a religious crisis in our lives. In *The Rebel,* Albert Camus has shown us that political and social criticism and rebellion often have their roots in what he calls "metaphysical rebellion." Metaphysical rebellion involves a radical questioning, perhaps even an overthrow, of once-accepted beliefs about the structure of reality which no longer seem clear and intelligible. When these foundations are shaken, the structures and institutions built upon them may also fall under attack, and their power may be seriously weakened or destroyed. In addition, Camus points out that metaphysical rebellion involves concepts of God, our understanding of ideas such as *knowledge* and *faith,* and basic frameworks of morality. Metaphysical rebellion implies religious crisis. By combining this latter insight with the idea that political and social criticism and rebellion are inextricably tied up with metaphysical rebellion, this book may help us to see some of the religious ideas that figure into our current state of metaphysical turmoil. Thus, the first way in which this book may be helpful is by aiding us to understand how reaction to our past shapes our present situation.

The second way in which this book fits into the picture we have described and in which it may be helpful to us is closely related to the first. As the book seeks to aid us in understanding some of our present circumstances, it may also enable us to catch some insights about what we need to do to move toward solutions for our problems. In the context of an examination of philosophical and theological positions from the past, against which many are rebelling, we may find and begin to develop positive suggestions that will be useful and crucial to us in forging the fresh thought patterns that we need. One lesson that should be remembered is this: If one looks, he can gain positive insights from the past, even while rebelling against it.

In summary, this book concentrates on understanding some of the ideas of important figures in the history of philosophy and theology, and our exploration of these ideas will combine two tasks: (1) We will seek to understand why past statements no longer seem adequate for us as they stand; (2) we will seek to appropriate and develop insights from these statements that may be useful and crucial to our attempts at fresh philosophical construction. Now, with these introductory statements of purpose on the ground, we have two main objectives in this chapter. The first is the answering of a question: What is the philosophy of religion? The second is a more detailed examination of some contemporary problems and their relation to the history of philosophy and theology.

What Is the Philosophy of Religion?

Today we speak of the philosophy of science, the philosophy of art, and the philosophy of mathematics, as well as the philosophy of religion. Thus, one way to begin to answer the question "What is the philosophy of religion?" is to indicate the goal and structure of "philosophy of ——" investigations in general. In the broadest sense, the goal of such investigations is to take a subject or a cultural phenomenon that is more or less well defined and to look into its features closely and critically. Such a statement, however, can be made about a wide variety of inquiries, and it is not sufficient to bring out the distinctively philosophical qualities that we need to see. An economist, for example, might inquire about the features of science or religion in a critical fashion, but his interests in these areas might not be centrally philosophical. The questions that the economist might ask are likely to be very different from those of a philosopher. While an economist may be concerned with science or religion in terms of its impact on world finance, a philosopher will be peculiarly interested in issues such as the following: (1) Are the assumptions and claims present in the aspect of life under investigation adequately grounded, and how do they fit with tested insights from other dimensions of our experience? (2) What are the implications concerning the fundamental structures of reality that are contained in these assumptions and claims, and what evaluation of these implications is in order? "Philosophy of ——" investigations pursue these issues, and as a philosopher works on these questions, he engages in a study that is both more general and aimed deeper (that is, directed toward ultimate foundations) than what the economist qua economist does with science or religion. This is not to say that what the philosopher does is necessarily better than or even more significant than what the economist does, but it is important to see that there is a difference in the tasks that are performed.

The questions noted above suggest that as the philosopher investigates science or religion, one of his jobs is to be a critic. As we have already suggested, critical questioning is a vital part of philosophy. Philosophy probes our beliefs and life styles, seeking to test their adequacy and to uncover the ground on which they stand. The philosopher asks for clarity. He also asks for credentials to warrant the claims we make. The philosopher always has some elements of doubt and skepticism in him; he is rarely willing to take things at face value.

At the same time, however, in the best philosophy the intent is not to be critical or skeptical for the sake of those things alone. Rather the intent is to criticize existing views so as to be able to construct ways of looking at our experience and our world that are more adequate, clearer, and better able to unify our experience into meaningful patterns. We live in a world that is vast and rich. It contains experiences and phenomena of widely differing kinds. Thus, one problem we face is this: How are we to make sense of all that there is? How, if at all, can human experiences be made to fit together? Mere criticism of existing beliefs and structures will not give us the overview that we need. Unless philosophy is to have only the effect of tearing down, it also needs to offer something in place of what has been removed. To paraphrase Immanuel Kant, if construction without criticism is blind, it is also true that criticism without construction will ultimately leave us with a sense of emptiness and negation. Philosophers who pursue questions of the kind noted above will accentuate criticism and construction to different degrees. We will see this variation in emphasis with respect to the nine men we will be studying in the forthcoming chapters. Nevertheless, it is clear that both criticism and construction must be present if philosophy is to serve men well.

Having made some suggestions about the significance of the idea of "philosophy of ——" investigations, we can now turn our attention more directly to the concept of "the philosophy of religion" itself. Among other things, this focus will enable us to indicate how we will restrict our study so as to keep its size manageable.

To speak of "the philosophy of religion" is to speak of a general category that can involve a plurality of emphases. That is, a philosopher can devote his energies to a wide variety of topics involving religion and still be a philosopher of religion. For example, his work may concentrate on a particular religious tradition, or he may engage in tasks that require a comparison of various religions. He may be interested in the ways that myth and symbol function in religion, or he may be primarily concerned with the problem of how we can verify claims that are made within religious traditions. Or his energies may be devoted to attempting to define what constitutes religion in general, or what the value of a particular religious doctrine may be.

Thus, the philosophy of religion is a flexible concept. It can be broadened or restricted depending on the interests of the philosopher in question, and the only universal restrictions that seem to hold with respect to its use are the following. To fit into the category of the philosophy of religion, an investigation (1) needs to raise at least one of the fundamental questions previously noted, and (2) it needs to start with and remain tied to human claims (both positive and negative) concerning both the experience of what is holy, sacred, divine, and ultimate in power and value, and the nature of that which may be taken to have these qualities.

Some additional comments are in order concerning the second of these restrictions. Whenever we deal with religious phenomena, we work within a context where categories such as *holy, divine, sacred,* and *ultimate in power and value* are applicable. In fact, wherever these categories are applicable in giving an account of phenomena, we can say that these phenomena are religious in nature. The philosopher of religion may be primarily interested in trying to clarify and specify the meanings and referents of these concepts and in assessing the validity and value of experiences of that which is taken to have such qualities. It is important to remember, however, that these fundamental tasks cannot be performed without particular experiences and claims already on the ground. Man may be a philosophical animal, but he does not enter the world as a philosopher. He becomes a philosopher only after he experiences something about his world and himself and only after he forms and uses concepts in attempts to organize his world. To make the specific point that is needed in our context, men are religious before they are philosophers of religion.

The philosophy of religion starts with religious men, and the existence of religious men entails human experiences that are understood in terms of concepts such as holy, divine, sacred, and ultimate in power and value. But once these experiences and claims about them are on the ground, questions can be asked with the goal of clarifying, testing, and perhaps extending and relating the experiences and claims in ways that unify human existence. Philosophy starts with something given, namely, human experiences and claims, but philosophy then has important things to say concerning how the given can and should be taken.

On the other hand, if philosophy and the philosophy of religion in particular have an important part to play in judging, testing, and evaluating human experiences and claims, the philosopher also needs to strive to see that his judgments and theories are always open to human experiences so that his philosophical view does not become rigid and closed. If philosophy's accounts and interpretations become frozen and isolated, they will distort and reduce human experiences as they are actually lived through. Although the facts of our experiences do not always speak for themselves, and although they do not always speak clearly when they do speak, they may speak on some occasions in ways that indicate that our judgments and theories about experience, and not our experiences themselves, need to be altered or rejected. In the emotionally charged area of religious claims, we will do ourselves a disservice if we let experience go unexamined and uncriticized. But by the same token, our philosophical judgments and theories about experience will become undesirably abstract and restrictive if they do not "keep their ears to the ground."

These comments lead to some important conclusions. First, a philosophical theory is not an infallible account whose validity and truth are certain and absolute. Philosophical inquiry is open-ended and fallible, and, since experience may always outstrip philosophy, finality and completeness are not achieved by any single philosophical view. Second, the task of a philosophical theory is to provide a *hypothesis* that can illuminate and unify our experiences. Philosophical theories, like scientific theories, emerge out of our questioning of experience, and they are tested when we bring them back into contact with experience to see how well they illuminate and unify our lives.

Given the facts that the philosophy of religion is a broad category and that one small book cannot deal with all the problems that can be placed in that category, what issues will we select for primary attention? First, we will not deal with all the major religious traditions that exist today. Rather our studies will be restricted to developments in the West and the Judeo-Christian tradition in particular. Moreover, as we look at this tradition, we will concentrate on three fundamental questions, all of which bear on man's understanding of God and God's possible relation to human life.

The three issues are the following: (1) What knowledge, if any, can men have about God's existence? This area includes concerns about the possibility of proofs of the existence of God, the distinction between faith and reason, and the differences between philosophy and theology. (2) What may the nature of God and the nature of man be conceived to be, and how does our understanding of one influence our understanding of the other? This question will enable us to concentrate on a crucial contemporary issue, namely, how does our experience of *freedom* influence our understanding of man's nature and what are the implications of this experience for our understanding of the existence and nature of God. (3) What does man's experience of *evil* entail for our views about the existence and nature of God? Along with the experience of freedom, contemporary man's experience of evil in the world is one of the crucial elements in our present crises, both political and religious. Exploration of this third question may be especially useful in enabling us to see our current problems more clearly and to understand how we need to move to find sound solutions for them.

Our method for dealing with these questions will be to see what some major figures in the history of Western philosophy and theology have said about them. This historical orientation will help us to see how previous formulations of these issues and attempts to answer them may contribute to our present difficulties and still provide some important positive insights to guide us. Issues in philosophy and theology are like men in that they change through time and yet remain the same. By understanding the past, men can learn important things about who they are in the present and what they need to become in the future. Awareness of the history of philosophy and theology can play an important part in this task of understanding. Old formulations are not sufficient for our present needs, but we build upon those old formulations either consciously or unconsciously. Moreover, by building on them consciously, we may avoid dangerous pitfalls and troublesome confusions.

Now it will be well to shift our attention to a different issue, but one that is related both to our question "What is the philosophy of religion?" and to our explanation of the methodology of this book. In the preceding comments, references to both *philosophy* and *theology* have appeared. A discussion of the possible differences and relations between philosophy and theology in Western thought will further help to clarify the stance of the chapters to follow.

How does *philosophy* differ from *theology* in Western thought? We may be able to understand this distinction by looking at the extremes of a spectrum. At one end of our spectrum we encounter a man who asks questions about basic life assumptions and the structures of reality. However, this man is largely devoid of religious interests, and he asks his philosophical questions without addressing them specifically to religious phenomena. Such a man qualifies as a philosopher, and his investigations are philosophical in character. At the other end of our spectrum, we meet a man who sees his task as that of unpacking, clarifying, and affirming the doctrines of a religious tradition and its view of God without particular concern for the broad and critically oriented questions we have noted. Such a man may not rightfully be called a philosopher, but he certainly would be called a theologian and he would be understood as one who "does" theology. Thus, philosophy may be characterized more by the questions that it raises, while theology may be characterized more by the positive subject matter with which it works; namely, positive assertions about God and religion.

Now consider this question: When we look at the major figures in the history of Western philosophy and theology, where do they fit on this spectrum? The answer is that they are usually not at the extremes, but rather in a middle ground that involves a combination of the question-asking that is characteristic of philosophy and the interests in God and religion that are characteristic of theology. Most philosophers, and especially the great ones, have had something to say about God and religion, and by the same token most theologians, and especially the great ones, have been philosophical to some degree in their posing of issues. We can still characterize a man primarily as a philosopher or a theologian in terms of the questions he asks, the breadth of their scope, and the interests he has in God and the religious phenomena of life, but in many cases there will be a blending of philosophical and theological concerns in the same thinker.

What does this distinction mean for our particular understanding of the discipline that we call the philosophy of religion? The answer is that the philosophy and philosopher of religion will fall somewhere in the middle area of the spectrum we have set up. The philosopher of religion will be both philosopher and theologian, and his work will have content that is both philosophical and theological. There will be, however, numerous shades of gray in this middle area and a few brief comments about some possible positions that can be occupied will be useful.

One kind of philosopher of religion might look at religion and theology analytically and critically and reach the conclusion that religion is so full of problems and difficulties that men would be better off if they freed themselves from it and replaced it with some nontheological view. The critical and analytical investigations of such a thinker may be combined with constructive efforts, but the thrust is to move away from the content of the tradition or traditions which were originally under examination. Such a thinker is a philosopher of religion, combining philosophy and theology in his work, but he falls more in the direction of the philosophical extreme of the spectrum, because he ultimately rejects any positive identification with a religious tradition.

On the other hand, we might have a philosopher of religion who asks the critical questions that are characteristic of philosophy, but whose efforts to answer them, along with the resulting conclusions, keep him in a positive relationship to a religious tradition. Such a thinker may clarify, rework, or radically transform a religious or theological view that is already on the ground, but this move is different from rejecting all such traditions and recommending that something else take their place. A philosopher who approaches the problems of the philosophy of religion by clarifying, reworking, or radically transforming some religious or theological tradition, but without rejecting the tradition in question, could be called a *philosophical theologian.* His philosophical tendencies may make it impossible for him to accept the boundaries of a particular tradition without modification, but at the same time he works with the categories and concepts of a tradition so that a positive continuity is maintained. In that way he is a theologian in an affirmative sense.

In the chapters that follow, the perspective represented will be that of a philosophical theologian. That is, as we ask fundamental philosophical questions about some claims found in the Judeo-Christian tradition, our analysis will seek to move in the direction of renewing and perhaps transforming that tradition so that it can continue to be a genuine option as a style of existence for contemporary men. In a time when many men describe life in terms of feelings of meaninglessness and absurdity, philosophy can serve men well by striving to keep open a plurality of options for meaning and by striving to show that there can be a plurality of life styles without needless and destructive conflict. But perhaps some of these points concerning current feelings and options for meaning will be clearer if we look at several specific contemporary issues and their relation to the history of Western philosophy and theology.

Some Contemporary Problems and the History of Western Philosophy and Theology

We live in an age in which *freedom* and *evil* are central categories. First, awareness of freedom is at the heart of our self-understanding. In much of the literature and philosophy of our time there is an emphasis on the idea that we inhabit a world of change and process in which we are free and active forces in shaping both the world's course and our own existence. In spite of the fact that we sometimes sense severe limits on our power to move and act, we generally regard ourselves as facing a future that is open-ended rather than closed and fixed. There is a factor of indeterminateness in the existence that we confront, and we see ourselves making our existence determinate through our choices, decisions, and actions, all of which imply the pervasiveness of freedom in our self-awareness.

In addition, freedom is a central factor in our desires and hopes. All about us we hear voices saying that the evils of stifling moral, political, and religious frameworks must be removed so that creativity and free expression can reign. There is a widespread desire for increased and novel opportunities for action, for the freedom to "do one's own thing," and for the elimination of all barriers that repress us. Thus, not only do we seem to understand ourselves as beings who are free and responsible for ourselves, but also our desires and hopes are often expressed in terms of freedom. We find ourselves living with considerable power to shape our lives and our world, and we long for situations which increase our freedom to move and act and in which the chances for fulfillment and a meaningful life are maximized.

On the other hand, any sense of hope and optimism that our awareness of freedom may involve is moderated by our experience and the awareness of what seems to be a magnitude of real and possible evil and suffering unrivaled in human history. Our century has seen world wars, Auschwitz, and Hiroshima. Moreover, the spectres of mass starvation, total pollution of our environment, racial warfare, and nuclear disaster stand on our horizon as real possibilities. Men may have suffered and done evil before, but to many of us it seems clear that the magnitude of real and possible suffering and evil has reached a new high in this century.

Contemporary men live in an ambiguous world where feelings of optimism and hope, which are fostered by an experience of and a desire for freedom, often clash with feelings of impending doom, which are caused by our experience of an unprecedented magnitude of real and possible evil. If this brief description of ourselves is accurate at all, and if we bring it into our context of the philosophy of religion, then at least one interesting question presents itself: What is the relation of our awareness of freedom and evil to our understanding of the existence and nature of God?

One contemporary answer to that question would go in the following direction. It would say that there is a basic conflict between most of the traditional theological assertions about God and man's awareness of radical freedom and evil. This discrepancy exists because traditional assertions suggest that God is a being who is characterized by power, knowledge, and goodness that are absolute, unchanging, and complete. This sovereign and transcendent being sees our existence from the perspective of eternity, and from this perspective our existence is finished rather than open-ended, fixed rather than moving, and known as good in the highest degree possible despite the fact that even the most charitable judgments of most men suggest that our existence is only an ambiguously moving mixture of good and evil. These assertions about God are regarded by numerous contemporary interpreters as denying the validity and authenticity of basic experiences that we find ourselves living through undeniably. With God in the picture, our freedom, the open-endedness of existence, the meaning of our striving, and our sense of responsibility for ourselves seem to be questioned and made less real than we feel them to be. In addition, the contemporary mind boggles at the prospect of trying to reconcile (1) the claims that God's power and goodness are absolute and that this is the best of all possible worlds with (2) our experiences of radical elements of evil in existence.

This contemporary view emphasizes that we cannot honestly rid ourselves of our experiences of freedom and evil. These experiences stand at the core of our existence. Therefore, in order to eliminate the grating effect produced by comparing our experiences with the nature of God as complete, fixed, and absolute, the best course of action open to us is to eliminate God, to stop thinking of God in positive terms. In a world that is understood to be structured so that there is an incompatibility between the existence of God and our experiences of freedom and evil, God must go if our existence is to be intelligible at all.

An answer of this kind can be heard with some frequency today. It is characteristic of some existential philosophers (for instance Jean-Paul Sartre) and of many people influenced by them. Elements of this style of thinking can also be found in the positions held by some of the recent "death-of-God" theologians (for example, William Hamilton, Thomas J. J. Altizer, and Richard L. Rubenstein). Moreover, these views are perhaps factors underlying the general secularity of our age. The important issue for us, however, is this: What are some of the fundamental implications and problems contained in this contemporary answer, and how do they fit into our study of the philosophy of religion?

One of the important implications of this contemporary perspective involves some ideas concerning the history of Western philosophy and theology. The contemporary answer we have described suggests that it is not only the case that previous views are inadequate for our present needs, but that these views are in fact contributing directly to the difficulties that we face. If we were dealing merely with the inadequacy of the views, the polemical tone of much contemporary thought would not be so great. The polemical tone, however, is present precisely because it is felt that the older ideas are actively pushing us in a direction opposite from the one that we need to take if we are to make our existence intelligible at all.

Nevertheless, before we accept this contemporary assessment, we may do well to look again at our philosophical and theological heritage to be sure that the current critique is sound. Philosophers and theologians have been known to set up straw men in the past, and we might find that a similar thing is taking place now. Past thinkers have discussed the nature of freedom and evil and the relations of freedom and evil to God, and they have often done so with greater sensitivity than some contemporary criticisms might indicate. This is not to say that we possess a philosophical and theological heritage whose reintroduction into the present situation will solve all of our problems. No doubt there are inadequacies in past views that can be dangerous if they are not exposed. But these weaknesses can be exposed accurately and specifically only if we go back and look at our heritage again. We are, after all, trying to understand ourselves, but if our attempts to do so rest on misunderstandings of the past, it is hard to see that we will have gained genuine insight into our current predicament. Thus, one of our tasks in this: We need to look again at the past so that contemporary criticism can be evaluated adequately.

A second implication in the contemporary critique we have noted involves an understanding of the reasonable options for belief that may be open to us. Note that in the perspective that we have described above the following move occurs. A recommendation is made that man is better off without God, but this conclusion is drawn from the inadequacies contained in what is essentially one particular view concerning what God might be like. If, as is sometimes implied, this particular conception of God is our only available option, then one would certainly be hard-pressed to maintain the desirability of belief in God, for the God described does seem to grate against our experience by making freedom, the movement of existence, and the open-ended quality of life less real than we find them to be, and by making it extremely difficult to comprehend how God's goodness and power are compatible with the degrees of evil and suffering that we see about us.

However, if it is the case that a world with this kind of God is not the best of all possible worlds, it is also the case that we are not restricted to a single concept of God. There can be a plurality of concepts of God, some of which are more adequate than others when placed in the context of our experience. A study of the history of Western philosophy and theology may suggest insights that can be used as we attempt to construct philosophical and theological positions that are viable for us now. As we have suggested already, it is doubtful that past formulations can be taken over without modification or even radical change, but a return to the past may jog our minds in fruitful directions as we engage in our tasks of construction.

Now something needs to be said about an additional factor in the second implication of the contemporary critique we have been discussing. In reaction to a particular idea of God, some contemporary critics suggest that man is better off if he stops thinking in terms of God. Far from making existence intelligible, the concept of God adds to its unintelligibility because of the problems the concept causes when brought into contact with our experiences of freedom and evil. The implication here is that although we may never overcome the fundamental unintelligibility of existence, we can prevent needless confusions and problems by curtailing positive discourse about God. However, if such an evaluation is sufficient to prevent some thinkers from speaking positively about God, it may not be sufficient to do this for everyone. In fact, a renewal of philosophical and theological interest in trying to speak positively about God could have the effect of saving us from a sense of meaninglessness and absurdity, which can come not only from an inadequate conception of God, but also from a view that sees our world as devoid of God and as existing against a backdrop of silence that spawns a world of purposes but has no purpose itself.

Man, after all, seeks and hopes for fulfilling meaning and intelligibility in his life. In a time when these commodities seem scarce, philosophy has important humanistic tasks to perform in (1) developing new options for looking at existence, (2) renewing and transforming options that once provided real insight but which are, for one reason or another, falling into decline or being forgotten, and (3) helping us to see how a plurality of life styles can exist together without destructive conflict. Our continued existence and well-being depend on our ability to be good constructive philosophers. To accomplish these tasks, we will have to deal honestly with the fundamental experiences and feelings of our time. This approach will require a primary emphasis on freedom and evil. Wishful thinking and ungrounded speculations will not meet our needs, but a philosophical boldness that combines constructive efforts with a sensitivity to the facts of our current experience may help to preserve and improve human life.

If we live in precarious times because everything is being questioned, we also live in times that are philosophically exciting. The questioning of previous perspectives opens the doors for new ideas and creative efforts. Philosophical options are closed only if we choose to see the situation that way. We may ultimately exist in a world in which there is a huge gap between existence and its intelligibility and meaningfulness, but we also live in a time when the continuation of human life may well require us to indulge our hopes for the contrary and to get on with the task of philosophical and theological construction.

A Look Ahead

Taking account of our goals—(1) understanding some important aspects of our philosophical and theological heritage and assessing the adequacy of this heritage for our present needs, and (2) seeking to find and develop positive insights within our heritage that will be useful as we try to construct sound options for our own time— the chapters that follow will acquaint us with nine crucial figures in the history of Western philosophy and theology. We can place the men we will study into three general chronological groups. The first group includes Augustine, Anselm, and Thomas Aquinas, and it involves a span of time that extends from the fourth century A.D. through the thirteenth century. An examination of their ideas helps us to understand what we can call the "classical" statements concerning the existence and nature of God and his relation to the world. To a large degree these classical concepts are the ones that are presently under attack, and it is precisely this fact that makes it important to look at them, so that we can judge fairly whether these concepts are adequate any longer.

Gottfried Wilhelm Leibniz, David Hume, and Immanuel Kant constitute the second group, which involves a span of time running from the middle of the seventeenth century to the early years of the nineteenth century. The ideas of these men reveal both some important attempts to preserve the classical concepts and some attacks on them. The efforts of this group still exert influence today. This is especially true of the critical perspectives introduced by Hume and Kant. In many ways we live in a philosophical and theological context set by the critiques they developed.

The third group, which is essentially composed of nineteenth century figures, includes Søren Kierkegaard, Friedrich Nietzsche, and William James. A study of their views enables us to see the foundations of two philosophical trends that have been and are dominant factors in our own century. These are *existentialism* and *pragmatism*. Here too we may find a hostility to the classical concepts, but in the criticisms and the constructive claims presented by this final group we may find important foundations on which we can build.

Yesterday's problems are identical neither with those of today nor with those we are likely to encounter tomorrow. This is also true of yesterday's solutions. But if we understand where we have been, we may be able to see more clearly where we are, where we are headed, and where we ought to be going. Let us, then, reflect on the past with the hope that this will help us to find ourselves in the present and the future.

II

AUGUSTINE
AND THE
HUMAN PREDICAMENT

Augustine's Life

Augustine (354–430) was born in the small North African town of Tagaste. His father, Patricius, was a pagan, but his mother, Monica, was a Christian and she raised her son in the Christian faith. Augustine's parents wished to give him a good education, and in 370 he was sent to Carthage to study rhetoric. His student days reflected a pattern of interests and activities characteristic of many young men and women both before and after him. Hard work and success in his studies were combined with a questioning of the Christian faith and with an affiliation with the "new morality" of the day, the latter culminating in Augustine's taking of a mistress, who presented him with a son two years after his arrival in Carthage.

Although an account of Augustine's sexual experiences might be of considerable interest, our attention must be directed toward the changes in belief that led him from an initial rejection of the Christian faith to a revised understanding and a reacceptance of it. Augustine's young and inquiring mind was troubled by what he took to be a naive literalism in much of the scriptural interpretation he encountered. In addition, and perhaps more important, he was concerned about how one could reconcile Christian teachings concerning God's goodness and the goodness of his creation with the presence of evil and suffering in the world. In Carthage

Augustine found no satisfactory Christian solution to the problem of evil, but he did encounter and accept for a time metaphysical views of the Manichees, who offered a perspective that seemed more rational than the Christian teachings Augustine knew, especially where the problem of evil was concerned.

The Manichees attempted to account for the presence of evil in terms of a metaphysical dualism. Instead of regarding the world as ultimately dependent on a single God, sovereign and absolutely good, they asserted that there are two ultimate factors in reality. One is characterized by light and goodness, while the other is characterized by darkness and evil. These powers strive against each other eternally, and the world and human existence are products of this conflict. In human life, the duality and the striving of the powers are revealed in the differentiation and the frequent conflict between the soul and the body, the soul being a manifestation of light and goodness and the body being related to the force of darkness and evil. Thus the Manichees also advocated an ascetic style of life so that the goodness and light of the soul could be maximized and salvation could be obtained. Augustine found the metaphysical perspective of the Manichees attractive, but, since his interests at this time were more theoretical than practical, he did not feel obliged to submit himself to the ascetic demands of the Manichean teaching.

Having finished his work as a student, Augustine opened a school of rhetoric in Carthage, where he stayed until 383. During this time he continued to think in terms of the Manichean framework, although he became increasingly perplexed by problems that he found in this perspective (for example, the lack of a clear account concerning why the two fundamental powers were in eternal conflict). The failure of the Manichean philosophy to provide a rational solution for all his fundamental questions led to a gradual weakening of Augustine's adherence to its teachings, and by the time he left Carthage to teach in Rome and Milan he was moving toward a period of general philosophical skepticism. It seemed unlikely that the human intellect could push beyond finitude, fallibility, and error to clarity and certain knowledge, a conclusion that Augustine accepted reluctantly and not without a sense of despair.

This skeptical conclusion, however, was not Augustine's stopping point. In fact, his experiences in Milan began to bring the Christian faith back to life for him. Under the influence of Ambrose, the bishop of Milan, Augustine discovered that an allegorical interpretation of scripture was possible and that such an interpretation did much to remove the qualities of inconsistency and simple-mindedness that he had found in many of the interpretations he had heard earlier. Moreover, he became acquainted with the writings of some philosophers who worked within the framework of Plato's thought. These Neoplatonic writings, which included the *Enneads* of Plotinus (c. 204–270), influenced Augustine in at least three major ways: (1) by suggesting steps to overcome epistemological skepticism, (2) by helping him to think of God in less anthropomorphic terms than he had been able to do previously, and (3) by providing a new perspective on the problem of evil.

Some elaboration of the third point will be helpful. As Augustine understood the Neoplatonic position, its account of evil both avoided the problems of Manichean dualism and allowed for a reinstatement of the fundamental Christian claims of the goodness of God and his creation. Neoplatonism did this by suggesting that evil is a lack of being, an absence of goodness, rather than a positive force. That is, to say that evil is a lack of being or an absence of goodness denies the Manichean dualism by asserting that evil has no positive and autonomous existence as a fundamental power in reality. On the other hand, this same denial of the positive and autonomous existence of evil as a power seems to remove the problem of stating how an omnipotent and an absolutely good God could create or tolerate such a power.

One problem does remain, however. Even if we characterize evil as a lack of being or an absence of goodness, how do we reconcile the presence of these qualities with our understanding of the goodness of God and his creation? To give Augustine's answer to this question and to explore the problems that his answer entails will require a more detailed examination of his work, which will be provided in the next section of this chapter. For the present, however, we can briefly sketch the Neoplatonic suggestions from which he worked.

In the Neoplatonic perspective, man's existence and the physical world are understood as components in a hierarchical emanation from the fundamental source of being, which is usually called the One or the Good. That is, the One or the Good is a power or force which overflows to produce an exhaustive scale of kinds of being. The degree of reality possessed by any particular thing that exists is, then, directly proportional to its distance from the One or the Good. Moreover, being and goodness are directly related. The higher something stands on the scale of being the better it is and, insofar as something exists at all, it is good. On the other hand, evil is equated with nonbeing, hence with a lack of goodness. Evil is nothing positive or autonomous, but it is present as a lack or a deficiency. Furthermore, it is asserted that this presence of evil is compatible with the Good and the goodness of the existence that overflows from it. The creative overflowing of the Good actualizes all possible forms of goodness, but nothing in the hierarchy of being can duplicate the perfection of the Good itself. In contrast to the Good, everything manifests some lack of perfection, but, at the same time, to be created and to exist are goods in themselves. As we shall see, such an account is useful to Augustine because it lends itself naturally to the ideas that God is absolutely good and that what he creates is good and not evil.

With the help provided by his contacts with Ambrose and Neoplatonism, many of Augustine's intellectual difficulties with the Christian faith subsided. When these intellectual changes were coupled with what Augustine regarded as a conversion of his will, a change which replaced a deep sense of struggle between his intellectual understanding and some of his personal desires with a sense of harmony between his understanding and his moral orientation, Augustine was baptized by Ambrose in 387. The following year he returned to his native Africa, establishing a small monastic community in his hometown of Tagaste. At the same time, he devoted much of his energy to theological and philosophical writing, a task which he had already started to take seriously in the two years prior to his return to Africa. In 391, Augustine was ordained a priest, and in 395 he was made the bishop of Hippo. These added responsibilities did not, however, prevent him from writing, and by the time of his death in 430, when the city of Hippo was under seige by the Vandals, Augustine had secured himself a place of lasting importance as an interpreter and defender of the Christian faith.

Augustine continues to be a significant figure because the views he developed in his theological and philosophical writings are foundational factors in the mainstream of Christian tradition. In Augustine's lifetime, a plurality of views, some of them seriously conflicting, presented themselves as valid interpretations of the Christian faith. Much of Augustine's writing was directed against interpretations that he found to be inadequate and erroneous. His arguments against these views and his positive statements concerning the Christian faith were instrumental in establishing the Church's understanding of the lines between orthodoxy and heresy. Working in the intellectual turmoil of his own day, Augustine produced a set of ideas that in many ways became the normative foundation on which future Christian thinkers were to build.

Now we need to look in greater detail at Augustine's basic ideas concerning the three questions we posed in the first chapter: (1) What knowledge, if any, can men have about God? (2) What may the nature of God and the nature of man be conceived to be, how does our understanding of the one influence our understanding of the other, and how, in particular, does our experience of freedom bear on these issues? (3) What does man's experience of evil entail for our view about the existence and nature of God?

One of the best ways to see Augustine's position on these issues is to look at his dialogue *On Free Choice of the Will,* which he started in the winter of 387—388 while still in Rome, but which was not put in its final form until 395.[1] Thus, in the remaining pages of this chapter, we will concentrate on this work, seeking to describe the essence of Augustine's philosophical and theological position and to uncover some problems and useful insights that his views may contain.

Augustine's Position in "On Free Choice of the Will"

We have seen that Augustine's intellectual and spiritual journeys took him from a Christian starting point to a rejection of that perspective and then to a renewed and revised relationship with the Christian faith, which enabled him to become one of the chief spokesmen for and defenders of Christian doctrine. *On Free Choice of the Will* plays an interesting part in this development because, given the dates of its beginning and completion, the dialogue not only stands as one of Augustine's early efforts to instruct others, but it is also likely that his religious faith was deepened by the writing of the dialogue. Augustine surely knew what most great philosophers have known, namely, that writing, along with the meditation and reflection that are required to do it, is a valuable exercise in producing clarity and self-understanding. In addition, it is noteworthy that the chief problem on which the dialogue concentrates is that of the relationship between God on the one hand and man's freedom and experience of evil on the other.[2] Once Augustine could see what he took to be a satisfactory Christian account of the relations between these factors of existence, he was far on the way toward a reconciliation with the Christian faith.

The dialogue is set as a discussion between Augustine and an inquisitive friend named Evodius. It begins with Evodius asking Augustine to tell him "whether God is not the cause of evil."[3] Augustine wants to deny that God causes evil. He has set a question for himself with the goal of seeing whether a clear and defensible line of thought can be developed to substantiate the view that man's experience of moral evil does not compromise the absolute goodness and omnipotence of God. Augustine takes some fundamental claims about God and probes at them, trying to see whether what one is asked to believe is also intelligible. In seeking and showing the intelligibility of the Christian teachings, Augustine finds that human reason stands in a complex relation to faith. First, reason can help to prepare a man for faith, which always involves a conversion of the will as well as intellectual assent. Second, reason can also help to clarify and draw out the significance of what one has appropriated in faith. Finally, the relation of God and men to which faith points is regarded by Augustine as the proper resting point for reason. The content of faith provides the ultimate satisfaction for man as a rational being. Faith and reason, then, are not poles apart. Rather, they are complementary components, and the wholeness of life depends on their harmonious interaction.

This view is further revealed in the fact that Augustine's writings do not suggest that there is a sharp distinction between philosophy and theology. Instead, the two are mixed up together. Theological claims find clarifying support in philosophical analysis, and the natural culmination of sound philosophical thought is found in Christian teaching. Frequently, then, Augustine gives his reader the impression that he is sure of the answers to his questions before he asks them, but this is not to be confused with a blind assertion of the answers. Augustine's writings are largely attempts to develop arguments to show the intelligibility of the answers which he holds in faith. One may question the validity of Augustine's arguments, but to charge him with being narrowly dogmatic, as some readers are prone to do, is unfair.

To return to Evodius's original question concerning the possibility that God is the cause of evil, how does Augustine proceed to answer it? In the first of the three sections of the dialogue, we find that Augustine shifts the original question slightly by concentrating on two closely related issues: (1) What is involved in doing evil? and (2) Why do we do evil? These questions, while focusing on evil, shift the attention away from a direct consideration of God. Before God's relation to evil can be made clear, Augustine thinks that attention must be given to the nature of evil and its relation to human activity.

Augustine's approach to the first of these issues reveals the influence of Neoplatonism. Man exists in the middle range of a spectrum of being at the top of which is God and at the bottom of which is nonbeing. Not only is man dependent on God for his existence, but also man's nature is such that his well-being and fulfillment depend on a positive orientation toward God, an orientation in which one recognizes his dependence on God, and in which one responds to God's will in obedience, love, and service to others. The authenticity and the fulfillment of human existence are constituted by the realization and cultivation of one's relation to God. On the other hand, if one neglects and fails to cultivate this relationship, or if one willfully turns away from God, a course of action is pursued that produces distortion in the self and plunges one toward the end of the spectrum characterized by nonbeing. To turn from God is to turn away from the sustaining source of existence itself. Such an action leads to a loss of identity, a lack of recognition of one's identity as a creature of God. The results are fragmentation and disintegration of the self and a corresponding lack of fulfillment.

Augustine contrasts these two styles of life in terms of one's concern and love for what is eternal as opposed to what is temporal. Drawing again on a Neoplatonic line of thought, Augustine suggests that what is eternal is also the most real and of the greatest perfection. By orientating oneself toward the eternal features of existence (for example truth), one draws near to the source of all power and meaning and hence allows for the fulfillment that is natural to man as a creature of God. To turn toward temporal things (for example, material wealth, political power, sensual pleasure) and to make them the focus of one's "ultimate concern," to use Paul Tillich's term, is to concern oneself primarily with that which is changing and perishing, and hence of less reality, value, and sustaining power. In these circumstances, one may lose himself to dimensions of reality that stand lower on the hierarchical scale. The loss that occurs in these cases is characterized by Augustine as a lack of being and an absence of good. One falls short of what he could be, he stands lower on the scale than he needs to, and this may lead to disorientation for others as well.

It should be noted here that Augustine is not recommending total neglect of temporal things and concerns. The structure of our existence in the world requires us to attend to them. However, our attention should not be focused on the temporal to the exclusion or neglect of the eternal. Proper balance requires that priority be given to one's relationship to God. Temporal concerns will find their rightful place if this ordering is followed. On the other hand, an orientation that gives primacy to temporal concerns will bring out the qualities of lack and deficiency that we have noted, *and*

these qualities are the identifying marks of the evil that men do.
To do evil is to create a lack or a deficiency in oneself or in
others. It is to push oneself or others away from God and toward
nonbeing. But if the evil that men do is best characterized as a
lack of goodness or a deficiency in being which results from our
pushing ourselves and others away from God and toward nonbeing,
how do we account for the fact that this occurs at all? This takes
us to Augustine's second question, "Why do we do evil?"

Augustine's answer to this question is cast in terms of man's
will. Men are not creatures who are exhaustively controlled by
factors external to themselves. We have freedom, autonomy, and
power that help to determine how our attention will be fixed and
how our capacities for thought and action will be used. For
Augustine, human life is permeated by decisions, choices, and
responsibilities, all of which point to the presence of the will and
its freedom. Moreover, the doing of evil and the existence of our
capacity to choose freely are linked together. Thus, in Augustine's
view, one of the most important responses to make to the question "Why do we do evil?" is this: We do evil because we *freely
choose* to do it.

There are at least two important implications present in this
response. First, Augustine wants to make clear that there is nothing
necessary about man's doing of evil. The emphasis on free choice
rules out the view that men had or have to do evil. Men do evil,
but it results from free choices. Second, the emphasis on the
relation between human freedom and evil is an important factor in
Augustine's denial that God causes the evil that men do and experience at the hands of each other. The evil men do and experience
from each other does have a cause, but the cause is to be found in
the human will rather than in God.

To say that the reason we do evil is that we choose to do it
suggests another question that needs attention: Why do we choose
to do that which is evil? The factors here are complex, but the
considerations Augustine would point out include the following.
First, one's training and upbringing might have the effect of leading
one to attend primarily to temporal concerns and things. In such a
case the will might have a proclivity to choose to do evil, but
there would still be no necessity compelling its movement in that
direction. Another factor to consider would be that because of the
physical and sensory structure of our existence which necessarily
involves us to some degree in the natural world, our choices, while
free, may tend increasingly toward concerns involving our relation
to that temporal and changing world, rather than toward that

which is less immediate but eternal, immutable, and perfect. A third factor would be that the prospects of social prestige and political power may attract our attention and lead us to choose in their favor in a way that excludes priority for our relationship to God. Factors of this kind can influence the movements of our will, although Augustine wants to maintain that these influences are not exhaustive determinants of the will. Freedom of choice remains as an essential component in man's doing of evil.

One thing, however, is clear from the examples that we have cited. In Augustine's view, it will be difficult for men to avoid doing evil if they lack a proper relationship between understanding or reason on the one hand and will on the other. Without a sound grasp of the structure of existence and man's relationship to God in particular, the freedom of the will exists without the direction it needs. Without the guidance that a reasoned understanding of the Christian faith provides, there will still be freedom present in human life, but it will exist in a context of ambiguity and unclarity in which the chances of doing evil are maximized. On the other hand, however, movement toward such an understanding and the internal appropriation of it also involve the will. For example, in turning toward a rational search of one's own, or in cultivating insights obtained from others, or in praying to God for help, the will moves us. Augustine's understanding includes the view that the predicament of man is sometimes so severe that if one does succeed in moving in the right direction, this success will be due to God's gracious action within him. In some circumstances the human will becomes poisoned so as to limit severely its power to do what it should, but through God's grace even this situation can be transcended.

It should be noted that in some of his writings Augustine seems to push the severity of man's sinful condition and the graciousness of God to such extremes that man's freedom to do good at all is essentially denied. This extreme view emerges primarily when Augustine is arguing against those (for example the Pelagians) who defend a view suggesting that the freedom of the will to do good is not essentially influenced by past actions which may have been in the direction of evil. For Augustine, the effects of a man's sinful past can only be wholly set right by God, and Augustine's reaction, or overreaction, to the view that the will is really not influenced by the past emphasized the idea that the good is done only through God's action in men. However, this extreme view is not characteristic of *On Free Choice of the Will*. There the emphasis on man's autonomy is more marked. The will needs the illumination of reason if wise action is to occur, but the movement of the will is also crucial to the growth of right understanding. As long as a man lives, his reason and will are never totally incapacitated, and, although God's help is often required, men can grow toward achieving the right relation between reason and will that constitutes human well-being.

The answers that Augustine has given thus far concerning the relations between God, evil, and human freedom do not, however, satisfy Evodius completely. At the end of Book I, Evodius states the problem that bothers him:

> But I question whether free will—through which, it has been shown, we have the power to sin—ought to have been given to us by Him who made us. For it seems that we would not have been able to sin, if we did not have free will. And it is to be feared that in this way God may appear to be the cause of our evil deeds.[4]

If it is evil for men to miss recognizing, maintaining, and developing a right relationship with God, and if the freedom of the human will is the cause of any failure that occurs in this regard, then is it not the case that God, the creator of man's will, is directly responsible for man's plight, and hence less than absolutely good? Or, if we want to put the question in a less biased fashion, how are we to understand God's nature and his goodness in particular if he creates men with a freedom which entails the evil possibility of our falling away from him and which has also led to the actualization of that possibility?

Evodius's question cuts deeply and casts shadows of unclarity over some basic Christian claims. Augustine's understanding of the Christian faith requires him to say that God creates only that which is good. Human existence is one of God's creations, and it is good. Moreover, to be human is to be a freely willing agent, and it therefore follows that man's free will is also created by God as good. However, because sin and evil appear, and because they depend on the human will, Evodius has questioned the goodness of the will's existence, and this raises serious problems. If the goodness of the will's existence cannot be defended, we will be forced to say one of two things, neither of which Augustine wants to accept: Either God did not create the will, or, if God did create it, he should not have done so in the way that he did. We either call God's omnipotence into question by denying the full dependence of human existence on God, or we call into question his wisdom and goodness.

Augustine and Evodius choose to deal with the problem by maintaining and trying to clarify two fundamental claims: that God creates only what is good, and that God is the source of human freedom, which in turn is to be taken as a good and not as something that should be different from the way that God created it. However, their recognition of far-reaching implications of Evodius's question leads them to an examination of the foundations of their faith. In fact, the discussion is pushed back to the level of clarifying how men know the existence of God and the characteristics of his nature. Here again we see Augustine's efforts to bring faith and understanding into harmony.

Augustine begins his analysis of man's claims about God's existence by exploring some characteristics of man's self-awareness and knowledge of his own existence. By questioning Evodius, Augustine shows him that a man can have clear knowledge about his own existence, life, and understanding. Evodius knows that he himself exists because, even if he doubts his experiences or questions whether he is being deceived by Augustine's inquiries, an agent (that is, Evodius himself) must exist in order to doubt the experiences or to do the questioning. Moreover, Augustine points out that the clarity that Evodius now has about his existence entails both his aliveness and his capacity to understand. Dead things do not have awareness of themselves, and clarity of thought depends on a capacity for understanding. Thus, Augustine asserts, Evodius possesses certainty about three things; namely, that he exists, lives, and understands. Evodius is also willing to admit that understanding or reason is the highest capacity in man, and that it is the power that sets him above many other forms of existence on the scale of being.

These preliminary steps set the stage for Augustine's chief argument for the existence of God and for some important insights concerning God's nature. The argument is based on man's awareness of his rational capacity and its power to apprehend truths that are eternal. Although man's reason is subject to the defects of temporality and changeability, as is manifested by the fact that the clarity of its apprehension of truth can vary, Evodius acknowledges human reason to be our highest capacity. Moreover, Evodius is willing to consent to the following idea. If it can be shown that a reality higher than our reason exists—that is, an existent (1) that lacks the defects of human reason and hence possesses the qualities of eternality and immutability and (2) to which nothing could reasonably be granted to be superior—then this would be God and his existence would be demonstrated.

Evodius's consent to this idea gives Augustine an interesting base from which to operate. Their understanding of perfection or superiority is such that the presence of the qualities of eternality and immutability in a thing is sufficient to give it a higher position in the scale of being and perfection than anything which involves the qualities of temporality and change. In this context, therefore, finding the existence of something that is immutable and eternal will be sufficient to constitute a demonstration of God's existence. For example, if we find an existent, X, to be immutable and eternal, it will stand higher than human reason or anything else that is temporal and changing. Furthermore, unless we find some other existent, say Y, that is (1) eternal and immutable, (2) capable of being legitimately taken to be superior to X, and (3) capable of being designated as that to which nothing could reasonably be granted to be superior, then X will not only meet the requirements of eternality and immutability, but it will also meet the requirement of having nothing that can reasonably be granted to be superior to it. Hence, it will fit the specifications for being called God. Of course, if Y, or something still more perfect, should be found to exist, it would legitimately be called God.

Augustine thinks that if he can show that something immutable and eternal exists, this proof will be sufficient grounds to allow us to say with certainty that something exists which is legitimately called God. Now, given this framework, how does he proceed? Augustine is struck by the fact that human experience involves a content that is shared and communal. This characteristic exists to some extent in sensory experience, as for example, when we speak of seeing the same object. It is even more evident when we consider things such as the propositions of mathematics or some moral claims. Propositions such as "7 + 3 = 10" or "We should live justly" share or participate in one peculiarly interesting quality. Their truth is eternal and unchanging. The truth of these propositions is the same in all times and places, and we cannot deny their truth without setting up a massive grating effect in our understanding and without producing contradictions and a sense of falsity. Moreover, our experience of immutable and eternal truth does not allow us to say that we have conjured it up or created it. Rather, our experience of truth is one of discovery, of finding our minds moving toward it as something fixed, and of recognizing that its existence does not depend on our perception of it.

Augustine claims that in our encounter with this truth we come face to face with something that stands above human reason and that possesses the qualities of immutability and eternality that he is seeking. In addition, once he has gotten this far, he has met the formal conditions to which Evodius agreed, and Evodius is prepared to grant that they can say with certainty that God exists. Augustine's argument implies that eternal and immutable truth is God. Although this affirmation is not the only one that he makes about God, it is one of his most fundamental claims. Augustine takes eternality and immutability to be identifying marks of God. Hence, an encounter with eternal and immutable truth is an encounter with God, even though every man may not recognize immediately that this is the case.

Having argued that we can be sure that God exists, Augustine's efforts in *On Free Choice of the Will* turn next to clarify the idea that all good things come from God. The argument here rests on the basic idea that, with the exception of God, none of the good things that exist are sufficient to account for themselves. To exist and to be good imply the presence of form, but except in God, form is never totally self-generating. For example, a human life or a human species does not constitute itself. Its existence depends on something else, and this pushes our thought back toward the ultimate ground that is God.

Now that he has clarified the claims that God exists and that all good things come from God, Augustine is ready to look again at the nature of human freedom. The pressing question is this: Is freedom a good, and, if so, how? If he can affirm and explain the goodness of freedom, he thinks that this will clarify not only the claim that freedom comes from God but also the claim that it comes from him rightly.

It is clear that Augustine's answer to the first part of our question must be positive. His Neoplatonic background and his Christian commitment push him in the direction of saying not only that all good things come from God, but also that all things that exist come from God and are good. Evil, it will be recalled, is characterized by nonbeing. The real issue, then, is to say how freedom, which is real, is a good. Again, Neoplatonic metaphysics comes to Augustine's aid. If this metaphysical outlook suggests that everything is good insofar as it exists, it also allows one to say that there are different degrees of goodness in what does exist. Thus, just as there is a difference in perfection between a man and a stone, there may also be different degrees of goodness in the dimensions of human existence.

Drawing on this insight, Augustine suggests that freedom of the will is an *intermediate good.* This classification means that freedom of the will, which entails our responsibility for the use of freedom, is something without which a man cannot live rightly, since he would not, strictly speaking, be a man without the freedom. This explanation puts freedom higher on the scale of goodness than, for example, the possession of some physical comforts, which may be good but not essential for full human existence. On the other hand, however, the reality of freedom does permit evil to occur, and in that sense it is not as high in the order of goods as a virtue such as justice would be. When justice is present, it does not itself produce evil, but the presence of freedom may result in evil.

Thus, freedom stands as a good. It is essential to our humanity and its proper use is essential for our well-being. Uses of freedom may result in evil, which means that freedom is only an intermediate good. However, since freedom of the will is a necessary condition for human existence, it must be acknowledged as something which rightly exists as God created it. If evil enters into the picture, it is because of man's misuse of freedom. To blame God for such occurrences is to make a serious mistake.

These analyses leave Evodius convinced that the existence of freedom of the will can legitimately be called good, but he is still troubled by one particular aspect of the relationship between God on the one hand and man's freedom and doing of evil on the other. The problem arises because of Augustine's account of God's nature. Augustine regards God as perfection itself. Given Augustine's understanding of perfection, this means that God is characterized by completeness, self-sufficiency, absoluteness of power, knowledge, and goodness, as well as by the qualities of eternality and immutability that we have noted above. The point of particular interest here is the idea that God's knowledge of all existence is complete. God sees everything, including time itself, from a perspective of eternity that encompasses all being. If God did not have such a full knowledge of being, something would be lacking in him and he would be less than perfect. Evodius, however, is concerned that it may be impossible to reconcile this view of the completeness of God's knowledge with the idea that sin is committed or evil is done through free human choices and not by necessity. Thus, in Book III, Evodius asks and Augustine tries to answer a difficult and important question: "How can it be that God has foreknowledge of all future events, and yet that we do not sin by necessity?"[5]

Augustine wants to assert that there is no incompatibility between the claim that God's knowledge is full and complete and the claim that if men do evil they do so through free choice and not by any necessity imposed on them by God's foreknowledge. In

the next section of this chapter we will want to see whether
Augustine's assertion will stand, but first we must draw out his
position. Augustine believes that Evodius's feeling that there is an
incompatibility between God's foreknowledge and man's freedom in
doing evil can be removed if we are clear about the fact that
having knowledge of some thing or event is not the same thing as
being the cause of that thing or event. In short, Augustine's position is this: God knows what I will choose to do in the future,
whether my action be good or evil, but his knowledge neither
produces the action nor binds me in necessity so that I am forced
to do some particular thing. Rather, God knows my will as free.
He knows what *I choose.* God is not the cause of all that he fore-
knows, and he does not do all of the things that he knows will
occur.[6] Not only is it the case, therefore, that man chooses freely
and without necessity, but this view also allows Augustine to re-
emphasize the point that when sin or evil occurs it is man who is
responsible and not God. Moreover, Augustine can say that God's
punishment of wrong-doing is just. This punishment is simply an
additional instance of goodness in the scale of being that Augustine's metaphysical view entails.

These latter points push us to a final consideration regarding
Augustine's position in *On Free Choice of the Will.* How would he
respond to the question, "Did God create the best of all possible
worlds?" Augustine would give an affirmative answer. However, his
attempts to explain it lead to difficulties. If Augustine wants to say
that this is the best of all possible worlds, he has to reconcile this
claim with the fact that our world is one in which men do evil.
On the other hand, there is a strand of Augustine's thought that
tries to reconcile these factors without assuming the position that
our doing of evil is a necessary condition for the perfection of the
world. Men do evil because they freely choose to do it. There is
no necessity that operates here. To say that this is the best of all
possible worlds, then, is to direct our attention to the general
structure of the world. The world is created by God without initial
flaws. Men can introduce flaws through their sin but, if this does
occur, the justice of God is sure and through his mercy things will
be set right. Sin and evil will be dealt with and overcome, and
the good will prevail. This line of thought emphasizes the freedom
of men. It suggests that although every detail of the world may
not be as it should, the overall structure of existence makes it
legitimate to say that this is the best of all possible worlds, and we
can do so without committing ourselves to the notion that man's
doing of evil is either a necessary condition for calling this the best
of all possible worlds or really a good in disguise.

There is, however, another strand of Augustine's thought that must be remembered in this context, and it calls the first view into question. In Augustine's view, men deal with a creating God who is perfection itself. If this God created anything other than the best of all possible worlds, he would have thereby exhibited a mark of imperfection, but this is ruled out because of the perfection already ascribed to God. Now, given Augustine's position with respect to God's foreknowledge, it will not be possible to say that God was unaware that man's freedom would lead to evil choices and consequences. God's knowledge is complete. He has a total picture of all being, and if we are to call this the best of all possible worlds, as we must if we affirm Augustine's understanding of God as creator, then it would seem that we are talking about more than the general structure of existence. The details, after all, are known by God too, and if the totality of the details constitutes the whole that is the best of all possible worlds, then the details are themselves vital components in the picture. One is led to draw the following conclusion: Man's doing of evil is a necessary component in making this the best of all possible worlds.

A sense of conflict exists when these two lines of thought are brought together. We will examine it more fully in the next section, but now let us summarize the salient features of Augustine's positions with respect to our three main questions. (1) Augustine thinks that we can know with certainty that God exists. There is a harmonious relationship between faith and reason. Reason clarifies and gives assurance concerning what is taken on faith, and Christian teaching provides the content and the satisfaction for which reason longs. (2) Man exists in the middle ground of a hierarchical scale of being which has God at the top and non-being at the bottom. Man exists in a world of time and change, but through faith and reason he can know that God's nature is characterized by qualities such as immutability, eternality, self-sufficiency, and absoluteness of power, knowledge, and goodness. Moreover, man possesses freedom of the will. If properly used, this freedom brings man happiness through a right relationship with God. On the other hand, if improperly used, man's freedom plunges him toward evil, which is characterized as nonbeing. (3) Man's possession of freedom makes him, and not God, responsible for the evil that men do. God's goodness is protected in Augustine's theories. Although God has foreknowledge of human existence, Augustine argues that this neither causes man's sin nor makes it necessary.

Some Problems and Useful Insights in Augustine's Thought

What are the most pressing problems that a contemporary reader will find in Augustine's thought? Surely some of them involve his understanding of the relation between God's foreknowledge and man's freedom, and the implications of this relationship for an understanding of evil. Augustine states that there is no incompatibility between God's foreknowledge of human action and man's possession and experience of freedom. But is this the case? Is our contemporary understanding of the meaning of freedom fully compatible with the kind of God that Augustine describes?

In Augustine's view, God sees all being from the perspective of eternity. God creates and knows time in all of its detail. Moreover, God's knowledge involves the qualities of absolute clarity and certainty. Augustine's God does not operate with mere judgments of probability or good hunches about existence. His knowledge is not composed of fallible judgments that must be tested by future experience. On the other hand, our contemporary experience and understanding of freedom involve us in a world that we take to be moving, open-ended, and full of possibilities. To be living and free means that our existence is characterized by incompleteness and indeterminateness and that movement toward completeness and determinateness depends largely on our autonomous choices and acts.

It is difficult to see how this inescapable contemporary understanding of freedom is fully compatible with Augustine's God, who has absolutely certain knowledge of all temporal details, including those that are still in the future for us. Augustine's theory entails that God knows the totality of one's existence from eternity and with absolute clarity and certainty, and, no matter how one tries to avoid it, he is pushed to the conclusion that his life is complete before he has actualized it himself in time. Strictly speaking, our lives cannot be otherwise than God knows them to be, and our lives are constituted for God before they are constituted for ourselves. Moreover, to say that our freedom is left intact because God knows our wills as free is simply to introduce confusion. God's perspective from eternity means that God knows time completely. This means that, though we have not yet made tomorrow's choices and do not know with absolute certainty what choices we will make tomorrow, God knows these choices. This statement, in turn, means that tomorrow's choices are already set for us, *but in the contemporary world of freedom this is precisely what we experience not to be the case.*

If Augustine's claims concerning God's knowledge call our experience of freedom into question, they also create serious problems for our understanding of evil. Strictly speaking, if we do evil, Augustine's God, who knows from the perspective of eternity, sees our action prior to our acting. Since God's knowledge is complete and fixed, we could not do other than what God knows. The conclusion that presses on us is that we had to do evil. Even if one says that God really knows our choices to do evil, the fact remains that God knows the temporal sequence exhaustively and before we have experienced it in our own lives. Hence, God's knowledge seems to constitute our action. The evil action seems to be inescapable. In addition, this action appears to function as a necessary ingredient in the world's perfection. Augustine's God not only has exhaustive knowledge, but he creates the best of all possible worlds. The world that exists involves evil, and therefore evil appears as necessary to the perfection of the whole. These conclusions both question the adequacy of Augustine's view that God is not directly responsible for evil and invalidate our sense of moral responsibility.

Augustine's theory concerning God's knowledge does not allow for a contemporary understanding of freedom, which entails that factors of ambiguity, open-endedness, uncertainty, incompleteness, and indeterminateness are not merely the results of a clouded, finite intellect, but fundamental qualities that permeate existence. His view is also full of problems when it comes to developing a conception of evil that is compatible both with his claim that God is not directly responsible for evil and with our sense of moral responsibility. But even if it can be shown that Augustine's theory about God's knowledge is logically consistent with real experiences of human freedom and responsibility, it is unlikely that contemporary men will accept it as one that is really adequate. Logical consistency is not a sufficient condition for a sound and believable theory, theological or otherwise, and the contemporary mood concerning freedom and responsibility will not rest content with a view which, at the very least, seems strained in its attempts to handle basic components of our experience.

This objection suggests that an adequate theological framework will need (1) to allow our sense of freedom and responsibility to stand and (2) to interpret evil as contingent rather than as necessary. As it stands, Augustine's theory seems incapable of doing these things. This is the case because Augustine understands God primarily in terms of completeness, immutability, eternality, and self-sufficiency. A more temporal conception of God—one in which the possibilities of change, growth, and development of knowledge are present—would go far toward eliminating the grating effects that we have noted. Augustine, however, cannot think of God in these terms. His Neoplatonic metaphysical framework equates divine perfection with a lack of change and with completeness and eternality. Thus, if we need a conception of God that involves a greater measure of change and temporality, it is unlikely that it can be fully developed in terms of the metaphysical theory that Augustine uses.

One useful insight that we can gain from our study of Augustine is that an adequate contemporary perspective for interpreting experience and man's religious life in particular will need to give a more fundamental place to time, change, and freedom than Augustine's Neoplatonic framework allows. This does not mean, however, that every insight that Augustine develops within that perspective is invalidated. In particular, there are two fundamental points in Augustine's thought that are likely to be of great importance in our own constructive efforts. The first is Augustine's claim that human fulfillment and happiness depend largely on man's discovering and cultivating a relationship between himself and an ultimate source of existence that provides a framework of purpose and meaning in which he can live and grow. Man is a being who seeks for fulfilling meaning, and Augustine is right that this need eventually involves us in a search for God. If we live in an age that is less certain of God's presence than Augustine was, it is still the case that the realization of human fulfillment—physical, intellectual, spiritual, and moral—and the reality of God are intimately linked.

The other useful insight in Augustine's thinking is more implicit than explicit. In spite of his difficulties in handling man's freedom, Augustine clearly thinks that freedom is a good. This viewpoint suggests that freedom may be of considerable value and importance to God as well as to men. What Augustine's God seems to desire from men is freedom rightly used (that is, uses of freedom that bring men and God closer together). At the same time, consider one more aspect of Augustine's thought. While he is anxious to deny God's *direct* responsibility for man's doing of evil, Augustine never denies that man's freedom entails the possibility of evil and that evil can result from God's creation of human freedom. Thus, if freedom does result in evil, perhaps we could say that God is at least *indirectly* responsible for it.

Now, if we brought these ideas together, we would not have to go too far to develop a view that would stress the idea that freedom is a primary value for God. In fact, it could be a value so high that, in order to make possible the experience of seeing freedom extended widely and used positively and creatively, God would create a world that had the possibility, perhaps even the probability, of man's doing evil in it. A God who has power sufficient to deal with evil so that it will never ultimately frustrate him, and who is characterized by greater degrees of temporality and change than Augustine's total framework allows, might have such an interest. He might bring a world into being where the possibility or the probability of evil, wildness, ambiguity, and frustration are risks worth taking for the value that both God and man can know from an experience of the creative use of freedom. This God would not be identical with Augustine's, but he might be a closer match for the world that actually exists. In any case, Augustine's views leave us with a speculative suggestion that is worth pursuing and clarifying in our future thought.

III

ANSELM AND
THE ONTOLOGICAL
ARGUMENT

Anselm's Life and Augustinian Background

Anselm's life was less marked by inner turmoil than was Augustine's. Born in 1033 in Aosta, a town in northern Italy, Anselm decided at an early age that he would give his life to the Christian faith, and he did not swerve from his plan. Anselm was disciplined and bright, and in 1059 he went to the Benedictine monastery at Bec in Normandy, which was one of the great centers for learning at this time. In the following year, he entered the Benedictine order. From the outset, Anselm was a leader in the monastery at Bec, and in 1078 he was named abbot, the top position of authority.

Under Anselm's guidance, the intellectual reputation of the monastery continued to grow. This growth was largely due to his own writing. In the period 1076-1090, Anselm produced numerous works, among them the *Monologium* and the *Proslogium,* which contain his arguments for the existence of God, and dialogues such as *On Freedom of Choice* and *The Fall of Satan.* These dialogues deal with problems concerning freedom and evil, and we will examine them in addition to concentrating on Anselm's efforts to demonstrate God's existence.

When the position of Archbishop of Canterbury was left vacant,

Anselm went to England and took the post in 1093. He served there until his death in 1109. Although he was busy handling relations between Church and State, Anselm still found time to study and write. *Cur Deus Homo* is one of the works that is thought to have been produced during his term as Archbishop of Canterbury. It is Anselm's attempt to answer a crucial question in Christian thought: Why did God become man? This effort to state how Christ atones for human sin stands as one of the landmarks in the history of Christian theology.

Like Augustine, Anselm's philosophical and theological thinking was not formed in an intellectual vacuum, but was influenced by his knowledge of previous theories. This time, however, it is Augustine himself who provides the framework. Although Anselm does not merely reiterate Augustine's views, there are at least three major ways in which Augustine influences Anselm's perspective. First, Anselm essentially adopts his position on the relationship between faith and reason. Some of Anselm's contemporaries in the Church held the opinion that attempts to provide arguments demonstrating the rationality of the Christian faith not only led to fruitless conflicts but were also undesirable manifestations of human pride. Anselm, however, took the Augustinian line that faith and reason were both compatible and mutually supporting.

Anselm's famous statement from the *Proslogium* is: "For I do not seek to understand that I may believe, but I believe in order to understand. For this also I believe,—that unless I believed, I should not understand."[1] Anselm affirms his belief that the Christian claims are true. His position is not one of having to be persuaded of their validity. Rather he desires to comprehend more fully how the claims can be true and what they are saying. To seek to understand the claims is to try to show how their truth is possible, and a part of Anselm's faith is that this task can be accomplished.

Moreover, the value of obtaining this rational understanding is two-fold. On the one hand, by showing that faith is compatible with reason, one helps believers to appropriate more deeply the claims that are involved. An intelligible faith sustains the human soul more adequately than one that is incapable of rational interpretation. On the other hand, obtaining a rational understanding of the claims of the Christian faith can also be helpful in bringing nonbelievers into a positive relationship with God. This is not to say that understanding is the same as faith, or even that understanding is a sufficient condition for faith. Anselm, however, thinks that without some rational understanding faith cannot exist at all.

If reason can benefit faith, Anselm also holds that belief in Christian teachings is a necessary condition for adequate rational understanding of the Christian faith and for obtaining reason's satisfaction in its quest to understand existence as a whole. Anselm thinks that belief in the truth of Christian teachings establishes a disposition in the believer that makes understanding possible. Without belief, the necessary disposition is lacking. For example, before I can begin to comprehend the love that God has for me, I must believe that he does love me. If I doubt or deny that God loves me, it is impossible to understand his love for me. For Anselm, adequate understanding of the Christian claims comes primarily in retrospect, and it depends on prior belief in their truth.

Moreover, Anselm accepts Augustine's view that God provides the ground for existence and the basic framework of meaning which makes life intelligible and significant. Reason finds its fulfillment in a right relationship to God, and this is mediated to men through Christian teachings. On the other hand, a defective relationship between man and God (that is, a distortion or lack of faith) creates an obstacle that precludes the possibility of satisfaction in reason's quest for intelligibility. Thus, like Augustine, Anselm not only sees no large gaps between faith and reason, but also his writings reveal no sharp breaks between philosophy and theology. Philosophical analysis clarifies theological doctrine, and theological doctrine provides the content that completes and fulfills philosophical inquiry.

The second major way in which Anselm's thought reflects an Augustinian influence involves his understanding of truth and value judgments. With respect to the former, Anselm holds that there are propositions whose truth is eternal. One of his examples is: "Something was destined to be."[2] No time can be conceived when this proposition came to be true or when it was not true. This suggests that the truth of the proposition is eternal. But how are we to account for this? Following Augustine, Anselm's answer is that the encounter with the eternal truth of the proposition is an encounter with God, who is the eternal self-sufficient ground of all that is. Anselm's conclusion is the same as Augustine's: One way to speak of God is to say that God is truth.

Anselm's analysis of our value judgments goes in the following direction. When we judge the value of things, events, or persons, we sometimes rank them with respect to their perfection or lack thereof. On the one hand, the fact that we judge the degrees of perfection of things, events, or persons implies that there is, in fact, an absolute and eternal standard of perfection to which we are appealing. Without grounding our appeal in such a standard, our value judgments become so relativized as to lose their significance. No reasonable man is willing to give up the view that value judgments are meaningful and that there are genuine differences of quality in things, events, or persons. Hence, the absolute and eternal standard of perfection must exist. Like truth, however, this standard is regarded by Anselm as a manifestation of God. Its absoluteness and eternality reveal it to be God himself. Again, Anselm's conclusion parallels Augustine's: God himself is perfection. This conclusion is important, because, as we shall see, Anselm will make a great deal of the relation between God and the idea of perfection in his ontological argument for God's existence.

The final Augustinian influence that we need to identify is present in Anselm's understanding of human freedom and our experience of evil. In the debate as to whether a conflict exists between the assertion that God is omniscient, knowing all temporal details from the perspective of eternity, and the assertion that men are genuinely free, Anselm holds the Augustinian view that the two assertions are fully compatible. He thinks that if an action or event is known by God and, hence, its existence is certain, this is not the same as asserting that the action or event is necessary. Since the event or action is not necessary (that is, it could have been different), freedom, Anselm argues, is preserved. Working in this context, Anselm is then able to say that man's doing of evil, while known from eternity by God, is not necessary. A man does evil through his free choices, and God's knowledge does not make them necessary. Again, however, it should be pointed out that Anselm's views do not merely repeat Augustine's thought. Anselm lived in a different time, and both the issues he found and the answers he developed were cast somewhat differently than they were for Augustine. Thus, as we look at Anselm's treatment of human freedom and man's experience of evil, we will watch for these differences and see whether he significantly reduces the grating effects that were produced in Augustine's handling of these phenomena.

Man's Knowledge of God's Existence

Before we consider Anselm's views concerning freedom and evil, we need to deal with his position on a different issue. What knowledge can men have about God? The most important aspect of Anselm's answer is this: We can have certainty about God's existence. Human reason is capable of demonstrating that God exists; in particular, this can be done by reflecting on the concept of God. In the *Proslogium,* Anselm tries to prove the existence of God in this way. His effort is known as the *ontological argument* for God's existence. The fact that Anselm's attempt has been a continuing source of philosophical and theological debate from his day to the present testifies to the importance of the ideas he developed.

In the Preface to the *Proslogium,* Anselm says that he had long searched for "a single argument which would require no other for its proof than itself alone; and alone would suffice to demonstrate that God truly exists . . . and whatever we believe regarding the divine Being."[3] Anselm had argued for the existence of God in his earlier work, the *Monologium,* but taking these arguments to be undesirably complex, he continued to look for one that was simpler. Anselm's discovery of the ontological argument seemed to fill the bill.

By noting three of the arguments Anselm develops in the *Monologium,* we can make the approach of the ontological argument stand out more clearly. First, Anselm asserts that it is clear that the goodness of things in the world must be caused. This means that one of two alternatives must hold: Either a single thing is the cause or many things are the causes. If the first option holds, we have a unitary source of goodness which is dependent on nothing else for its goodness and which can only be designated as goodness itself. If the second option holds, it too ultimately points toward the single source. If we say that there are many causes of the goodness in things, these causes themselves participate in goodness, and this fact points toward the existence of a single, common source, goodness itself. Anselm equates this source with God. God is the ultimate ground of all good things. Their existence pushes us to the recognition of the reality of God.

The second argument follows a similar line, although it concentrates on existence rather than on goodness. Taking it as evident that the existence of things in the world entails their being caused, Anselm sets up another disjunction: Either there must be a single ultimate cause or there are multiple causes. If the first part of the disjunction holds, we have a cause that is uncaused, self-sufficient, and the source of all power. This is God. If, on the other hand, we say that there are multiple causes, we are ultimately forced to reduce the multiplicity to the single, ultimate cause. Multiple causes must either support each other or exist independently. Anselm argues that the first possibility cannot hold because something that is supported cannot be the cause of that which supports it, which would ultimately be true on the "mutual support" hypothesis. If, on the other hand, there are multiple causes with independent existence, it will still be true that they share something in common, namely, their power to be causes. This shared power points to the single, ultimate cause, which is the source of all existence and power. Once more, we arrive at the conclusion that God exists. He is the grounding cause of all that is.

The third argument, which was alluded to in the first section of this chapter, moves from the fact that we rank things in the world according to their degrees of dignity or perfection. Anselm regards it as clear that our value judgments are intelligible. Moreover, this intelligibility depends on the reality of an ultimate standard, perfection itself, which is either unitary or plural. If we acknowledge this standard to be unitary, then we in fact assert God's existence, since ultimate perfection is an identifying mark of God. On the other hand, if we should say that a plurality of things share ultimate perfection, we also require a single source to account for the fact that the perfection is shared. The fact that there is something shared pushes us toward God as the ground of all perfection.

What is the chief contrast between these arguments and the ontological argument? The arguments we have noted thus far move from a consideration of things in the world to a consideration of properties such as goodness or perfection and then reach the conclusion that God exists. On the other hand, the ontological argument moves directly from a consideration of the concept of God to the assertion of God's existence. The approach is based on internal reflection on an idea rather than on empirical judgments concerning the natural world. The two approaches, however, are related in Anselm's treatment in that the concept of God with which he works in the ontological argument is largely the same as the concept that emerges in the arguments of the *Monologium* (for example, the idea that God is perfection itself).

There are two things to do in examining Anselm's ontological argument. The first is to look at the argument proper, which is presented and developed in a few pages near the beginning of the *Proslogium*. The second is to look at the argument in the broader context provided by the *Proslogium* as a whole. Only if the second task is combined with the first will we have a full grasp of the function of the proof in Anselm's thought.

To start with the first task, what is the line of thought that constitutes the ontological argument for God's existence? Anselm begins with the idea that when we talk about God, the concept of God has a meaning that can be grasped. Anselm asserts that God is understood to be "a being than which nothing greater can be conceived."[4] For Anselm, this statement means not only that God is the greatest possible being but also that God is perfection itself. Anselm notes, however, that some people who hear, and who seem to understand, this idea of God may still deny his existence. The concept of God may be in their understanding, but they may still assert that God does not exist. Moreoever, it would seem legitimate to do this, since having a concept in one's mind does not assure the existence of the thing to which the concept refers. A painter, for example, may think of a painting, but it does not follow that the painting has any existence other than as an idea in the painter's mind.

But is it true that the existence of a concept in one's understanding never directly implies the existence of that to which the concept refers? Anselm's answer is negative. There is one crucial case where the presence of a concept in our understanding directly points to the existence of the concept's referent. This case involves the concept of God. Anselm's position is this: "That than which nothing greater can be conceived, cannot exist in the understanding alone."[5] It must exist in reality as well as in idea. To deny this assertion is to fall into contradiction. That which can be conceived to exist, but does not exist, cannot be that than which nothing greater can be conceived. Thus, to think of a being than which a greater cannot be conceived, and to have an accurate understanding of the meaning of our thought, is to think of a being whose status in existence is more than that of an idea.

Anselm develops the line of thought further. In fact, building on what he has stated already, Anselm presents a second argument which arrives at the conclusion that God "cannot be conceived not to exist."[6] How is this conclusion reached, and what is its significance? Anselm arrives at this conclusion by coupling two main ideas. First, he claims that it is clear that a being whose non-existence is logically impossible is greater than one whose nonexistence is logically possible. From this claim it follows that a being than which a greater cannot be conceived must be one whose non-existence is logically impossible. The second idea is that God is a being than which a greater cannot be conceived. Thus, if we are thinking clearly, we find that it is really impossible to conceive that God does not exist. This means that God is not a being who could have come into existence or who could perish. Moreover, his existence depends on nothing beyond himself. God's perfection entails that God's existence is *necessary*, and Anselm takes this to be one of the fundamental attributes of God. Thus, Anselm claims not only to have shown that God does exist, but he also argues that God's existence is necessary, which is sufficient to separate God from all the other forms of being that we know.

Anselm's ontological argument was controversial from the outset. Some of the most significant criticisms brought against it came from one of Anselm's contemporaries, a monk named Gaunilo. Gaunilo raised at least two difficult objections to the argument. First, he states that if Anselm's argument is sound, we could prove the existence of many things simply by thinking about them, a possibility that Gaunilo thinks absurd. The example that Gaunilo presents to illustrate his point involves the conception of an unusual island. This island is conceived to be better than any actual land we know. Now, Gaunilo asserts, if we follow Anselm's view that perfection entails existence, it follows that the island in question must exist. If it does not exist except in the mind, it will simply not be as good as the lands we know exist. Gaunilo, however, finds this argument unreasonable. An unwarranted leap is made in going from the idea of the island to the assertion of its existence. An idea of something is of a different order than the actual existence of what one is thinking about. Just as the mind boggles at the claim that the hypothetical island must exist, Gaunilo thinks that one really can prove the existence of a being which is conceived to be the greatest conceivable being and, hence, one whose existence seems to be necessary. There is still a big difference between the thought of a necessarily existing being and an actual referent for that thought.

Anselm's responses to this first criticism are instructive. Gaunilo forces Anselm to make it clear that proving the existence of God, who is (1) a being than which a greater cannot be conceived, is different from proving the existence of a being which is either (2) the greatest thing of a certain type or (3) greater than all other beings. The three categories are not absolutely identical with each other. It is possible that what can be conceived not to exist is (2) the greatest thing of a certain type or (3) a being which is greater than all other beings. Moreover, if that which is conceived to be either (2) or (3) can be conceived not to exist, then it may be the case that the being that is so conceived does not exist in fact. That is, Anselm agrees with Gaunilo on a basic point. If we are conceiving that which is either (2) or (3), it does not follow with full clarity that anything exists to fit the conception. Anselm thinks that there is enough doubt about the referents for ideas (2) and (3) to make it unwarranted for us to say that from the conception of that which is either (2) or (3) it follows that something exists to fit the conception.

Anselm then proceeds to call Gaunilo's attention to the fact that the demonstration of God's existence does not move from the conception of the greatest being of a certain type or from the conception of a being which is greater than all other beings. God certainly is the greatest of all beings, but the argument moves instead from the concept of a being than which a greater cannot be conceived. Anselm asserts that the uniqueness of this concept lies precisely in the fact that, when one reflects on it carefully, he discovers that the presence of the concept in the mind requires that there must be something in existence that fits the concept. If this is not the case, then one simply is not thinking of a being than which a greater cannot be conceived. The perfection that is referred to in this concept requires existence, and, moreover, existence that is necessary.

Thus, Anselm continues to assert that there is one crucial case where reflection on a concept in the mind allows us to have certain knowledge of the existence of something that fits the concept. The possibility that this may be the case has concerned philosophers for generations. Many have argued that the evidence is overwhelming that (1) thought about something and (2) the existence of that thing are radically different and that we delude ourselves if we think that they are ever related in the way that Anselm's argument suggests. On the other hand, no matter how many times men have claimed to put Anselm's argument permanently to rest, revivals of interest in its validity have occurred. Anselm's argument meets one test of greatness; namely, it has the power to lure men back to it over and over again.

Now consider a second criticism that Gaunilo brings against Anselm's argument. It will enable us to make a transition to an examination of the part that the ontological argument plays in Anselm's thought in the *Proslogium* as a whole. Gaunilo thinks that one of the major reasons why Anselm's argument fails is that men do not really have an adequate understanding of the concepts involved. We lack a full understanding of God, and, when we hear concepts such as "a being greater than all others" or "a being than which a greater cannot be conceived," we are not sure what to think. It is not certain that these ideas are really "in our understanding" with any clarity. On the other hand, before we can prove the existence of something, a basic requirement is a clear grasp of the thing whose existence we are trying to demonstrate. Faced with this charge, Anselm makes two important responses. One of them is presented directly to Gaunilo, and the other is implicit in the development of the *Proslogium* as a whole.

The direct answer to Gaunilo is this: It is not the case that we lack the understanding required to make the argument work. While it is true that we do not understand God completely, we do know enough to recognize that it is correct to say that he is "a being than which a greater cannot be conceived." Moreover, Anselm denies Gaunilo's implication that no meaning is conveyed when we use the concept of "a being than which a greater cannot be conceived." The concept is significant, and one can grow in learning its ramifications. Even the fool who denies existence to "a being than which a greater cannot be conceived" has some understanding of the concept, and, building on that understanding, he can be brought to see that it entails the existence of a being who fits it. Thus, Anselm's conclusion is that, even though we find God to be beyond full comprehension, we can grasp enough about him to understand that he exists and that his existence is necessary.

The second and implicit response that Anselm makes to Gaunilo involves an elaboration of the idea that God transcends full human comprehension. Anselm and Gaunilo are in agreement on this point, and Anselm's thinking about this is clarified by the direction in which the *Proslogium* moves. This direction, in turn, tells us some interesting things about the ontological proof as a factor in Anselm's theology. If a person looks at the *Proslogium* as a whole, he is struck by the fact that the ontological argument is actually only a small portion of a larger meditation on this question: What is God like? The formulation of the ontological argument at the outset of the *Proslogium* tends to give the reader the feeling that Anselm is quite sure what God is like and that this can be grasped conceptually. This mood is even sustained for a time in the chapters that follow after the ontological argument. Anselm begins to spell out the attributes of God. God is whatever it is better to be than not to be. He is the self-sufficient cause, omnipotent, just, eternal, and unrestricted by space and time.

However, as Anselm makes these statements about God, another note begins to creep into his thought. Forced to reflect on the nature of a being who radically transcends the boundaries and limits of human experience, Anselm begins to wonder whether human understanding is capable of grasping God after all. At one point he reaches this interesting conclusion: "Therefore, O Lord, thou art not only that than which a greater cannot be conceived, but thou art a being greater than can be conceived."[7] Anselm's meditation has taken him on a dialectical path that he finds more than a little unnerving. The certainty and clarity that seemed to characterize the formulation of the ontological argument are replaced by expressions of concern such as the following: "I tried to rise to the light of God, and I have fallen back into my darkness . . . What art thou, Lord, what art thou? What shall my heart conceive thee to be?"[8]

Anselm becomes increasingly impressed by the transcendence of God, and both he and the reader of the *Proslogium* come to understand more clearly the difficulty of forming an adequate conception of God. This growth of awareness suggests that the movement of thought in the *Proslogium* is not much different from that of many Platonic dialogues. Plato's dialogues do not always end up with clear and definite conclusions, but they always carry the reader through a process of thought that heightens his awareness and understanding. When they finish the *Proslogium,* both Anselm and the reader may know more about what God might be like than they did at the outset, but neither is left with an absolutely clear and complete comprehension of God. Thus, when Gaunilo points out that men do not understand God fully, it is altogether likely that Anselm sees this much better than his critic.

If this analysis is correct, what does it say about the ontological argument itself? Two points can be made. First, if we take the *Proslogium* as a whole, the ontological argument is not an isolated element, but rather a link in a dialectical chain. The goal of Anselm's meditation is not only to see whether God's existence can be demonstrated, but also to obtain an adequate comprehension of what God might be like. This objective takes him through an initial stage, where he claims that the concept of God as a being than which a greater cannot be conceived entails God's necessary existence, to a later stage where his reflection on the implications of the argument both help him to say more about God and, at the same time, leave him with a new awareness of the difficulty and complexity of forming an adequate conception of God.

This development leads to our second point. Does Anselm's new awareness affect his assurance that he has demonstrated the existence of God? If we focus on the text itself, the most obvious answer would be a negative one. Anselm remains confident that he has shown that something exists which can be described as "a being than which a greater cannot be conceived." On the other hand, however, we can conjecture that Anselm's work in the *Proslogium* and his encounter with Gaunilo may have left him with an element of uneasiness about the significance of the argument. With his heightened awareness of the complexities involved in grasping God's nature, Anselm may have ended up less sure of what God is like than he might have thought possible when he began to meditate deeply on the nature of "a being than which a greater cannot be conceived." The ontological argument leaves Anselm with the assurance that his meditation has led him to something real, beyond himself, and unique, but just what has been encountered is not crystal clear. In this sense, Anselm may have felt that he both knew more and knew less than he thought he could when the argument first came to mind.

Let us summarize Anselm's answer to the question "What knowledge can men have of God?" It is clear that Anselm thinks that we can know that God exists and that God's existence is necessary. Anselm also feels that we are on sound ground in ascribing to God attributes such as omnipotence, self-sufficiency, goodness, and immutability. The attributes of God that Anselm stresses are largely the same as those emphasized by Augustine. However, as a result of his meditation on God's perfection, Anselm introduces a greater degree of transcendence into God's nature than is the case with Augustine. This suggests that the attributes ascribed to God always fall short of giving us a total grasp of God's nature. The terms that we apply to God are intelligible, and they take us far in increasing our understanding of him. Nevertheless, our thought about God always has its limitations. Now we must leave the difficult and fascinating problems of the ontological argument in order to concentrate on Anselm's views concerning man's freedom, the evil that men do, and the implications of these phenomena for our understanding of God.

Freedom and Evil

A discussion of three themes in the dialogues *On Freedom of Choice* and *The Fall of Satan* will enable us to see Anselm's basic position on human freedom and the doing of evil. The themes are: (1) Anselm's definition of freedom of choice, (2) the relation between evil and nonbeing, and (3) the relation between God's knowledge and man's freedom.

In *On Freedom of Choice,* Anselm asserts that the proper definition of freedom of choice is "the ability to keep uprightness of will for its own sake."[9] What is the significance of this idea? First, when Anselm seeks to define freedom of choice, he wants to grasp that which is shared by all beings who possess the capacity to choose freely. By working in this way, Anselm can strip away some qualities that are not essential for freedom of choice. The search is for the common core without which freedom of choice would not exist.

At the outset of the dialogue, Anselm and the student with whom he is discussing the problem decide that the ability to sin does not belong to the essential definition of freedom of choice. This discovery is very interesting because it would seem to be important to affirm that in men, at least, freedom to choose and an ability to sin or to do evil are, in fact, closely bound together. Even Anselm wants to assert that sin or evil would never manifest themselves without freedom of choice playing a part. How, then, can the basic definition of freedom exclude the ability to sin?

An essential definition of freedom of choice captures only those characteristics that are shared by the beings who possess this freedom. Anselm holds that, in addition to men, God and the angels also possess freedom of choice, but "since God and the good angels are unable to sin by free choice, the 'ability to sin' does not belong to the definition of free choice."[10] This means that the ability to sin, which is an aspect of freedom in man, is an accidental quality (that is, a nonessential quality) of freedom. To understand why this is the case, however, one needs to see more clearly why Anselm denies this ability to God.

At this point, Anselm's interpretation involves his conception of the perfection of God. It would seem that the denial of the ability to sin would not only have the effect of limiting God's freedom, but might also imply that man's freedom is greater than God's and that, hence, man is greater than God. Anselm, however, denies these conclusions. God is actually more free than men because he lacks the ability to sin. If this ability is used and sin occurs, as is the case with human freedom on some occasions, then the effect is that one's freedom to do the good may be restricted. The ability to sin, though a part of human freedom, is really a threat to freedom in the positive sense, which is the ability to keep uprightness of will for its own sake. For Anselm, it is a greater good, a higher degree of perfection, for a being to possess only the ability to choose the good rather than to couple this capacity with the ability to sin. Choosing evil is not an aspect of perfection. Hence, having the ability to choose evil is no perfection either, and, since God is perfect, he will not possess the ability to choose evil. God may lack an ability possessed by man, but God's freedom is greater and more perfect than man's for it is in no danger of being lost through misuse.

But how does freedom of choice get linked with "the ability to keep uprightness of will for its own sake?" Anselm's answer follows from his rejection of the idea that the ability to sin or to do evil is an essential aspect of freedom of choice. If one leaves that ability out of the picture, the natural thing to say is that freedom

is the ability to do the good and the just, and this means nothing
other than to do the right things and to do them for the right
reasons. Having an "upright will" involves these things. Anselm,
however, speaks in terms of our having the ability to *keep* uprightness of will *for its own sake.* How are we to interpret these aspects
of the definition of freedom? First, to have the ability to keep
something suggests that one already possesses that which is to be
kept. Here "to keep uprightness of will" means that one receives a
will that is upright. The human will is created this way by God,
while God's will is "given" upright in the sense that it simply is
this way from all eternity. To be God is to be an uncreated,
necessarily existing, omnipotent, and upright will. Freedom, then, is
the ability to keep the will upright and, moreover, the ability to
do this for the sake of uprightness itself.

    The latter qualification points to an additional factor in
Anselm's understanding. The possession of an upright will, which
involves doing the right things for the right reasons, is the foundational condition for good actions. Unless we act for the sake of the
will's uprightness, we have no assurance that we do what is good
or that we do the good for the right reasons. In fact, if we act
from a different motivation, we are likely to do the wrong things
or to act for the wrong reasons, and, in either case, the uprightness
of the will is reduced.

    The idea that the uprightness of the will can be reduced or lost
leads to some other important concepts. First, it enables us to
clarify further some of the differences between God and man. In
God's case, the ability to keep uprightness of will for its own sake
means that it is God's nature to be directed toward the good. God
is a being who chooses, but his choices are always marked by the
qualities of (1) being directed toward what is good and just and
(2) being made only because they are good and just. God is not
motivated to act except in terms of the good and the just. There is
never a gap between God's ability to keep uprightness for its own
sake and his use of the ability. There is always absolute harmony
between (1) God's ability to choose the good and the just and (2)
his choices. In fact, this is true of God to such an extent that
Anselm simply asserts that God lacks the ability to sin or to do
evil directly. Man, too, has the ability to keep uprightness of will
for its own sake, but he differs from God in that he can lose the
uprightness of his will, which is given by God. Men sometimes do
the wrong things, and they sometimes act for the wrong reasons.
This is simply to say that, unlike God, men have the ability to sin
and to do evil.

Second, if freedom of choice is defined as the ability to keep uprightness of will for its own sake, and if a man can lose the uprightness of his will, does this mean that he also loses his freedom? Anselm's answer is a qualified no. If uprightness has been lost through sin, then freedom is impaired in the sense that a man is no longer in possession of that which he is to keep. If one is really to exercise an *ability to keep,* that which is to be kept must already belong to him. On the other hand, Anselm does not think that the loss of the will's uprightness totally annihilates the power to choose or the *ability to keep* uprightness. That is, man is never stripped of the power that would make possible the keeping of the uprightness, if the uprightness were there. Restoration of the will's uprightness is ultimately possible only through God's grace, but a man always retains the ability to keep uprightness, even when he is in the depths of sin.

Working within a framework that takes God to be omnipotent and perfect and that regards God as creating only that which is good, how does Anselm deal with this question: Why does man's freedom involve the ability to sin and to do evil? Anselm does not answer this question directly, although, as we will see shortly, he does try to show that God does not directly cause man's doing of evil. However, there is an implied answer to the question in Anselm's understanding of the relation between freedom of choice and uprightness of will, and the implied answer leads to some interesting problems.

At one point in *On Freedom of Choice,* Anselm speaks about Satan and Adam: "They had freedom of choice for the sake of having uprightness of will." [11] Here freedom of choice, which in the cases of Satan and Adam involves the ability to sin, is a condition for continued possession of uprightness of will. Uprightness of will is not so much a fixed property as a quality of acting and, moreover, a quality of acting that is maintained only by making right choices from among a plurality of possibilities which include options that would be wrong or evil to pursue. Thus the ability to sin seems to be essential to man's freedom, even if it is not to God's. As a result, Anselm's thinking leads to the following problem, which remains unresolved. If the ability to sin plays an essential part in man's free choice, why is this not the case with respect to God? Or, if the ability to sin is nonessential to God's free choice, why is it essential to man's free choice? To put the latter question in a different way: Why did God not create us with a less risky form of freedom, namely, with a freedom that does not contain the defect of the ability to sin? It is not clear that we had to be created with the ability to sin in order to be free. This necessity would only be the case if the definition of freedom of choice required that the ability to sin be included. If that is the case, however, Anselm's definition is called into question.

Anselm's views on the nature of evil and on the issue of whether God's exhaustive knowledge makes evil necessary are more clearly defined, although they too involve problems. Anselm's God does only what is good. Moreover, everything that exists in the world depends on God for its existence, and therefore everything that exists in the world is good. On the other hand, however, sin and evil are factors in our experience, so how are they to be handled? Since everything that exists in the world is good, the only available alternative is to say that evil is nonbeing or nothing. Anselm illustrates the meaning of this idea by suggesting that evil is like blindness. Blindness is really a lack of sight. We only speak of blindness where a capacity to see has been lost. When we think about what we are referring to when we talk about blindness, we recognize that it is logically, if not always temporally, subsequent to the fuller and higher capacity of sight. In the same way, evil is the privation of good, and it can appear only because the good has prior existence. The term "evil" does not refer to a thing or a power. If we think that the term does work in this way, our confusion is probably due to our tendency to think that nouns name things or powers and that whenever a noun is used a thing or a power is denoted. The term "evil" functions differently than terms such as "table" or "freedom of choice," although our linguistic habits may not make this immediately clear.

Anselm protects God's goodness. God does only what is good. He does not create evil directly, although Anselm is less troubled than Augustine about admitting that God's action may indirectly lead to nonbeing and to evil by permitting other actions that have these results. Thus, at one point in *The Fall of Satan,* Anselm says that God "gives an evil will by not prohibiting it when He can . . . ."[12] God does not himself do the choosing of evil, and he does not approve the evil act, but he may "give an evil will" in the sense of allowing the will to act in this fashion. Nevertheless, Anselm thinks that this latter fact is not sufficient to remove the claim that God's goodness is absolute.

The claim that God does not do our choosing for us leads us to a brief consideration of Anselm's position on the relation between God's knowledge and man's freedom. Anselm's ideas on this issue are basically Augustinian, but some of his emphases are different from Augustine's. Anselm stresses the idea that "what is able not to happen cannot be known with certainty by rational inference."[13]

He takes human choices and actions to be instances of "what is able not to happen" (that is, no particular choice or action is necessary). This flexibility precludes the possibility that the future can be "known with certainty by rational inference." I cannot deduce with certainty what the future will be by looking at the past and the present. Anselm seems to be saying that the future is really open-ended, and he *is* saying this as far as temporal and finite minds are concerned. His restrictions on knowledge, however, do not eliminate the claim that God's knowledge is exhaustive. If God's knowledge were only temporal, he would be subject to the limitations of rational inference, but God's knowledge is of a different order. He sees things from an eternal perspective. This means that he grasps the totality of being as though it were all in the present and that his knowledge does not depend on rational inference, which is a temporal process. Thus, Anselm says, "The foreknowledge of God is not properly called foreknowledge. For all things are always present to Him, and so He does not have *foreknowledge* of future things, but *knowledge* of present things." [14]

Not only does God know my life in its completeness, which includes knowing my sin and the evil that I may do, but this knowledge is understood by Anselm not to be incompatible with my freedom of choice. I sin or do evil when I use my freedom of choice improperly, and the fact that God has exhaustive knowledge of my existence does nothing to impair my freedom. God sees all my choices as present, but he sees them as my choices and as choices that might have been different. My choices are free in the sense that they are mine and in the sense that they did not have to be what they were.

Anselm is unwilling to compromise God's omniscience, and the result is that the grating effect produced by Augustine's theology is reproduced in Anselm's thought. Even if God's knowledge of me is of *something present to him,* as contrasted with *something that is yet to be,* it is still the case that God's knowledge of me is *complete and certain.* It is hard to see that this completeness and certainty are compatible with my own experience of freedom. This experience involves incompleteness, open-endedness, and uncertainty with respect to myself, and it is not adequately grasped in a view that equates freedom with a lack of necessity concerning the content of God's knowledge. The completeness and certainty of God's knowledge from the perspective of eternity still include my temporality, and that means that there is a sense in which God knows what I will do before I do it. Where that is the case, God's knowledge constitutes my existence, and I am robbed of autonomy.

Anselm makes it no easier than Augustine to avoid the conclusion that God's knowledge not only shapes me exhaustively but also makes inescapable the evil that my life may involve. The options are clear: Either we must deny the full validity of our experience of freedom so as to accept Anselm's position on God's knowledge, or we must make changes in that position so that we can better accommodate our experience of freedom.

Let us summarize Anselm's most important points concerning our basic questions: What may the nature of God and the nature of man be conceived to be, how does our understanding of the one influence our understanding of the other, and how, in particular, does our experience of freedom bear on these issues? What does man's experience of evil entail for our view about the existence and nature of God? Anselm thinks that both God and man are free, but God's freedom is perfect, since it does not include the defect of the ability to sin. In addition, Anselm protects God's goodness. God creates all that exists, and all that exists is good insofar as it exists. Evil, on the other hand, is nonbeing, a privation of the good, and it is not created by God. When human freedom is not used to maintain the uprightness of the will, evil results. Although men do evil, it is not necessary that they do it. Man's doing of evil is always linked to his free choices, and man's freedom is not impaired by the fact that God has exhaustive knowledge of human existence. Thus, the appearance of evil does not need to be a threat to the belief in God's existence and goodness.

Some Problems and Useful Insights in Anselm's Thought

We have already pointed out that Anselm's treatments of freedom and evil do not satisfactorily resolve several problems. Two important examples are the following. First, Anselm's removal of the ability to sin from the definition of freedom is not coupled with an adequate statement concerning why God creates human freedom so that the ability to sin is essential to it. Second, in spite of Anselm's denials, his treatment of God's knowledge has the undesirable effect of producing the feeling that human action is totally constituted by God and that man is robbed of autonomy so that any evil he does could not have been avoided.

One interesting point to see is that these problems about freedom and evil push us back to issues that are inextricably bound up with Anselm's ontological argument and its context. Anselm's position on issues concerning freedom and evil is largely dictated by the conception of God that emerges from the *Proslogium*. His reflection on what God might be like results in a view that stresses God's transcendence but still attempts to grasp God's nature primarily in terms of qualities such as absolute goodness, completeness, immutability, eternality, self-sufficiency, omniscience, and omnipotence. Linking these attributes as Anselm does, qualities such as temporality, incompleteness, and change are excluded from God's nature. But precisely these qualities need to have a place in God if we are to remove the grating effects produced by bringing Anselm's conception of God into contact with our inescapable experiences of freedom and with our concerns about evil. If we are to preserve the validity of the belief that our experience of freedom is not a hollow sham, and if the evil that we do and experience is to be regarded as genuinely contingent, we will need to introduce elements of temporality, incompleteness, and change into our conception of God in a way that Anselm will not allow.

These latter points suggest still another interesting problem: Is Anselm's view about the nature of God the only one that can be made to fit with the idea of a being than which a greater cannot be conceived? Or is it possible that if we bring our experiences of freedom and evil to bear on the idea of such a being, we might emerge with a different description of God than the one provided by Anselm? Anselm, after all, did not meditate in a vacuum when he began to fill in the concept of a being than which a greater cannot be conceived. He worked in an Augustinian and Neoplatonic framework that already tipped the scales in a particular direction when it came to specifying God's perfection. Our situation today differs from Anselm's in that we are perhaps less sure that we have an adequate metaphysical framework in which to operate. But this lack of stability may be precisely the stimulus we need to begin developing a fresh view about God and existence that will fit with the experiences that we are living through.

Anselm was bold enough to try to say what God is like. We may not be able to accept his view of God without reservations, but perhaps we can profit from the example of his boldness. The clash between traditional views of God and contemporary experiences can prove to be merely a destructive conflict or it can be a fruitful tension that produces an understanding of existence which increases human fulfillment. It will not be the latter, however, unless many of us take up Anselm's task of trying to think clearly about what God might be like. Our age is not one that will grant itself the luxury of thinking that God's existence has been proved or even that it can, in principle, be proved. We are, in fact, a people who are generally skeptical about the possibility of proving anything with finality and completeness. On the other hand, however, we also live in an age that seeks and needs an understanding of existence that is intelligible and believable and that can help men to find meaning and to live with hope. A boldness that results in fresh thinking about the relations between God, the world, and men may take us far in developing options that have these qualities.

IV

THOMAS AQUINAS AND MAN'S KNOWLEDGE OF GOD

Thomas's Life and the Influence of Aristotle

For many years, the writings of Thomas Aquinas have served as the intellectual foundation for the official teachings of Catholic Christianity. As a result, Thomas is now regarded by many as conservative. In his own time, however, he was an intellectual innovator. The philosophy and theology he developed reflected fundamental changes in the patterns of thought that characterized many of his contemporaries. Who, then, was this man? What changes did he introduce, and what is there in his thought that leads many contemporary students to think of his philosophy and theology not only as conservative but also as fundamentally inadequate for dealing with our experiences and problems?

Thomas was born near Naples. His exact birthdate is uncertain, but available records place it near the beginning of 1225. He received his early education at the nearby Benedictine Abbey of Monte Cassino. Later he studied at the University of Naples and, while still in his teens, he came under the influence of the Dominicans. Thomas entered this order in 1244, but his action met stiff resistance from his family, who wanted him to join the Benedictines at Monte Cassino. In fact, the pressure from his family was so severe that he was kidnapped by his brothers and held as a hostage for a time to prevent his becoming a Dominican. Thomas won out, however, and by 1256, after study in Paris and Cologne, he was licensed to teach theology.

Unlike Augustine and Anselm, Thomas never became a bishop, but he was a very important figure in the medieval universities and in the intellectual life of the Church. This is true largely because he devoted much of his energy to harmonizing Christian teachings with Aristotelian philosophy. As we have seen, Augustine and Anselm used a Neoplatonic framework to develop their ideas. Neither of them knew much about Aristotle, but in Thomas's day metaphysical options were broader. Brought to Spain by Arab scholars in the twelfth century, Aristotle's works and Arabic commentaries on them became more widely available to Christian thinkers than they had been previously. Aristotle's philosophy sparked the interest of Christian scholars for at least two reasons. First, to some men Aristotle seemed to be a threat to Christian faith. Not only did Arab scholars use Aristotle as an ally in expounding their Mohammedan faith, but also some of Aristotle's specific metaphysical views seemed to clash head-on with Christian doctrine. For example, Aristotle taught that the world was eternal and uncreated, and this idea conflicted with the Christian doctrine of creation. Thus, even though the teaching of Aristotelian natural science and metaphysics was banned at some Christian centers of learning, Christian scholars had to know something about Aristotle in order to combat the "errors" of Mohammedan thought and Aristotelian philosophy.

The second reason for Christian interest in Aristotle was more positive. As some men studied Aristotle, they saw that his natural science and metaphysics might bring valuable insights to Christian doctrine. The Platonism that grounded most Christian theology led to a tendency to play down the importance of empirical knowledge about the natural world. As the teachings of Augustine and Anselm indicate, the dominant theological mood was largely introspective. Observation of nature was less important than reflection on the eternal truths that could be discovered by the intellect alone. Aristotle's philosophy brought a more empirical and naturalistic perspective into the open. Although it cannot be said that these elements were entirely lacking in the Platonism of Augustine and Anselm, Aristotle's interest in nature and empirical observation turned the attention of many thinkers and helped to stimulate the feelings that nature was intelligible and that it was important to understand it more fully.

The introduction of Aristotle's empirical and naturalistic orientation seemed both to call for a fresh statement of Christian doctrine and to provide the insights and the categories that would make such a statement possible. Thus, a growing number of Christian scholars began to synthesize Aristotle's philosophy and Christian teachings. The most extensive and successful effort in this direction was that of Thomas Aquinas. His writings, including the *Summa Contra Gentiles* (c. 1258-1260) and the *Summa Theologica* (c. 1265-1272), on which we will be drawing in the forthcoming pages, reveal a brilliant mind which sifted and synthesized, extended and elaborated Aristotle's teachings so as to state the Christian faith in a way that took account of the best knowledge available and the crucial needs of the day. When Thomas died on March 7, 1274, his work was still controversial, but his views gradually assumed a normative position for all of Catholic Christianity.

Two additional points about Thomas's writings are in order. The first involves the structure of the two *Summas* mentioned above. Both works are long and complex. They are intended to be summations of Christian philosophy and theology, and their scope runs from broad metaphysical speculation to minute points of Christian doctrine. The *Summa Theologica,* which Thomas left unfinished, is intended mainly for those who already think within a Christian framework. Therefore, it relies more heavily on appeals to Scripture and earlier Christian thinkers than is the case with the *Summa Contra Gentiles,* which was directed primarily to Mohammedans and those influenced by Arabic interpretations of Aristotle. Using a form shared by numerous medieval works, the *Summa Theologica* consists of a series of articles in which Thomas poses an issue (for example, whether it can be demonstrated that God exists), summarizes important positions that have been held on the topic, and then gives his own views. The *Summa Contra Gentiles* does not follow this elaborate form, but it shares the argumentative quality of the *Summa Theologica.* In both of the *Summas,* Thomas is concerned to refute positions that he takes to be erroneous, whether they come from non-Christian sources or from within the Church.

The second point to note about these writings involves Aristotle's influence on Thomas. Thomas was struck by the fact that Aristotle's work was both genuinely philosophical and non-Christian. These features raised the question of the relation between philosophy and theology, and Thomas's writings speak to this question in greater detail than those of Augustine or Anselm. Following the insight that Aristotle is a philosopher but not a Christian theologian, Thomas asserts that there are some fundamental differences between philosophy and theology. On one hand, the philosopher, strictly speaking, begins and ends with that which can be known through reason. On the other hand, the theologian works primarily within the context of revelation. He uses reason, but he moves within the boundaries of principles that are revealed and which he accepts on authority and faith. The theologian can use philosophical arguments to oppose what is said against revelation and to clarify that which belongs to the sphere of faith. Nevertheless, these uses of philosophy will not be sufficient to make a theologian a philosopher, since the theologian will still be operating in the context of revealed truth.

Thomas holds that there are some truths (for example, the mystery of the Trinity) which are solely within the domain of revelation. We can argue from them and show that they are not contrary to reason, but demonstration of their truth through reason is impossible. On the other hand, there are some truths that are genuinely philosophical in the sense that they are not directly revealed to men by God but are rather discoverable and demonstrable through rational inquiry alone. There is, however, a third group of truths where philosophy and theology overlap. That is, some truths, such as the existence of God, are both revealed and capable of being established by reason. Thus, although philosophy and theology have fundamental differences, they come together at some important points. *Natural theology* is the name that Thomas gives to this area of overlap.

Thus far Thomas's analysis supports the view that Aristotle can be a genuine philosopher even though he is not a Christian. Philosophy, while never ultimately in conflict with Christian doctrine, seems capable of standing on its own. Thomas, however, issues some qualifications on this point, and his final position reveals a close affinity with Augustine and Anselm. Thomas not only wants to hold that philosophy and theology are never ultimately in conflict, but he also asserts that revelation and faith supplement reason. Human fulfillment and the quest for meaning in which reason participates ultimately require a relationship to God and an understanding of his nature which are only possible through revelation and faith. God's grace and man's faith complete and perfect that which can be known through rational investigations of nature. By himself Aristotle is not sufficient for salvation. But

Aristotle coupled with God's revelation and man's faith can do the job.

Thomas's distinction between philosophy and theology makes it clear that human reason has some basic limitations. What knowledge, then, can men have of God without the aid of revelation? To what extent can we conceptualize accurately what God is like, and how should we proceed on this task? Moreover, what will our best grasp of God's nature entail for our understanding of freedom and evil? Thomas speaks to all of these questions in detail. As we explore his answers, we will see that he both differs from his predecessors, Augustine and Anselm, and shares many of their conclusions, including some that result in difficulties similar to those we have noted in previous chapters.

The Existence and Nature of God

Like Augustine and Anselm, Thomas thinks that we can demonstrate the existence of God, but he does not regard Anselm's ontological argument as adequate. What, then, is Thomas's approach to God, and why does he reject the ontological argument? To answer these questions, some attention must be paid to Thomas's understanding of the nature of man and the structure of human knowledge. Utilizing some distinctions from Aristotle, Thomas holds that when we deal with material things we are involved with a composite of form and matter. Ultimately the form of a thing is the structuring principle that makes the thing what it is. Matter, on the other hand, refers to an underlying element of potentiality that is capable of receiving a plurality of forms. In our practical encounters with physical things, we never deal with pure form nor with matter isolated from form. Rather, what we encounter is a unified thing, but the distinction between form and matter can and must be made in order for basic phenomena to be intelligible. Fundamental change in things is an example. A material object can be transformed or radically altered so that we no longer regard it as the same object. In such cases, however, something stays constant, and this is matter. The change that has occurred is then accounted for in terms of an alteration of form.

Thomas's account of the distinction between body and soul in human existence reflects this form-matter relationship. Thomas rejects the Platonic and Augustinian tendency to regard man as a soul inhabiting a body in a way that suggests that there are two separate entities involved. The emphasis in Thomas's theory is on the unity of man. This leads Thomas to assert that the human soul is the form of the body. The soul is the principle of vital functions, sensation, and intellectual operations. In combination with the matter that it informs, the human organism is produced. The human being that inhabits the natural world is neither form alone nor matter alone, and thus it is neither body alone nor soul alone. In order to maintain his doctrine of immortality, Thomas does hold that not every intellectual function of the soul is intrinsically related to the body, but, when he is considering man as a part of the natural order, his emphasis is clearly on the unity of body and soul, matter and form, in man.

This emphasis is further revealed in Thomas's account of the structure of human knowledge. Thomas is an empiricist in the sense that he believes that all our knowledge originates with sense experience. He does not believe that our knowledge is restricted to sense experience, but one meaning of the idea that the soul is the form of the body is that the functioning of our intellect depends on sense experience. There are no innate ideas in the mind, but rather the proper function of the human intellect is to learn and know from an original sensory encounter with the natural world. Even the soul's knowledge of itself, which is the result of reflection on its action in the world via the body, depends on this original encounter.

This empirical slant in Thomas's understanding of human knowledge has important ramifications for his arguments concerning God's existence and for his position on the possibility of accurate conceptualization of God's nature. Consider, for example, Thomas's rejection of Anselm's ontological argument. Thomas does not want to reject Anselm's conclusion that we can demonstrate that God exists. What he does reject is Anselm's method of arriving at this conclusion.

Anselm's argument moves from reflection on the concept of God to the assertion that God exists. Thomas raises at least three objections to Anselm's reasoning, all of which involve the attempt to move from an idea in the mind to existence beyond the mind. First, he suggests that Anselm's argument is inconclusive because not everyone may agree with Anselm's definition of God as that than which nothing greater can be conceived. Other ways to define God may be possible, although it should be pointed out that it is unlikely that Thomas himself would disagree with Anselm's definition. Second, even if everyone should agree that this definition of God is proper, a definition is not sufficient to demonstrate existence in reality as well as in idea. Here Thomas reiterates Gaunilo's principle that a conception in the mind is never sufficient to guarantee existence beyond the mind. Thomas thinks that, if we hold Anselm's definition of God, it is true that we will *think* of God as existing, but it does not follow that God does exist beyond the mind.

The third objection is a slight recasting of the second. Thomas suggests that Anselm's argument entails that the proposition "God exists" is self-evidently true for men. That is, simply on the basis of our possession of an idea of God, and without reference to anything else, we can know that God exists. For Thomas, a proposition is self-evidently true when the predicate or the quality being attributed to the subject is necessarily contained in the essence or the nature of the subject (for example, as would be the case in the proposition "A man is an animal"). Thomas takes this to mean that before we can know that a proposition is self-evidently true we must know the essence or the nature of the subject under discussion. Moreover, he thinks that in Anselm's case we would have to have an immediate nonsensory grasp of God's nature or an innate understanding of his essence in order to know that the proposition "God exists" is self-evidently true. However, Thomas's empirical slant denies this possibility. Thomas believes that all our knowledge is grounded in sense experience, and, since God transcends the sensory order, we do not possess and cannot obtain the direct grasp of God's nature that is required to make Anselm's argument work.

These objections are interesting because they may say more about Thomas than they do about Anselm. Anselm had already taken some steps to counter the first two objections that Thomas proposes. With respect to the first, Anselm's argument does not rest on the claim that everyone will immediately accept his definition of God, but only on the claim that, if any person thinks carefully and critically about what he means when he speaks about God, he will find no sound reason to disagree with Anselm's formulation. Second, Anselm might point out that Thomas has missed the uniqueness of the concept of God and that he has simply begged the question in asserting that there are no instances where conceptualization in the mind gives certain knowledge of the existence of the concept's referent. In the third place, Anselm might argue that Thomas has not conclusively demonstrated that it is impossible to move from meditation on the idea of God to a grasp of God's nature sufficient to make the argument work. Even if one accepts Thomas's principle that all our knowledge is grounded or originates in sense experience, the possibility of this apprehension of God may not be eliminated. Anselm's argument does not depend on our having a concept of God prior to or in isolation from sense experience. The concept of God can come to us in any number of ways, but Anselm's point is that once we have the concept, meditation on it is sufficient to bring us certain knowledge of the reality of God.

Thus, if it is the case that we are left with some uncertainty about the validity of Anselm's ontological argument, we also ought to have some uncertainty about Thomas's claim to have demonstrated the argument's invalidity. Thomas's analysis does show, however, his commitment to the view that any valid attempts to demonstrate the existence of God will have to move to God from our empirical experiences of things in the natural world, rather than from meditation on ideas alone. This viewpoint is what Thomas stresses when he says, "It remains, therefore, that man is to reach the knowledge of God through reasoning by way of the likenesses of God found in His effects."[1]

Although he rejects Anselm's ontological argument, Thomas thinks that God's existence can be demonstrated by reasoning from empirical data. We may not apprehend God immediately, but a rational analysis of phenomena in the natural order pushes us to an affirmation of God's reality. In the *Summa Theologica,* Thomas states that God's existence can be demonstrated in five ways.[2] We will look briefly at each of these arguments. Before we do so, however, it will be well to point out that, in addition to starting from perceptible things and events, the arguments share several other features. First, each rests on the principle that there must be a final stopping point in any chain of explanation. Infinite regresses of causes or explanatory principles are ruled out. Moreover, the arguments also depend on the idea that the point of final rest cannot be within the series for which one is accounting. Rather, this point must be both outside the series and different in nature from it or any of its members. Finally, each argument arrives at a principle (for example, a first efficient cause or an absolutely necessary being), and Thomas asserts that each of these ultimate factors, which are needed to account for natural phenomena, are actually manifestations of one God.

The first argument starts with our experiences of motion or change. Following Aristotle, Thomas interprets motion or change in terms of the transformation of potentiality into actuality. A thing cannot be moved unless it has a potential for movement, and for this potential to be actualized, something actual must set the thing in motion. In addition, since it is impossible that the same thing can be simultaneously actual and potential in the same respect (for instance, something cannot be actually hot and potentially hot in the same respect at the same time, or I cannot be actually sitting and potentially sitting in the same respect simultaneously), it is apparent that "whatever is moved must be moved by another."[3] Moreover, if that by which something is moved is itself moved, as is the case in our experience, then a third mover must be posited. An infinite regress of these moved movers, however, is unintelligible, and hence is to be rejected as an adequate explanation of movement. Thus, our experience pushes us to assert that there must be a first, unmoved mover, which men recognize as God.

A few additional remarks concerning Thomas's understanding of the need for a *first,* unmoved mover will help to clarify the argument. When Thomas argues that the infinite regress is unintelligible, he is primarily referring to the idea that all relationships of dependency must have a stopping point. That is, there must be something on which other beings are dependent but which is itself not dependent on anything else. Thus, the unmoved mover is *first* in the sense that everything is dependent on it and it is dependent on nothing. By placing the emphasis in this way, Thomas does not restrict firstness to a temporal quality. In fact, following Aristotle, Thomas admits the impossibility of proving the nonexistence of a series of moved movers going back infinitely into the past. That is, it cannot be demonstrated either that the past is finite or that there was a time in the past when no moved movers existed, although Thomas accepts on faith the Christian teaching that the world has not always existed. Even if it is impossible to demonstrate these points, however, Thomas thinks that the series of moved movers, whether finite or infinite, requires something beyond itself to explain its existence. A first unmoved mover, a creator who is ultimate and independent and whose existence is necessary rather than contingent, is required.

Similar considerations operate in Thomas's second argument, which concentrates on cause and effect relationships in general. The natural world functions in terms of efficient causality. That is, everything that we directly encounter in the natural order is an effect of a cause that has produced it. This means that, strictly speaking, nothing in the natural order can be the cause of itself. To meet the conditions necessary for causing itself, the thing would have to exist prior to itself, which is an absurdity. On the other hand, it is not intelligible to rest with an infinite series of efficient causes in the natural order. An ultimate grounding is required, and therefore there must be a first efficient cause, which, again, men recognize to be God. God stands as the ultimate and necessary source of all the cause and effect relationships we know.

The third argument focuses on the nature of existence itself and utilizes a distinction between necessary and contingent existence. In the natural order we see that things come into existence and perish. Such beings are contingent. If we should assert, however, that contingent existence is the only kind of existence, we find ourselves in trouble. Any existent which is contingent, and therefore capable of nonexistence, has also come into being and hence at some juncture did not exist. Moreover, Thomas asserts that, if it is possible for everything not to exist, then at some time there was nothing in existence. If this were true, however, there would be nothing in existence now, because contingent beings cannot generate their own existence. But clearly things do exist now, and this means that there must be something that exists necessarily. Furthermore, there must be one ultimate necessary being. This conclusion is generated by the fact that any necessary being either has its necessity caused by another necessary being or it does not. However, just as was the case with efficient causes, it is impossible that there can be an infinite regress of necessary beings, and therefore we are forced to acknowledge the existence of one ultimate necessary being, which is God.

Again, some additional comments are needed to bring out Thomas's position in this argument. One of the interesting components of the argument is Thomas's assertion that if it is possible for everything not to exist, then at some time there was nothing in existence. Earlier in the proof, when Thomas speaks of the possible nonexistence of things, the implication is that he is speaking about particular entities or things. But when he argues that if it is possible for everything not to exist, then at some point there was nothing in existence, he shifts from a consideration of individual things to a consideration of all individual things whose nonexistence is possible. It is also possible for the totality of individual things whose nonexistence is possible not to exist. Coupling this possibility with the principle that something is capable of nonexistence only if there is a point at which it did not exist, Thomas concludes that if every existent thing is contingent, there must have been a time when nothing existed. If there was ever a time when nothing existed, nothing could exist now. However, by virtue of the fact that contingent beings exist now, we know that there must be one ultimate necessary being which is their source.

Thomas's fourth argument is inspired by Augustine and Anselm as well as by Aristotle. It moves to God from the degrees of truth, goodness, and like properties in the things of the natural order. When we judge things comparatively with respect to such positive characteristics, we do so in terms of something which is the maximum of the quality of perfection in question. Now, Thomas asserts, that which is the maximum of the quality we are noting must be the cause of the quality in all the things that possess it. Here we see an idea stressed by Augustine and Anselm; namely, that possession of a quality of perfection (for example goodness) in a contingent being ultimately requires a noncontingent grounding which is that quality itself. Moreover, Thomas argues that whatever is supreme in goodness or truth is also supreme in being, and whatever is supreme in being is the cause of being in all things that exist. If these things are not the case, then the conditions that are required to make basic comparative judgments intelligible are eliminated. But such judgments are intelligible. Thomas's conclusion, then, is that we are pushed to acknowledge one ultimate cause of goodness, truth, and being, and this is God.

The last major argument for God's existence that Thomas presents in the *Summa Theologica* is often called the *teleological argument* or the *argument from design*. We live in a world in which things that lack knowledge (for example, natural bodies) still function in patterned and ordered ways. As Thomas puts it, they "act for an end."[4] Moreover, this order occurs with such regularity that it is unthinkable that it is due to chance. The presence of pattern or design in that which lacks knowledge points to the reality of a transcendent directing intelligence. That which lacks knowledge cannot be said to move itself toward an end or toward the fulfillment of a purpose, but some intelligent being must exist through whom "all natural things are directed to their end; and this being we call God."[5]

In the *Summa Contra Gentiles* there is also an argument from design, but it is cast in a slightly different way from that in the *Summa Theologica*. First, Thomas argues that things that are "contrary and discordant" cannot be maintained through time as parts of a single order unless there is a governing intelligence whose plan makes their coexistence possible. In our world we find that things of widely diverse natures do exist and they they exist together in one order. "There must therefore be some being by whose providence the world is governed. This we call God."[6]

If Thomas's arguments are valid, he has shown that there is (1) a first, unmoved mover, (2) a first efficient cause of all that exists, (3) one ultimate necessary being, (4) an ultimate source of being and all perfections, and (5) an intelligence that governs the universe. Moreover, he thinks that each argument points to the existence of a single reality, whom men will acknowledge to be God. It is worth noting that in the context of the demonstrations themselves, Thomas does not argue much for the validity of the idea that all the arguments point to one God. However, his later discussion clarifies his reasoning on this point. Moving from the conclusion of the third argument, namely, that there is one ultimate necessary being and that men will recognize this being to be God, Thomas suggests that the qualities noted in the conclusions of all the other arguments will be found in the one ultimate necessary being of the third proof. Thus, the arguments can all be taken as pointing to one God.

If we start with God as the ultimate necessary being, we can assert that such a being will contain no unactualized potentiality. To deny this would be to assert that God could become other than he is. Thomas takes this introduction of contingency to be sufficient to deny the original claim that God is the ultimate necessary being. If God can really become other than he is, there is a sense in which his existence is not necessary. This conclusion entails either that he is presently less than the ultimate necessary being or that he possesses the capacity to become less than the ultimate necessary being, which is a defect that is incompatible with the existence of the ultimate necessary being. God, therefore, must be pure actuality. Thomas understands this assertion to mean that there is no difference between God's nature or essence and God's existence (that is, we cannot speak of God's nature without implying that he exists; God's essence is to exist fully). Moreover, if a being is fully actual, this means that it is perfection itself, since if it lacked any perfection, it would involve the potentiality of being greater or of having something added to it. In addition to involving the power to be the first, unmoved mover and the first efficient cause of all that exists, this being's perfection, which is the ultimate source and norm for all other manifestations of perfection (for example, goodness, truth, and the like), also includes the knowledge required for the governance of the universe. Thus, the existence of God as the ultimate necessary being, which is the conclusion reached by Thomas's third argument, implies the qualities designated in all the other arguments. Thomas takes this implication to be sufficient evidence for asserting that each argument points to one God.

Thomas describes God in terms similar to those used by Anselm and Augustine. Not only is God fully actual, immutable, eternal, simple, incorporeal, and infinite, but he is also absolutely good, omnipotent, omniscient, just, and loving. Thomas recognizes, however, that his understanding of the nature of human knowledge requires him to say something about the accuracy and the significance of our statements concerning God's nature. We can move from an analysis of the natural world to definite knowledge of the existence of God, but Thomas is unwilling to admit that we have the intellectual power to grasp God's nature directly. Thus, on what grounds are we justified in speaking about God's nature and in describing him with the terms noted above in particular?

Thomas thinks there are two fundamental ways that we can follow in speaking about God's nature. Both move from our understanding of things in the natural world to a description of God, and although neither gives us an exact and exhaustive comprehension of God's nature, each gives us trustworthy insights. The first way, known as the *via remotionis* or the *via negativa,* is to learn something about God by coming to recognize what he is not. For example, if we say that God is incorporeal (that is, not corporeal), we can distinguish him from many other beings and we may move closer to a precise understanding of how he differs from everything else that exists. Negative differentiation is not identical with positive affirmation of attributes, but it moves us in a fruitful direction.

One further point about the *via negativa* is important. When we deny a quality to God, we are not denying it to him because he lacks any perfection. Rather, our intention is to point out that God far exceeds any perfection that the quality may designate. Our denial of a quality to God is a way of specifying his nature by indicating his superiority to the limited perfection of things in the world. Thus, if we say that God is not corporeal, we are saying neither that he is less than a body nor that he lacks any perfection. We are saying instead that he is more than a body and that he lacks the imperfections that are entailed in being corporeal.

Working in this negative way, Thomas asserts that God is not only incorporeal, but also immutable, to cite but two examples. We are justified in saying that God is incorporeal because an ultimate necessary being must be fully actual, while every corporeal being entails some degree of potentiality. We can say that God is immutable (that is, not changing) for similar reasons. If God is not immutable, then he can change. But change is possible only where potentiality is present, and the presence of potentiality in God is incompatible with his being fully actual. To say that God is incorporeal and immutable does not give us a direct, positive grasp of God's nature, since he ultimately transcends our understanding. Nevertheless, these assertions about God are proper, and they focus our attention in the right direction.

Not every predicate that we apply to God functions in the negative manner that we have just described. Some predicates, such as goodness or wisdom, function more affirmatively and directly in our descriptions of God. Our problem, however, is this: Since the qualities that we attribute to God are primarily experienced by us as they are found in things in the natural world, and since the terms that we use to describe God positively are also used to describe creatures, how can we show that our positive claims about God are legitimate? God, after all, transcends his creation, and this suggests that positive claims about God may not be possible. Put another way, we seem to face the following dilemma: Either the positive qualities that we attribute to God are legitimately applicable only to creatures, in which case our positive descriptions of God are invalid, or we are forced to empty the attributes of the meaning they have when applied to creatures, in which case our speech about God is likely to be devoid of meaning.

Thomas takes a middle path on this issue, and his answer includes the second way of speaking about God's nature. On the one hand, Thomas accepts the idea that no quality that we attribute to God is predicated *univocally*. For example, when we say that God is good, the term "good" does not convey exactly the same meaning as when we say that Socrates is good. On the other hand, the term "good" is not used *equivocally* in this situation. When we say that God is good and that Socrates is good the meaning of the term "good" is not completely different in the two cases. Qualities can be attributed to God *analogically*. In analogical predication, an attribute is assigned to two different things on the basis of a resemblance between them. An attribute that functions in this way does not carry an identical meaning in both of its applications, but there is a common core or direction of meaning that is involved. Moreover, Thomas thinks that there is a firm basis of resemblance between God and man which makes analogical predication possible. Creatures have a real relation to God. They depend on him for their existence, and Thomas interprets this relation as entailing the fact that the creatures reveal qualities of the creator. Thus, when we see qualities of perfection in creatures, we can attribute these to God analogically. In doing so, however, we must be clear about the fact that we are not saying that the creature has the quality in an eminent fashion and that God has it only secondarily. On the contrary, we are saying that God has the quality in the highest degree and that the presence of the perfection in creatures points us back to the absolute perfection of God.

Like his use of the *via negativa,* Thomas's understanding of analogy makes it clear that man's knowledge of God's nature is not exact or exhaustive. In this life we do not encounter God fully, but always incompletely through the mediation of the natural world. Nevertheless, Thomas is firmly convinced that we can know the existence of God through his effects. Moreover, he thinks that we are justified in affirming that God's nature can be at least partially grasped and that the description of God provided by Christian teachings is both essentially accurate and adequate for our needs. But now let us turn briefly to another question: How does Thomas account for man's experiences of freedom and evil?

Freedom and Evil

Thomas's use of Aristotle does not force him into radical disagreement with Augustine and Anselm as far as a basic description of God's nature is concerned. He differs from Anselm and Augustine more in his methodology than in his conclusions about what God is like. Nevertheless, there are some interesting variations that emerge in Thomas's discussion of freedom and evil.

We can begin by elaborating on God's relation to the world. Thomas emphasizes the idea that God created this world freely and not out of necessity, which implies that other worlds are at least logically possible and that God's power is sufficient to have brought any of them into existence. At the same time, Thomas affirms the absolute perfection and goodness of God. Now consider the following question: Is this world the best of all the possible worlds? It would seem that Thomas's answer ought to be affirmative, for if God did not create the best of all possible worlds, the absoluteness of his goodness would be compromised. Interestingly enough, however, this is not the line that Thomas takes. The freedom of God seems to have precedence over the idea that God *must* create the best of all possible worlds to be consistent with his absolute goodness. If the latter idea is given priority, God acts necessarily, but Thomas takes God's freedom and omnipotence to allow the theoretical possibility that God could have created a better world than this one. "Yet God could make other things, or add something to the present creation; and then there would be another and a better universe."[7] In fact, however, God chose this particular world, and, since his will is immutable, no real change is possible.

One of the interesting implications of Thomas's view is this: If we say that God is good and that he had to create this world because it is the best possible world, then we may not only be compromising God's freedom, but we may also be calling his goodness into question. That is, Thomas seems to be aware of the fact that it is not too difficult to imagine a world that would be better than the one that presently exists. If we take this world to be the best manifestation of God's goodness, we may be inclined to say that God is not so good after all.

Thomas's insight on this point, however, raises other questions. For example, if this is not the best of all possible worlds, then why did God create it? Or to put the issue in a slightly different way, if, as Thomas asserts, God's will and goodness are not in conflict, how can God avoid creating the best of all possible worlds? Thomas does not answer these questions clearly, although he offers some apologies for his inability to do so and goes on to treat some related issues. It is clear that Thomas cannot allow conflict in God and still maintain God's unity, so the path is not open to say that this world exists because God's will dominates over his wisdom. In fact, it is really not possible to say precisely why this world does exist. To think that one could say why it exists would be to presume an understanding of God's nature that it is not possible for us to achieve.

We can be sure, however, that this is a good world. God, who is goodness itself, does not create evil. To do so would be contrary to his nature. Moreover, since evil is actually a lack or a privation, Thomas holds that it is not possible, strictly speaking, to create it directly. To regard it in this way would be to confuse it with a positive entity, which is precisely what it is not. Thomas is not saying that evil is an illusion. Evil is real, but its reality is that of a lack or a privation and not that of a positive thing.

What, then, makes evil appear? What is its relation to man's freedom and to God's knowledge? To start with God's knowledge, Thomas couples the denial of God's direct creation of evil with the traditional affirmation that, since God's knowledge is exhaustive, he knows all evil, both possible and actual. God creates with full cognizance of evil; he permits evil to have a place in the world, but he does not create it directly. Nevertheless, Thomas is sensitive to the fact that if God creates with full knowledge that evil will be present in the world, there is a sense in which it is natural to say that God's permitting of evil makes him responsible for it.

Thomas develops and qualifies this idea along the following lines. In creating our particular world, God produces a world that involves a capacity for violent natural processes, suffering, destruction, sin, and death. Moreover, he knows the precise occurrences of these phenomena. To the extent that another world was possible, God is responsible for the reality of these phenomena in the existing world. This is not to say, however, that God's choice of this world is dictated by a desire or specific choice of these evils. God does not want them for their own sake; he merely permits them to exist. But this qualification raises an additional question: Why does God permit them to exist? Thomas's analysis and the problems it entails move in the following direction. First, he suggests that the evil is permitted because the very nature of the things in the natural order entails a capacity for destruction, suffering, and death. Two objections, however, can be raised against this view. First, it seems possible to say that the capacity might exist without requiring actualization of evil, or at least without requiring the vast appearance of evil that we experience. These points, in fact, are precisely what Thomas emphasizes with respect to human freedom. Thus, to say that a certain capacity is entailed by the mere existence of a thing is not sufficient to account for the actualization of the evils in question.

Second, since Thomas has already admitted that God could, in principle, have created a world that is better than this one, and since it seems that one likely candidate for such a world would be one in which evil is at least less rampant than we presently find it, one finds himself pushed in the direction of thinking that, if Thomas's God chose this world, he also chose directly the evil that it contains. The difficulty for Thomas is that the completeness of God's knowledge in creating really makes it impossible to draw a viable distinction between (1) God's being responsible for evil in the minimal sense of permitting it and (2) his being responsible for evil in the stronger sense of producing it in the act of creating.

Thomas, of course, tries to escape from the full force of this charge by arguing that in the case of beings with freedom (for example men) God's knowledge is knowledge of the use of freedom. Hence, this knowledge does not cause what it knows. As we saw with Anselm, however, this idea rests on a weak and inadequate sense of freedom. In Thomas's view, freedom is merely equated with a lack of absolute necessity, and freedom is in no way taken to undercut the exhaustiveness of God's knowledge. But it is precisely this completeness of knowledge in God that reintroduces a sense of determination that is incompatible with man's experience of freedom. God's immutability precludes any change in his being. Theoretically speaking, God can see the possibility of things other than those that exist, but practically speaking, the world and every man's existence are complete and fixed in God's knowledge. Thomas's theory pushes toward a theological determinism that not only robs men of the validity of their experience of freedom, but also implies that the evil we do and encounter is fixed and unavoidable. Nothing could be more antithetical to our experiences and basic hopes than these views. Even acknowledging the possibility that if we had a sharper intellect, we would see that the conflict between our experiences and hopes and Thomas's God is apparent rather than real, it is doubtful that many contemporary men will find the implications of this aspect of Thomas's doctrine of God to be either desirable or believable.

Some Problems and Useful Insights in Thomas's Thought

Since our exposition of Thomas's views on basic issues concerning freedom and evil has already pointed out some unsolved difficulties in his theory, let us merely summarize the basic problems and then look briefly at some insights that emerge from his work. The problems that Thomas leaves us are essentially the same as those that emerge from Augustine and Anselm: (1) Thomas's God, who is characterized by completeness, immutability, and eternality (that is, nontemporality), seems incompatible with our sense of freedom. Merely equating freedom with a lack of absolute necessity is not sufficient to prevent the conclusion that Thomas ultimately reduces freedom to a form of theological determinism. (2) Thomas's attempt to distinguish between God's permitting evil and his direct causation of it fails to be convincing. Again, this failure is largely due to his description of God as complete, immutable, and nontemporal. In spite of Thomas's objections, the presence of evil and its quantity and quality seem to be fixed from eternity by God's knowledge and will.

The issues above suggest some insights that can emerge from our study of Thomas. These insights present themselves in the form of problems. By seeing the difficulties in Thomas's theory, we are made aware of still other basic questions that need attention if we are to obtain a view of God that is adequate for our present needs. One such issue is this: Faced by the difficulties entailed by Thomas's views on freedom and evil, how is our thinking about God to be shaped? Should we take an existing theological theory as normative, or should we regard our own fundamental experiences as normative in the sense that no theological theory can be viable unless (1) the integrity of these basic experiences is preserved, and (2) they are understood to be foundational factors in our attempts to understand what God might be like. If we follow Thomas's professed methodology, it is clear that we have to move from the world to God, from our experiences to a viable theological theory. Thomas claims that he does this, but another question that we should ask is this: Has he really moved from the world and experience to God, and, if so, why does his theory end up with the grating effects that we have noted? Moreover, even if we regard God as radically transcending the world, does every sound theory about God have to entail the emphasis on completeness, immutability, and nontemporality that Thomas finds so necessary?

There is still another point that needs attention. When Thomas says that this is not the best of all possible worlds and that God could have created a better one, he both hits on a contemporary feeling and raises a crucial question for theologians today. Why did God select this world from among the possibilities available to him, and what does the existence of this world say about God's goodness? Thomas claims that this world is the result of God's goodness, but he does not explain very clearly why this world was chosen over some others that might be regarded as better. Thomas's lack of clarity on these issues leaves us uneasy. But in producing this uneasiness in us, Thomas gives us this insight: If we are now to have a religiously adequate view of God, we must say more than Thomas does about God's goodness and his purposes in creating.

People today are likely to be more interested in intelligible treatments of these issues than in attempts to prove God's existence. We live in an age that is generally skeptical about the possibility of proving the existence of God, and almost every contemporary student who reads Thomas's proofs of God's existence finds them inconclusive. This tendency is largely due to the fact that the student is not prepared to admit the self-evidence of a fundamental assumption underlying the arguments. Thomas's arguments rest on the premise that an infinite regress of causes or reasons is ultimately unintelligible, and hence ultimately impossible. If one questions that assumption, Thomas's arguments cannot get off the ground. Until one is convinced that the assumption is valid, the proofs will never be fully convincing.

We know that certainty is scarce in most areas of life, not only in relation to our claims about God's existence. Thus, without much lamenting, contemporary men will accept the idea that God's existence cannot be finally demonstrated. But accepting this notion does not rule out the possibility that men can have a lively interest in what God might be like. Moreover, if an intelligible account of God's nature can be given, this could be sufficient to stimulate both belief in his existence and religious commitment. Thomas's proofs and his discussion of God's nature give us one possible view of God, but this view is not the only one that can exist and it may not be the most adequate for our present needs.

Thomas helps us to see once more that a theory which emphasizes God's completeness, immutability, and nontemporality to the exclusion of qualities such as open-endedness, change, and temporality will clash with our understanding of some of the most basic and obvious features of our world and lives. However, if we take seriously Thomas's belief that we know God through his effects, and if incompleteness, change, and temporality are qualities of existence that are marked in our experience, then perhaps we must also take seriously the idea that those qualities are basic to God's nature too. A theory about God that incorporates such an emphasis would, I think, take us far in the direction of a believable view of God.

What could be the central advantage of developing such a view? My answer is that it could provide the basis for a pattern of meaning that would help men to find lasting significance and structure for their lives in a world where many claim that human existence is legitimately described only in terms of its ultimate absurdity, unintelligibility, and meaninglessness.

Our discussion of Augustine, Anselm, and Thomas gives us a feeling for basic elements in classical Christian theology. In the next three chapters, we will find Leibniz, Hume, and Kant examining many of these fundamental teachings. Leibniz will be more an apologist for his predecessors than either Hume or Kant, but all three of these philosophers will help to make us aware of issues that we must face now if we are to avoid the conclusion that, for us at least, God is dead.

V

LEIBNIZ AND
THE PROBLEM OF EVIL

Leibniz's Life and The Context of the "Theodicy"

As we turn to Leibniz, we enter an era that is vastly different from that of Augustine, Anselm, and Thomas. At the same time, however, we will see that there are basic points of continuity in the philosophy and theology of Leibniz and his predecessors. Some of these differences and points of continuity between the medieval period and the "modern" orientation that Leibniz represents can be grasped through a brief account of Leibniz's life.

Gottfried Wilhelm Leibniz, the son of a professor of philosophy, was born in Leipzig in 1646. While still a boy, he learned Greek and studied Thomistic philosophy. He entered the University of Leipzig at fifteen. There his studies introduced him to the works of Hobbes, Descartes, Kepler, and Galileo. Much in these writings was critical of the medieval tradition, but Leibniz's study of "contemporary" philosophy and science did not result in a radical rejection of earlier views. Instead, his disposition and training prepared him to play a part similar to that of Thomas. That is, Leibniz brought together medieval ideas and the newest science and metaphysics of his day, and, by making some alterations, produced an influential philosophical position of his own.

Philosophy, however, was only one of many tasks that concerned Leibniz. After his studies at Leipzig, he went to Jena and

Altdorf to study mathematics and law respectively, taking a degree
in law in 1667. He refused a teaching position at Altdorf in order
to enter the world of politics. As a diplomatic representative of the
Elector of Mainz, Leibniz lived in Paris for a time and also traveled
to England. He continued his mathematical work, and in 1676,
while in Paris, he discovered the infinitesimal calculus. Leibniz's discovery and the subsequent publication of his findings touched off a
serious quarrel with Isaac Newton. Newton had done some writing
on the infinitesimal calculus prior to Leibniz's discovery, but
Newton had not published his ideas immediately. Consequently,
when Leibniz published his findings before Newton, a bitter contro-
versy ensued concerning the priority of discovery.

After his return to Germany, Leibniz was employed by the
Duke of Hanover primarily for the purpose of writing a history of
the ducal family. Leibniz failed to complete the history, but he did
find time to work on many other fascinating projects. He founded
learned societies and in 1700 became the first president of the
Society of the Sciences in Berlin. He made proposals to unite
Catholics and Protestants, and, when these failed, he developed
plans to unite various Protestant groups. He even approached Louis
XIV of France and Czar Peter the Great of Russia with a proposal
for unifying Europe. Moreover, by the time of his death in 1716,
Leibniz had produced some philosophical writings of lasting
importance.

The *Theodicy,* which we will explore in some detail, is one of
these works. It is Leibniz's statement on the fundamental problem
of the relations between God's goodness, man's freedom, and the
reality of evil. Leibniz shares a basic interest with the men we have
already studied; namely, he wants to defend the view that neither
the omnipotence nor the goodness of God is jeopardized by the
fact that evil appears in our world. This position leads him to
defend other ideas that we have noted before: (1) Neither God nor
man acts by absolute necessity; (2) God permits evil, but he does
not create it or cause it directly; (3) God always chooses what is
best. These points of similarity between Leibniz and some of his
predecessors ought not, however, obscure the fact that he
develops his ideas in his own way within an intellectual context
that differs from that of Augustine, Anselm, and Thomas. Leibniz,
after all, lived in the astronomical and physical universe of Coperni-
cus, Galileo, Kepler, and Newton, and his philosophical and
theological thought was influenced by men such as Hobbes,
Descartes, Spinoza, and Luther in addition to the earlier figures
whom we have encountered.

What is the place of the *Theodicy* in the context of Leibniz's philosophical work? The *Theodicy* was published in 1710. Not only is it one of Leibniz's few book-length pieces, but it is also one of the few works that he published in his lifetime. Leibniz wrote much of his philosophy in letters, articles, and brief works such as the *Monadology,* which was written in 1714, but left unpublished until 1840. The latter work is probably the one for which Leibniz is best known. It is a condensation of his mature philosophical views, sketching his famous doctrine on *monads.*

Leibniz holds that the basic elements of the world are indivisible, self-contained, self-developing entities—monads—which are created by God, the only necessary and uncreated being. Although some basic features can be shared, no two monads are identical in the powers and potentialities that they possess. Moreover, each goes through a process of development to achieve the end or the goal which helps to constitute its nature. In Leibniz's view, monads do not exert causal influence on each other, but they are not absolutely cut off from one another. They affect one another through God's planning and mediation. In bringing the world into being, God creates each monad with all of the others in mind. In addition, each monad, from its own particular perspective, reflects the entire universe within itself. This principle accounts for the fact that the world appears differently from different perspectives and yet is also one. Leibniz understands God's creation to manifest a "preestablished" harmony in which the greatest possible variety of beings and the greatest possible order of beings are combined. Such a world is the best of all possible worlds in the sense that God could devise none better.

God plays an important part in Leibniz's metaphysics, but the details of his activity are not spelled out very clearly in the *Monadology.* The *Theodicy* does better on this score, especially where problems about freedom and evil are concerned. Leibniz wrote the *Theodicy* largely to refute the contentions of Pierre Bayle (1647–1706), a French philosopher who maintained that faith and reason are not always in harmony and that, in particular, it is not possible to obtain a sound account that shows how a perfect (that is, omnipotent and absolutely good) God and evil can coexist. In the *Theodicy,* Leibniz argues at length against Bayle's views on these issues, and this work will be the major touchstone for our discussion of Leibniz's philosophy.

Like many important philosophers, Leibniz emerges as an interesting mixture of the new and the old. He lived in a time of scientific and mathematical innovations to which he himself contributed. Unlike Augustine, Anselm, and Thomas, his public life was directed more toward secular affairs than toward religious matters. Philosophically he was in touch with contemporary issues. On the other hand, his thought is not correctly characterized as breaking radically with the views of Augustine, Anselm, and Thomas. Leibniz holds much in common with them, and he can be regarded as an apologist for their views. In making this assertion, however, it must be noted that philosophers are like Leibniz's monads: Two are never identical. Thus, we will find that Leibniz shifts and treats classical statements in his own way.

The Relationship between Faith and Reason

The first major issue that Leibniz takes up in the *Theodicy* is the relationship between faith and reason. In the discussion of this topic, he articulates some basic principles that govern his treatment of God's relation to freedom and evil. At the outset, Leibniz says:

> I assume that two truths cannot contradict each other; that the object of faith is the truth God has revealed in an extraordinary way; and that reason is the linking together of truths, but especially (when it is compared with faith) of those whereto the human mind can attain naturally without being aided by the light of faith.[1]

Leibniz is closest to Thomas at this point.

There are differences between what is believed through faith and what is known through reason, but there is no ultimate conflict between the two spheres, and there are areas of overlap (for instance, the existence of God is demonstrable as well as being revealed). Moreover, reason, the linking together of truths, is not only central to philosophy, natural science, mathematics, and logic, but it also plays an important part in theology, which is the investigation of the truths of revelation. In all cases, the task of reason is to indicate the validity or the invalidity of the premises from which we begin, to draw out the implications of our basic premises, and to show the relationships between our ideas. The goal is to obtain finally demonstrable conclusions wherever possible. In some cases, we must rest with conclusions that are merely probable, but this stopping point is not the most desirable.

In the *Monadology*, Leibniz says that truths can be divided into two kinds. First there are truths of reason. These truths can be known a priori (that is, without testing in sense experience), and they are characterized by their logical necessity. A truth is logically necessary if its denial produces a contradiction. For example, the proposition "An equilateral rectangle is a rectangle" is logically necessary, since I cannot deny it without contradicting myself. On the other hand, there are truths of fact. These truths are contingent. They can be denied without producing a contradiction. Moreover, Leibniz holds that apart from one exception, assertions of God's existence, all true propositions that assert the existence of things are truths of fact and not truths of reason.

There is more, however, to say about the truths of fact. For Leibniz, there is a sense in which even the truths of fact are necessary, which is to say that they are also truths of reason. This concept is brought out in the *Theodicy* where Leibniz says that the truths of reason are actually of *two* kinds. First, there are the logically necessary propositions, which we have noted. In addition, there are truths that are founded on what Leibniz calls "moral necessity."[2] The truths of fact are ultimately grounded in this manner. That is, Leibniz believes that nothing exists without a sufficient reason (an ultimate and final reason) for its existence. The sufficient reason for a thing's existence is ultimately its fitness for existence. For example, we see that nature functions in terms of physical laws, but we can ask why these laws exist. Leibniz's answer is that they exist because they are supremely fit for existence. They are vital factors in God's creation of the best of all possible worlds.

If there is a "moral necessity" in the second kind of truths of reason, we must still be careful to distinguish this necessity from logical necessity. The distinction rests in this fact: In cases of moral necessity, both God and men could conceive of states of affairs other than those that actually exist without falling into the absurdity of contradiction. One practical difference that this distinction makes for Leibniz is that God cannot be conceived as being under any absolute necessity to bring this particular world into being. Leibniz establishes God's freedom in creation by saying that, in principle, other worlds could have been created.

Nevertheless, following Leibniz's treatment in the *Theodicy,* all truths, strictly speaking, are truths of reason. God not only knows the logically necessary truths, but he also operates on the principle of sufficient reason, which means that he grasps a priori and chooses in terms of the ultimate fitness of things for existence. Men, on the other hand, do not always possess an a priori grasp or an exhaustive empirical account in terms of the principle of sufficient reason. Men can see that certain things exist, and they can always reason to some empirical understanding of the fitness of these things for existence, but they are not capable of seeing things in the a priori and detailed fashion that characterizes God. In Leibniz's universe, a man can know that everything is ultimately intelligible and rational and that every truth is really a truth of reason in the broad sense of the *Theodicy*, but, practically speaking, no man comprehends all truths as truths of reason.

The existence of the world rests on (1) God, (2) the principle of noncontradiction, and (3) the principle of sufficient reason. These three factors are bound up together inextricably. As we will see shortly, the principles of noncontradiction and sufficient reason play important parts in Leibniz's demonstrations of God's existence. At the same time, an account of God's nature and his creation further reveals a fundamental bond between God and these principles. To say, as Leibniz does, that there is unity and order in God and creation is to say that God's being and action reveal the principle of noncontradiction. To say that God and his creation are good is to say that God operates in terms of the principle of sufficient reason. These principles would not exist apart from God, but the very existence of God makes them binding in existence. They are themselves an aspect of God's being, and no claim that conflicts with either of these foundational principles can possibly be true.

These latter comments take us to two more issues. Leibniz treats one of them directly at the beginning of the *Theodicy* while the other takes us back to the *Monadology*. The first issue is this: What should be done when objections are brought against fundamental articles of faith (for example, the doctrine of the Trinity) with the intention of showing that these articles are not true? Leibniz makes the following points in response: (1) Articles of faith cannot be demonstrated by reason. (2) Nevertheless, no truth is contrary to reason. Therefore, if an objection is brought against a truth, it will be possible to show either that the objection is flatly false or that the objection has only the force of probability behind it and need not be taken as a sufficient reason to give up belief in the article of faith. (3) Thus, the proper way to proceed against objections brought to bear on articles of faith is either to demonstrate their falsity or to show that their force is only based on some degree of probability and, hence, need not be absolutely binding on the believer. If, on the other hand, one should discover that an objection is demonstrable, then the proper position to hold is that the article of faith is false and inauthentic. In the *Theodicy*, Leibniz uses this approach extensively to complement his attempts to demonstrate that this is the best of all possible worlds.

Recognizing that one might hold on faith the truth that nothing which happens in the world is contrary to God's goodness, Leibniz takes up many possible objections against this belief and tries to show either that they are false or that they lack sufficient power to be absolutely binding on the believer.

Now let us consider the second issue. God plays an important part in Leibniz's philosophy, but what evidence is there that God exists? Leibniz thinks that reason can demonstrate that God exists and that he is wise, omnipotent, and entirely good. Introducing variations, Leibniz draws on arguments developed by previous thinkers. One example is his use of the ontological argument. Leibniz thinks that previous statements of this argument are headed in the right direction, but they are not absolutely conclusive because they assume rather than demonstrate the *possibility* of God's existence. Now, for Leibniz, possibility is measured by the principle of noncontradiction. That is, something is possible if its conception does not involve a contradiction. Thus, the task that Leibniz sets for himself is to show that the idea of God as the all-perfect being does not involve a contradiction.

To demonstrate this argument Leibniz points out that the impossibility of God's existence would lead to an absurdity. If God's existence is impossible (that is, contradictory), then the existence of everything else, including possibilities, is impossible as well. This follows because one of the things that we mean when we speak of God is that he is not only a necessary being, but also the being on which all else depends. Therefore, if God's existence is not possible, nothing is possible. But it is absurd to say that nothing is possible. We know that things have been and are possible by virtue of our existence and experience. Thus, it must be the case that God's existence is possible. Having argued that this is the case, Leibniz asserts that the ontological argument is fully valid. The conception of God as the all-perfect being entails real and necessary existence for God. In addition, God's existence and perfection entail that he is wise, omnipotent, and entirely good.

We can mention briefly two other arguments that Leibniz uses in demonstrating God's existence. One is an argument that we have seen earlier in Augustine's works. There are necessary truths whose denial involves a contradiction. These truths are known by us a priori, and they do not depend on the full actuality of the things under consideration. For example, if we think of a figure that is bounded by three straight lines, it is necessarily true that this figure will have three angles. Moreover, this truth in no way depends on the physical existence of triangles. Truths of this kind, however, are not sufficient to account for themselves. They require an adequate metaphysical grounding which is itself absolute and necessary. God's understanding is the only grounding that ultimately meets these requirements, and, therefore, God exists.

The final argument has closer affinity to Thomas's proofs. Leibniz argues from the existence of contingent truths or truths of fact to the existence of God. In this argument, he appeals to the principle of sufficient reason, which means that explanations couched in terms of infinite regresses are ultimately incomplete and inadequate. Leibniz acknowledges that within a series of contingent beings one might go to infinity in developing a causal explanation. To explain X, one might refer to Y, and to explain Y, one might refer to Z, and so on to infinity. At no point in such a series do we meet a being that does not require something else to explain it. In short, we never reach the point of having a sufficient account of the series itself. But, since everything does have a sufficient reason, something must finally account for the series. Since the series to be explained ultimately includes every contingent being, no contingent being can stop the regress and provide the sufficient reason. Therefore, we are pushed to affirm that there must be a necessary being who is the ultimate ground of all contingent existence.

Leibniz takes this being to be God, and he asserts that this ultimate, necessary being must have certain other fundamental attributes. He must, for example, be supremely intelligent. Since the existing world is contingent and since an infinite number of worlds were equally possible, Leibniz believes that the necessary being must have known and understood all of them in determining which one to actualize. This position also implies the perfection of God's power. He brings one world into being by willing it, but his power is sufficient to bring any possible world into being. Moreover, God's supreme goodness is manifested by the fact that his knowledge includes knowledge of the good, and it is in terms of this knowledge that his will moves in creation. Thus, God not only actualizes one of the possible worlds, but also the world that he chooses is the best.

We have seen enough of Leibniz's thought to know that he draws on the past and introduces novel ideas of his own. Like his predecessors, Augustine, Anselm, and Thomas, Leibniz affirms that men can demonstrate the existence of God. However, his emphases on the concept of possibility and the principles of noncontradiction and sufficient reason give his arguments a distinctive turn. In addition, although Leibniz basically accepts the distinction between faith and reason set down by Thomas, his discussion of the different kinds of truth goes beyond the accounts that we have noted previously. Finally, Leibniz is not inclined to overturn the classical view that God is best described by stressing his absoluteness of power and goodness and his completeness of knowledge. However, Leibniz combines these qualities with ideas such as (1) God's choosing from among infinite possibilities, (2) God's interest in balancing maximum variety and maximum order in creation, and (3) preestablished harmony in creation. The result is a philosophy with a unique flavor. Now we must move to a more specific consideration of the relations between God's power, goodness, and knowledge on the one hand and the realities of freedom and evil on the other.

The Nature of God, Freedom, and Evil

If we consider three questions, we will cover the main points of Leibniz's *Theodicy* and gain some insights about his understanding of the relations between the nature of God, freedom, and evil. The questions are: (1) What does Leibniz mean when he says that God created the best of all possible worlds? (2) What are the general categories of evil, and how does God relate to each? (3) What is Leibniz's view of freedom?

In answering the first question, it is important to note that Leibniz is committed to two fundamental ideas. The first is that God is absolutely perfect. Among other things, this means that God's acts are always good. Leibniz's position is clear: "Nothing can come from God that is not altogether consistent with goodness, justice and holiness."[3] To this it must be added that God is ultimately the ground of all that is. Thus, *everything* that exists is consistent with God's goodness, justice, and holiness. This doctrine, however, must not be confused with a position that would say that everything that exists is intrinsically good or good in itself. Leibniz is also committed to a second idea, namely, that there is evil in the world. Destruction, suffering, and sin are not good in themselves. Taken by themselves, we would be fully justified in saying that they ought not to exist.

On the other hand, the position that Leibniz defends pushes us to say that although evil ought not to exist considered in itself, there is still a sense in which it ought to exist, for the world that exists is the best of all possible worlds. Put another way, what Leibniz is committed to defend is the view that *the best of all possible worlds is a world in which there is evil.* Again, Leibniz states his position clearly: "It is true that one may imagine possible

worlds without sin and without unhappiness, and one could make
some like Utopian or Sevarambian romances: but these same worlds
again would be very inferior to ours in goodness."[4]

How does Leibniz (1) develop the view that this is the best of
all possible worlds and (2) defend the view that the best of all
possible worlds contains evil? The development of (1) occurs
primarily by reflecting on God's action in creating, while the
defense of (2) comes largely via refutations of objections that claim
to show that this world is not the best of all possible worlds.

Turning first to the development of Leibniz's central idea, we
need to recall a point noted earlier, namely, that God picks one
world from an infinity of possible worlds. (Leibniz uses the term
"world" to mean "the whole succession and the whole agglomeration
of all existent things, lest it be said that several worlds could have
existed in different times and different places."[5]) More than his
predecessors, Leibniz emphasizes the vastness of the possibilities
available to God in creating. Possibility is limited only by the
principle of noncontradiction. God does not act out of necessity,
so, theoretically speaking at least, he has the freedom and power to
actualize any one of the worlds. Nevertheless, God is ultimately
moved by his wisdom, and thus he creates the best of the possible
worlds. Practically speaking, this means that only one particular
world could really exist, namely, the one that is absolutely the
best. If no possible world were absolutely the best, God would
have created nothing at all.[6]

We can clarify Leibniz's position still further by drawing on his
maxim that "God wills *antecedently* the good and *consequently*
the best."[7] First, God grasps *antecedently* (that is, prior to the
actualization of any possible world) all of the possibilities, including the prevention of every evil, and he is drawn toward the actualization of each possibility only and precisely insofar as each is
good. But a difficulty arises. Even for God, not everything that is
possible and toward which he is attracted by virtue of its goodness
is *compossible* (able to coexist in the world). For example, it is
possible that it is a good for me to be awake at time X or to be
asleep at time X, but, strictly speaking, both possibilities cannot be
actualized together. The effect that this principle has for God is
that he must make a selection from among the goods that are
possible. Moreover, the selection that God makes will be governed
by his goodness and wisdom. *Consequently,* the choice that God
makes in creating is that of *the best combination of compossibles.*
Or to put it another way, since some goods must be left out of
existence, God chooses *the least defective combination of*

compossibles. Leibniz thinks that this selection will result in the best of all possible worlds, which contains both the greatest possible variety of goods and the greatest possible degree of harmony and order.

The best possible world, then, does not contain every conceivable good. Second, it is the case that this world can and even must contain some evil. This is true because God cannot duplicate his own perfection in creating. To do so would be to create himself, which is an impossibility. Therefore, any world that God creates will lack some of the perfection of God himself. Insofar as it lacks some perfection, it involves some evil. The created world will be a good world, but every possible world contains some defects which may result in destruction, suffering, and sin.

Leibniz believes that no objection can ultimately stand against the view that our world is the best of all possible worlds and that evil is compatible with the best of all possible worlds. The argument from God's action in creation makes it clear that this is the best of all possible worlds and that it must, in fact, contain some evil. If, however, objections should still be posed after the analysis above has been presented, Leibniz offers a variety of other suggestions calculated to show that the difficulties cited are not sufficient to invalidate his claims that (1) God's perfection is complete, (2) this is the best of all possible worlds, and (3) the reality of evil is compatible with both (1) and (2).

We can mention two examples of these suggestions. First, if someone persists in objecting that the presence of evil in the world shows that this is not the best of all possible worlds or that God is imperfect, it can be pointed out that experience itself tells us that the presence of some evil is a prerequisite for undeniable and fundamental goods such as the overcoming of suffering and tragedy and the achievement of success in the face of risk. Furthermore, it is well known that some experience of evil is actually beneficial for making the goodness of things stand out. For example, men do not fully appreciate health until they experience illness. Suffering, tragedy, and risk might be eliminated. If they were, however, some basic goods could not be actualized, and the existent world would be less than the best one possible.

Second, faced by the proposition that evil actually outweighs the good in this world, which makes it totally implausible to believe that God is perfect or that this is the best of all possible worlds, Leibniz asserts that this point of view is far from binding. The vastness of our universe precludes us from knowing all that exists. For example, life that is virtually free of suffering and destruction may be present in areas of our universe unknown to us. Leibniz thinks that our perspective is usually too narrow when we think about good and evil. If we reflect broadly and carefully about our own existence and domain, we will find that even there the good outweighs the evil. Thus, Leibniz asserts:

> Had we not the knowledge of the life to come, I believe there would be few persons who, being at the point of death, were not content to take up life again, on condition of passing through the same amount of good and evil, provided always that it were not the same kind: one would be content with variety, without requiring a better condition than that wherein one had been.[8]

Now consider our second question: What are the general categories of evil, and how does God relate to each? Leibniz says, "Evil may be taken metaphysically, physically and morally. *Metaphysical evil* consists in mere imperfection, *physical evil* in suffering, and *moral evil* in sin."[9] We have already encountered metaphysical evil. It is simply the imperfection that is involved in our finite existence. It has its roots in the fact that while God can create a world that is the best possible, he cannot create one that duplicates his own perfection. To do so would be to create himself, which is impossible. For Leibniz, the origin of all evil has its source in this ultimate metaphysical fact.

Two further comments about this metaphysical evil need to be made. First, metaphysical evil is equated with imperfection, and imperfection is present where something is lacking in the being in question. Evil, then, is essentially a lack, a privation, rather than a positive entity. The impact of classical theology on Leibniz is clear at this point. Second, if created existence is intrinsically imperfect in contrast to God and, hence, involves evil in the form of privation, Leibniz seems to say that God is directly responsible for causing metaphysical evil simply through his choice to create, which was not, after all, necessitated. Leibniz deals with this point in a way similar to Thomas. Since metaphysical evil is, strictly speaking, a lack, it is not directly caused or created in the way that a positive entity is. God's relationship to metaphysical evil, then, is that he permits it or cooperates to allow its existence in the world as a component that cannot be avoided in realizing the undeniable goodness of the actualization of the best of all possible worlds. God's will is directly motivated only by the good, never by evil. Thus, if evil appears in the world, it is present only because it could not be avoided in God's choice to actualize the goodness of this world. To this extent, and only to this extent, God may be said to be responsible for metaphysical evil. But this in no way refutes God's absolute perfection or the fact that this is the best of all possible worlds.

Now what is God's relation to moral evil, which Leibniz equates with sin? Moral evil originates in the intrinsic imperfections that human existence involves. Men, for example, possess a finite intellect. Hence, at times they see things confusedly, and as a result the human will does not always move as it should. Improper movement of the human will, which results from confused perception and understanding, constitutes sin for Leibniz. But since these limitations exist only through God's creative action, is it not the case that God is really the direct cause of human sin when it occurs? Leibniz's answer is negative. We have already seen that God does not will metaphysical evil directly, but only permits it or cooperates to allow its existence. Moreover, there is a basic difference between metaphysical and moral evil. If creation occurs, metaphysical evil cannot be avoided, for some privation of perfection is found in all created beings. Moral evil, on the other hand, is in principle avoidable in the world that God has created. Even with the unavoidability of metaphysical evil in creation, moral evil is not necessitated. Thus, Leibniz holds that if this moral evil occurs, it is due to man's freedom. "... God wills moral evil not at all ...."[10]

Leibniz's position will not allow him to stop here, however, and by drawing out his perspective, we see one of the curious features of his position on evil. At the same time that Leibniz disclaims God's direct responsibility in moral evil, he continues to say that this is the best possible world. The latter position implies that this world would be less than the best possible world if anything about it were different. This means that if moral evil were missing, the world would be less than the best possible. Moreover, Leibniz understands that God wills to bring this world into being, and this concept suggests, as we saw with Thomas, that Leibniz's idea that God only *permits* moral evil is misleading. On close inspection, the *permitting* appears more and more like a form of *willing*. Consequently, it is not clear that Leibniz can demonstrate a difference between them sufficient to exonerate God from responsibility for man's sin.

There is an additional problem connected to the one just noted. Leibniz says that moral evil is avoidable, but, since it results from the intrinsic imperfections of created existence (that is, the finitude of man's intellect and will), one wonders whether it is really avoidable after all. We seem to be playing with a stacked deck of cards, and it appears all too likely that moral evil is avoidable only in the minimal sense of not being absolutely necessary. If sin is the virtually unavoidable result of defects over which men have no control, God seems to be more responsible for human sin than men are.

Leibniz believes that physical evil (suffering, sorrow, and misery) is primarily the result of moral evil. Here the idea of a "result" must be taken in more than one way. Physical evil can be the result of my sin in the sense that my action can cause suffering in others or in myself either through my direct physical action or through activity that leads to circumstances which later result in such effects. In addition, Leibniz suggests that physical evil can result from moral evil in the sense that God himself can inflict suffering as a just punishment for sin and as a means to direct men toward the achievement of good states of affairs. God does not will physical evil absolutely (that is, for its own sake), but Leibniz does imply that God is more directly connected with its causation than he is with respect to moral evil. Claiming that physical evil can function as a means to that which is good and that God would only inflict such evil on these terms is, of course, Leibniz's way of arguing that the existence of physical evil is fully compatible with our assertions that God is absolutely perfect and that this is the best of all possible worlds.

Our discussion of evil in general and moral evil in particular leads us to our third major question: What is Leibniz's view of freedom? Not only is Leibniz aware of the general criticism that man's freedom and God's foreknowledge are incompatible, but also he sees that his own theory requires some elucidation if basic confusions are to be avoided. As we shall see, the elucidation results in the reduction of human freedom to a form of determinism, and this, in turn, gives added force to the view that God's relation to moral evil is really more one of willing than that of merely permitting or cooperating to allow its presence.

Leibniz makes two central claims: (1) In God's knowledge, the future is as the present. For God, our future is set and known with certainty in every detail. (2) Man's will is exempt from necessity and constraint. Now, if you put those assertions together as Leibniz does, what doctrine of freedom emerges? The basic answer is that freedom is nothing more than the lack of absolute necessity. Human actions are "free" in the sense that alternative actions can be conceived without contradiction. But this in no way rules out the fact that God knows human existence exhaustively and with certainty. Neither does it rule out the fact that specific human actions are *hypothetically necessary* factors in making this the best of all possible worlds. That is, if God creates, which, Leibniz asserts, is God's choice in the sense that it is not absolutely necessary that he create, then his nature requires him to create the best of all possible worlds. Only one particular combination of components will constitute the existence of the best of all possible worlds. God knows this, and he has in fact created a world in accordance with his knowledge. Thus, this existing world is hypothetically necessary, and since it includes specific human actions, they too are hypothetically necessary.

Even Leibniz's argument that some of these specific actions originate in the human will does not eliminate the fact that they are determined to occur via God's action in creating. Real alternatives are open only in the theoretical sense that a different course of action could occur without contradiction. These restrictions do not bother Leibniz, however, since he is content to interpret freedom in this way. This concept of freedom is true even with respect to God. Even though Leibniz talks about God's grasping of an infinity of possible worlds and the fact that God has power sufficient to create any of them, the freedom left to God is minimal at best. Practically speaking, Leibniz thinks that God's knowledge and goodness are such that God has only one real alternative, namely, to create the best of all possible worlds. Existence is a good, and God's nature as good leads him to create. Moreover, God's knowledge and goodness lead him to create the best of all possible worlds. Leibniz speaks of the "inclination" of God's will in these matters so as to suggest that an additional step—a free movement of the will, a free choice—is required to initiate the action. But by the time God's will gets into the act, the inclining forces operative on it have effectively removed all courses of action except one. Where only one course of action is really open, it is dubious whether one should speak in terms of a *free* choice.

In men, as well as in God, "[t]here is always a prevailing reason which prompts the will to its choice, and for the maintenance of freedom for the will it suffices that this reason should incline without necessitating." [11] Leibniz believes that men are created so that in their finite way they function in terms of the principle of sufficient reason. Although we are finite creatures in whom habits, desires, and emotions play an important part in shaping conduct, we also possess an intellect which leads us so that we always choose what appears to be the best. Leibniz interprets this relationship between the will and the intellect to mean that the will is not coerced but only persuaded. Although we always do what we understand to be the best, the will still chooses freely.

Once again, however, it appears that Leibniz gives freedom with one hand and takes it back with the other. His account allows for the theoretical possibility that my action at time X could have been different in the sense that an alternative is not logically contradictory. But, practically speaking, the emphasis of his theory is such that by the time my will gets into the act, the inclining factors (that is, my intellect, habits, desires, emotions, and the like) have already exerted such influence that the course of my will is rigidly fixed and without real alternatives. The reduction of human freedom to determinism is complete.

Leibniz's treatment of freedom has disturbing implications for our understanding of the evil that men bring about. Although he claims that this evil occurs only through an improper use of the human will, it is also a hypothetically necessary factor in the existence of the best of all possible worlds. When God chooses to create, this evil follows automatically. Leibniz's theory does not provide a believable view of responsibility. A theory that holds men responsible even though alternatives were really unavailable is not going to strike many men as either attractive or intellectually binding. A believable theory of responsibility requires a more radical sense of freedom, namely, one in which there is a plurality of real options from which to choose.

Leibniz draws out and clarifies implications that were in the views of Augustine, Anselm, and Thomas. All of these men speak about man's freedom and his responsibility for evil. In the end, however, necessity and determinism emerge on top. The conception that these philosophers have of God's nature and perfection makes this inevitable. Where perfection is understood so as to give primacy to completeness, immutability, and eternality, the open-endedness, change, and temporality required for adequate conceptions of freedom and responsibility are lacking.

Some Problems and Useful Insights in Leibniz's Thought

If we ask whether the theory in Leibniz's *Theodicy* is adequate for us as it stands, the answer, I think, must be negative. Leibniz's determinism may be a possible theory, but it is not a believable one because it grates so sharply against our moral and religious sensibilities. A world in which evil is unavoidable to the extent that Leibniz's theory requires will not fit with our experience of freedom and responsibility or with our religious hopes. Leibniz thought that he was making traditional doctrine intelligible and believable, but the contemporary understanding of freedom and responsibility is too radical for his theory to work now.

There is also a more general reason why Leibniz's theory will not be attractive to many people today. Leibniz is primarily an apologist for traditional Christian theology. That is, he starts from the traditional teachings and tries to show that they do, in fact, fit and illuminate human experience. There are two difficulties with his approach as far as contemporary men are concerned. First, from our perspective, Leibniz goes farther in the direction of forcing experiences to fit his theory than he does in showing that the traditional teachings actually illuminate experiences without distorting them. Second, in starting with the traditional teachings, Leibniz makes some assumptions that are presently the very points under scrutiny. An apologetic approach to theology is possible when people are agreed on first principles and assumptions, but in a time such as ours, when we are uncertain about what can and should be assumed, an apologetic stance is not likely to have much power.

Leibniz assumes that the principle of sufficient reason is a basic metaphysical fact, but is this necessarily the case? Many contemporary thinkers would not agree. Leibniz adopts the classical conception that God's perfection entails the exclusion of incompleteness, change, and temporality from his nature. But is this the only way that God's perfection can be conceived? Perhaps there is no single doctrine of divine perfection from which one diverges only at the expense of being irrational or in error.

These latter considerations have implications for still another of Leibniz's ideas. Leibniz operates with the category of "the best of all possible worlds," and he assumes that there is ultimately one actual state of affairs that fits this category. Such an outlook depends on the Greek conception that existence is ordered in terms of one fixed and absolute standard of value, which ultimately orders all things so that it is possible to speak of "the best of all possible worlds." But in our time, the truth of such a rationalistic framework is not apparent to all men who think critically. Could it not be the case, for example, that there are in fact plural standards of value and that a fundamental condition for any priorities that may hold among them is that of being chosen for a place of priority. Perhaps there is no world that is absolutely the best of all possible worlds. Rather it may be the case that a plurality of worlds is possible and that one is created not because it conforms to a standard that makes it intrinsically and absolutely the best, but because God happens to favor one set of value priorities over another that is equally possible.

Leibniz would argue that such a God is not sufficiently rational. But that charge will hold only if one accepts the assumption that rationality entails ultimate agreement on and acceptance of a single, fixed course of action. Other conceptions of rationality are possible. One such possibility may include the idea that reason often leaves us with a plurality of sound options from which we then can choose simply because we prefer one over the other. One's preference may be a reason for choosing, but not one that is absolutely binding on everyone's intellect or that rules out the possibility that a choice in terms of some other preference could be equally good.

The inadequacies of Leibniz's theory can lead us to this insight: We may do better if we conceive of God with the higher degree of freedom implied by the statements above. God himself ultimately sets the value priorities in terms of which he chooses, and his choice is not bound by any standard that is intrinsically the best. His creation of a world, then, is not the creation of the best possible world, absolutely considered, but only the creation of one world that he happens to judge good. This world is the best of all possible worlds, given the particular standard of value that God chooses. From another possible value perspective, however, this world may not come off so well.

Men and God may disagree in their evaluations of the worth of the existence of this world. In Leibniz's view, this disagreement reveals the presence of human error and the finitude of the human intellect, which prevents a clear view of the facts. A more radical view of freedom offers a different interpretation of this situation. Now men might disagree among themselves and with God as to the worth of the existence of this world simply because they can legitimately choose to employ different standards of value in judging. Humanly speaking, it is all too clear that not everyone finds this to be the best of all possible worlds, even in Leibniz's sense that the best of all possible worlds is that which is least defective. Many contemporary men do not find it difficult to conceive that much suffering and doing of evil could be eliminated without detracting from the quality of existence. On the contrary, such eliminations would, from their point of view, be a vast improvement.

If there is a sense in which we can conceive of a better world, then perhaps the major task of the philosophical theologian today is to try to say why God might create a world that can become the mixture of good and evil that we experience. What qualities of such a world might interest God especially, and why might he be motivated to create on the basis of these interests? Such issues cannot be adequately handled from Leibniz's apologetic stance. Rather, what is required is an attempt at fresh construction that moves from experience in the world to a doctrine of God. Such an enterprise may have a plurality of results, but one significant view of God could emerge by placing an emphasis on freedom and on Leibniz's idea that God creates a world in which the variety and the order of existence are in fruitful tension with each other.

Variety of existence, freedom, and order and structure all characterize our world in fundamental ways. These qualities could be basic clues to God's goal in creating. This goal might include a primary emphasis on God's establishing an order with widely varying forms of being as a context in which freedom can exist and be used creatively. This goal might be of special interest to God because (1) the creation of such a world produces something that is itself free, powerful, creative, moving, and ordered and (2) this world uniquely portrays the creator himself.

Two further points might be added to this construction, the first bearing on God's knowledge. God may know all the things that are possible, but in a world that contains genuine freedom his knowledge will have a quality of incompleteness and temporality. For example, in such a world, God does not know human lives as completely actual until they actualize themselves in time. Where freedom is concerned there is no clash with God's foreknowledge because God's foreknowledge is only knowledge of possibilities and probabilities.

The second point draws out factors of importance with regard to evil and God's appraisal of the significance of achievements in the use of our freedom. Our world of freedom can contain radical evil. In fact, violence, destruction, and moral injustices of many kinds frequently accompany the freedom that exists. In our world, both God and man will have to share responsibility for the evil that is actualized. Men are genuinely responsible for what they do with the freedom they possess. But surely God is responsible for much of the wildness and the difficulty that characterize the circumstances in which freedom exists and that produce suffering and failure. In addition, however, we could say that the presence of such factors may help us to define God's purposes with respect to man's freedom. For God, the significance of the results of man's use of freedom may be determined largely by the degree to which creative human achievement occurs in the face of adverse odds. God may, for example, place greater value on a seemingly small creative achievement accomplished in spite of great difficulty than on an apparently greater result achieved in the face of minimal adversity.

Now, consider a final point. It may be precisely in this context that the traditional Christian claim that God is also characterized by love can once again have power by creating hope. God's love is not always obvious, but it may be the backdrop for our existence. God creates a predominantly self-sustaining universe, but he remains present, watching with concern to see what will be accomplished in a world where the best success is far from cheap. He sees and experiences a world in process that is a mixture of good and evil. He leaves men largely in silence, but he gives them a promise grounded in love, namely, that waste, destruction, suffering, and death are not to be the final facts of existence.

Could these suggestions be developed into a viable view of God for our time? That depends not only on the energies and talents of the thinkers who may choose to wrestle with them, but also on some theoretical considerations that are raised by Hume, the next philosopher we will discuss. Leibniz's theory leaves us with the challenge to think creatively, but Hume's philosophy will force us to be critical as well.

VI

HUME AND
NATURAL THEOLOGY

Hume's Life and Skepticism

Our study turns a corner in coming to David Hume. All the men we have encountered thus far believe that God's existence can be demonstrated either by an appeal to a priori principles or by observation of the world's structure. They also claim that the God whose existence is proved can be shown to be omnipotent, omniscient, and absolutely good. Hume, on the other hand, is skeptical about all of these points. Our contemporary doubts about the possibility of final demonstration of God's existence and nature are due largely to Hume's influence. Who, then, was this man, and what is the nature of the skepticism that characterizes his philosophical position?

Hume's brief autobiography indicates that he was born in Edinburgh in 1711. His father died when he was still an infant, leaving the family a small estate. Hume was a successful student, and as a young man he developed a strong interest in literature and philosophy. He was inclined to pursue a scholarly career of research and writing, but was temporarily diverted from this course of action by his family, who thought that he was well suited for the legal profession and persuaded him to study law. This unsuccessful venture lasted only a short time. Faced by financial needs, Hume went to Bristol and worked in the business world for a few months. However, this occupation, too, was distasteful to him. Thus, at the age of twenty-three, Hume accepted a small allowance from his family and traveled to France to study and write. He stayed there until 1737 and wrote *A Treatise of Human Nature.* Hume had high hopes for the work, but its publication aroused little interest.

Although he was discouraged by the poor reception of the *Treatise,* Hume continued to write. In 1741-42, while in Scotland, he published *Essays, Moral and Political.* This work was a success, and Hume was encouraged to proceed with a revision of his *Treatise.* In the meantime, he applied for a professorial chair in philosophy at the University of Edinburgh, but his reputation as a skeptic and an atheist blocked the appointment. Shortly afterwards, Hume accepted a post as private secretary to General St. Clair, accompanying him on an ill-fated venture against the French. Later, when St. Clair was appointed a British Ambassador to Vienna and Turin, Hume went along as one of his assistants.

In 1751, final revisions of the first and third parts of the *Treatise* were published under the respective titles *An Enquiry Concerning Human Understanding* and *An Enquiry Concerning the Principles of Morals.* At about this same time, Hume wrote his *Dialogues Concerning Natural Religion.* The *Dialogues* set out his position on God's existence and the nature of religion. However, upon the advice of friends who were concerned about the radical nature of his views, Hume withheld the *Dialogues* from publication. Under a provision of Hume's will, they were published posthumously in 1779.

Between 1752 and 1757, Hume served as Librarian to the Faculty of Advocates in Edinburgh. Having the resources of this library at hand, Hume wrote a history of England. This work was not only long but also controversial. In any case, as a result all of Hume's writings became better known, and they were widely praised in some circles. Praise was especially strong among intellectuals in France, and when Hume went there in 1763 as a secretary to the British Ambassador he received a warm welcome. Hume returned to London in 1766, bringing Rousseau with him, although relations between the two soon became strained. After serving three years as an Undersecretary of State, Hume retired to Edinburgh, where he died in 1776.

What are the dominant themes in Hume's philosophy, which struck many of his contemporaries and friends as controversial, radical, and even dangerous? One way to begin an answer to this question is to explore the nature and function of Hume's skepticism (that is, the position that denies the validity of some or all of our claims to have genuine knowledge). In the *Enquiry Concerning*

Human Understanding, Hume draws a distinction between *antecedent* and *consequent* skepticism. His analysis leads him both to accept and to reject some things in these positions. Hume finds his example of antecedent skepticism in the philosophy of René Descartes (1596–1650). Seeking to find a point of certainty from which he could deduce other equally certain truths, Descartes had proposed the use of methodological doubt. By questioning the validity of beliefs, Descartes hoped to discover at least one basic feature of our existence that could stand unchallenged and hence qualify as the point of certainty he needed. Utilizing his methodological doubt, Descartes thought he had discovered his point of certainty in the very experience of doubting. Although one can doubt and be mistaken about the existence of the world or even the existence of one's body, doubt about one's fundamental existence cannot be sustained. No matter how much I doubt, my own existence is a condition that must hold for my act of doubting to occur. Since doubting is a form of thinking, Descartes expresses his famous insight in the following form: *"Cogito, ergo sum"* ("I think, therefore I am").

As Hume understands it, then, antecedent skepticism is a component in a broad philosophical program. It is equivalent to a radical methodological doubt, and it claims not only the possibility and necessity of calling into question everything that in principle can be doubted but also that such moves are prerequisites for finding truths that are grounded in certainty. Hume's reaction to Descartes's use of antecedent skepticism constitutes a severe attack on this program. If, on the one hand, our doubt is as radical as Descartes demands, we can and will question the veracity of the faculties used to draw out Descartes's conclusion about his own existence. On Descartes's principles, these faculties must be regarded as suspect. We must have simple faith in their veracity if we are to accept Descartes's claim to know his own existence with certainty. But since this claim for knowledge now rests on some assumptions about our faculties, we can no longer properly regard it as absolutely certain. Descartes's program is an impossibility. If we call everything into question, we cannot legitimately claim to have knowledge. If we leave something as an assumption in order to claim that we have knowledge of matters of fact and existence, we give up the possibility of certainty.

Some elaboration on the last point will enable us to see Hume's position more clearly. Hume thinks, "All the objects of human reason or inquiry may naturally be divided into two kinds, to wit, 'Relations of Ideas' and 'Matters of Fact.' "[1] Relations of ideas (for example, that three times five is equal to half of thirty) can be known to be true a priori. Such truths are demonstrable and absolutely certain because their denial results in contradiction, *but they tell us nothing about matters of fact and existence.* On the other hand, knowledge of matters of fact and existence is neither obtainable a priori nor is it demonstrable and absolutely certain. Hume bases this view on the principle that, "Whatever *is* may *not be.* No negation of a fact can involve a contradiction. The nonexistence of any being, without exception, is as clear and distinct an idea as its existence."[2] Knowledge of matters of fact, then, can come only through empirical experience and never without the quality of fallibility.

Although Hume rejects antecedent skepticism as developed by Descartes, his emphasis on the fallibility of human knowledge in matters of fact leads him to see that a less radical version of antecedent skepticism can be helpful in avoiding error, prejudice, and blind dogmatism. Before accepting claims as true, some skepticism about their validity will encourage us to test and verify them as best we can. This approach will not give us absolute certainty where matters of fact are concerned, but it can help us to find sound beliefs.

If antecedent skepticism is a methodological tool, consequent skepticism appears historically as the result of particular philosophical inquiries. Moving from the discovery that our faculties (that is, our senses and reason) are not always devoid of error, the conclusion is drawn that genuine knowledge is an impossibility. What is Hume's response to this perspective? He begins by dealing with skepticism involving the senses. Some philosophers have pointed to common phenomena (for example, the bent appearance of an oar under water or the variations in the appearance of objects seen at different distances) as clear instances of the untrustworthiness of the senses. These occurrences are then taken as casting sufficient doubt on sense experience in general to invalidate claims to knowledge based on sensory data. Hume thinks that this is neither the only nor the most reasonable conclusion to draw from these experiences. His position is that these examples suggest only that we may need to correct the immediate evidence of the senses by reason and by taking account of factors such as the nature of the medium involved, the object's distance from us, and the conditions of the sense organs.

Other difficulties, however, are not settled so easily. Although we have a natural inclination to think that our senses give us a

trustworthy access to a real external world, philosophical questioning can cast serious doubts on the rational grounding of this belief.
How, for example, can we show that our senses give us an accurate
accounting of the world, or, even more devastating, how can we be
sure that there is a real external world? The mind, after all, seems
to have nothing present to it but perceptions—representations of
objects—which may not be accurate and which may not connect
with a real external world.

The skeptical philosopher can even turn reason against itself.
Objections can be raised against our trust in reason by pointing out
the contradictory opinions that men claim to be self-evident or
justified by reason. Moreover, critical examination suggests that our
use of basic rational principles is not and cannot be adequately
grounded. The major example that Hume draws on here is our use
of the relation of cause and effect. We will explore his analysis of
causality in more detail later on, but, briefly stated, one of his
major points in this context is that we lack sound arguments to
show that the constant conjunction of phenomena observed in the
past will continue to hold in the future. Much of our reasoning
about experience rests on the assumption that these relationships
will hold, but reason has no way to see whether this belief is
absolutely justified.

Hume finds that consequent skepticism is more difficult to
refute theoretically than the antecedent skepticism of Descartes.
Nevertheless, Hume argues against total consequent skepticism by
pointing out two main factors about it. First, if pushed to an
extreme, such a skepticism can result in no good. Its effect is
utterly debilitating. It would so undermine man's confidence that
all action would be curtailed. Second, man's natural inclinations
and beliefs are sufficiently strong that they simply will not be
destroyed by a confrontation with consequent skepticism. This
skepticism, in a word, is practically impossible. Man's natural
desires to live and act make the practical orientation take precedence over the possible objections that reason may raise about the
senses or even about itself.

On the other hand, an encounter with consequent skepticism has
a healthy cathartic effect on the human spirit. It impresses on us
the fact that practical conviction is not the same thing as rational
demonstration and certainty, and it leads us to a sharper awareness
of the contingency and precariousness of existence. As with antecedent skepticism, then, Hume acknowledges that we can learn
something from consequent skepticism even if we refuse to adopt

the position in its entirety. Not only do we need to be careful about the assumptions and beliefs that we hold as we start an investigation, but we also need to be aware of the limits of our senses and reason in drawing conclusions. All things considered, a *mitigated skepticism,* which regards knowledge claims as fallible and which places an emphasis on empirical testing and the need to look for error, is the best stance to take.

One further point needs to be made about the skepticism that Hume recommends. He thinks that our claims about matters of fact are always fallible. Our knowledge of matters of fact is always grounded in empirical experience, and the possibility of error lurks there continually. Nevertheless, by staying within the realm of our empirical experiences, by seeking evidence there and by testing our hypotheses, we may be able to avoid serious mistakes. At the same time, however, if we make broad philosophical claims about existence that go beyond our capabilities to support or refute them with empirical evidence, our thinking is sure to have a misleading effect. It will lead us to think that we both have a capacity to know and actually do know matters of fact that are really beyond us. The results of such thinking can only be confusion and error. Life is filled with enough uncertainty and difficulty already without introducing claims for knowledge that are unwarranted because they lack a sound empirical grounding.

But these considerations raise a new question: What conditions need to hold before Hume thinks we are justified in claiming to have knowledge of matters of fact? To answer this question, we must explore his theory of experience. By doing so, we will lay the groundwork for his critique of natural theology.

Hume's Theory of Experience and Analysis of Causality

Hume's theory of experience starts with the idea that all of the contents of our conscious experience can be broken down into two categories, namely, *impressions* and *ideas.* Hume says that the term "impressions" refers to "all our more lively perceptions, when we hear, or see, or feel, or love, or hate, or desire, or will."[3] Impressions differ from ideas not so much in content but rather in the forcefulness and vivacity with which they strike us. Ideas, on the other hand, are either images based on the memory of impressions or thoughts about the impressions, the latter often involving our faculty of imagination, which allows the production of ideas which may have no direct correlate in the sphere of impressions. Nevertheless, all ideas are ultimately derived from impressions.

Hume elaborates and clarifies the relation between impressions and ideas by stating that both can be divided into two categories in terms of their *simplicity* or *complexity*. A complex impression is composed of simple impressions. Moreover, every simple idea originates in a simple impression to which it corresponds directly. A complex idea, on the other hand, need not come directly from a complex impression to which it corresponds. Instead, complex ideas can be developed from a variety of simple or complex impressions, or they can be made from simple ideas.

All human experiences and thoughts have their ultimate origin in impressions of a sensory nature. There are two important ramifications to note concerning this crucial point in Hume's theory. The first involves our understanding of the meaning of terms and propositions, especially those used by metaphysicians. Despite the fact that all our thinking originates with impressions, thought can carry us far away from the original starting points. In fact, Hume suggests, we can move so far that the terms we use and the assertions we make may lack clarity or significance. The test for clarity and significance is simply to see from what impressions the terms and propositions in question are derived. By showing the connection between (1) terms and propositions and (2) impressions, or by discovering an essential lack or confusion of connection, we can indicate the presence or absence of clarity and significance in the terms and propositions we are examining.

The second implication of Hume's claim that all experience and thought have their ultimate source in sense impressions is essentially related to the first. Sense impressions are the given factors of experience, and the structure of our experience is such that we can never have full clarity and absolute certainty about their origin. Although we can think about these fundamental sense impressions, we can never get the objective distance from them that we need to examine their ultimate grounding. Any claims to such a perspective or to explaining these origins definitively will be unwarranted metaphysical speculations.

We can, however, do more with respect to ideas. Not only is it possible to obtain a valid theory concerning their origin, which Hume himself claims to have produced, but also it is possible to describe how ideas get organized in our experience. Analysis of experience indicates that men have two faculties, memory and imagination, which play vital parts in our mental processes. Memory allows us to retain impressions with exactness, although with less vividness than in the original instance. Imagination allows us to order and arrange ideas in a variety of ways. The possibilities available on this score are, however, regulated by three general principles of association. Our ideas tend naturally to follow or to be associated with one another when their referents or contents (1) involve a resemblance, or (2) are contiguous in time or space, or (3) are related in terms of cause and effect. Hume is disposed to believe that all the complex ideas which originate in our minds involve at least one of these three principles. He does not, however, offer a proof that his list of principles is exhaustive, nor does he claim to have an account of the origin of the principles. Like simple sense impressions, they are given factors in experience.

Hume is especially interested in the relation of cause and effect because, "[a]ll reasonings concerning matter of fact seem to be founded on the relation of *cause* and *effect*. By means of that relation alone we can go beyond the evidence of our memory and senses."[4] In addition to being one of the natural ways in which ideas are initially associated in the mind, the relation of cause and effect emerges as a basic reasoning principle in our conscious efforts to explore and understand our experience and world more completely. It is by thinking in terms of the cause and effect relation that we seek and assert connections between our immediate experience and the past and future. Obviously, the cause and effect relationship is of vital importance, and therefore it behooves us to be as clear as possible about the nature of the relation and the grounds that we possess for using it as we do. Hume is interested in appraising the validity of our reasoning as well as in obtaining a descriptive account of the foundational components of our experience and thought.

What, then, is involved when we employ the relation of cause and effect as a reasoning principle in our thinking about matters of fact, and can our use of the relation be shown to have a demonstrable rational foundation? Hume suggests that when we think of cause and effect relations between two or more things, we usually mean that one is immediately or mediately contiguous with the other and that the one we are designating as the cause is to some degree temporally prior to the other. These conditions alone, however, do not seem to suffice for the presence of a cause and effect relationship. Since it is conceivable that X can be contiguous with and temporally prior to Y without being the cause of Y, something more is required. Hume thinks that we add the idea that there is a *necessary connection* between X and Y in the situation where X is said to be the cause of Y. Without the addition of the idea that every event or thing must have some cause that necessarily produces it, the ordinary understanding of cause and effect relations would not exist.

Hume's analysis places great importance on the idea of a necessary connection. He probes at this idea to see the foundation on which it rests. Two approaches seem available for providing a rational base for the use of this concept: (1) One could argue that the use of the concept is valid on a priori grounds. (2) One could argue that the use is sufficiently grounded by an appeal to empirical experience.

Hume moves against the first alternative by arguing that it is neither intuitively certain nor demonstrable a priori that everything that begins to exist must have a cause. This proposition is a crucial factor in our idea of a necessary connection, and if we cannot show that every thing or event must have a cause, the concept of necessary connection is on shaky ground indeed. Hume makes short work of the claim that the proposition in question is intuitively certain. It is not intuitively certain because it is possible to think of something coming into existence without being caused and yet not fall into contradiction. Nothing in the idea of "coming into existence" necessarily entails the idea of "being caused to exist."

A similar fate meets attempts to obtain final proof of the principle that everything that begins to exist must have a cause. For example, it was argued that a denial of this principle leads to absurd results. If something started to exist without a cause, it would (1) have to cause itself or (2) be caused by nothing. Both alternatives are impossible. The first is impossible because it entails the absurdity of a thing's having to exist prior to itself in order to cause itself. The second is impossible, since it is clear that nothing cannot be the cause of anything. Since the results of denying the principle are absurd, the principle itself must be affirmed, in which case the idea of necessary connection is at least partially supported.

Hume, however, points out that these rationalistic arguments have a common defect. They assume the validity of the very principle that is in question. It is only absurd to say that something can come into being without having a cause outside itself if one is already committed to the principle that everything that comes into being must have such a cause. Hume takes this shortcoming to be sufficient to show that our use of the concept of necessary connection cannot be adequately grounded a priori by appeals to intuition or rational demonstration.

What, then, of the possibility of grounding our use of the concept of necessary connection by an appeal to empirical experience? First, Hume reminds us that the experience of any particular object or event does not force us to think in terms of a cause of the object or event. In itself, no experience of an object or event necessarily implies the existence of any other object or event. However, if we look at empirical experiences, we can begin to see how the idea of a necessary connection may emerge. In experience we frequently find that in addition to being contiguous and in temporal succession, phenomena are *constantly conjoined*. For example, on countless occasions we have seen one object hit a second object with the result that the second moves. Now, Hume suggests, when we find two objects related in this way through time, we attribute a causal power to the first, and we conclude that there is a necessary connection between the two.

Is such a move rationally grounded? Hume thinks not. Although it is the case that we may directly experience the constant conjunction of phenomena, he denies that there are any impressions that clearly correspond to the idea of causal power, which is crucial to the idea of necessary connection. Constant conjunction is not the same thing as necessary connection. Moreover, no matter how frequently the constant conjunction of phenomena may have been observed, it does not follow that the relationship will continue to hold. To think that this will be the case is to smuggle in a principle asserting the uniformity of nature. But such a principle cannot be demonstrated as eternally binding, since change is always conceivable. In addition, it cannot even be argued that the continuation of the uniformity of nature is a strong probability, since arguments concerning probability already assume some version of the principle of the uniformity of nature. Unless we assume some uniformity in nature, it makes no sense to say that anything is probable. Hume is certain that we do believe that nature is uniform and that this idea figures into our use of the concept of necessary connection, but this does not mean that either factor in our experience is based on sound reasoning.

Hume also dismisses the possibility that the idea of necessary connection could be directly grounded in internal feelings or states (for example, willing to move my arm and then seeing or feeling it move). Here, too, all that we really observe or feel is a constant conjunction of events, and the repetition of the conjunction of phenomena, no matter how extensive, is not the same thing as necessary connection. Hume's conclusion, then, is that the presence of the concept of necessary connection in human experience indicates a basic, but ultimately puzzling, fact about the human mind. From the constant conjunction of phenomena in our experience the idea of necessary connection is formed and comes to function as a powerful habit. Why it should be there is not fully clear. What is fully clear is that the idea is not rationally grounded. This conclusion means, in particular, that many of the uses to which the idea has been put in philosophy and theology are illegitimate. In fact, some of these illegitimate moves involving the concept of necessary connection and the relationship of cause and effect figure prominently in attempts to demonstrate the existence of God.

Let us summarize the ground that we have covered thus far. Then we will be prepared to explore the *Dialogues Concerning Natural Religion,* where Hume offers his critique of some traditional attempts to demonstrate God's existence and to show that his nature must be of a certain type. Hume leaves us in a world of uncertainty. Although he acknowledges that practical belief will win out, he argues that we have no certainty that there is a real world that directly corresponds to our experiences. In fact, the analysis of causality suggests that the world that we find ourselves inhabiting is largely a construction of our own minds. We think in terms of necessary connections, but Hume's investigation turns up nothing to suggest that this concept has anything more than a purely subjective origin. Hume's world is one in which the principle of noncontradiction holds, but it does not operate on the principle of sufficient reason. Not only do things or events fail to imply specific causes, but it is even possible to conceive of things or events as coming to be without having been caused at all. This world has a quality of looseness and radical contingency. Whereas Leibniz uses the principle of sufficient reason to imply a distinction between what is theoretically possible and really possible, Hume removes the principle of sufficient reason and puts all possibilities on a par. Within the boundaries of the principle of noncontradiction, literally anything can happen in Hume's world. Where matters of fact are concerned, he requires us to replace the concepts of certainty and rational demonstration with those of fallibility and practical belief. Now, in such a setting, what place, if any, is God allowed?

The Existence and Nature of God

Hume's *Dialogues Concerning Natural Religion* raise fundamental objections to claims that we can conclusively demonstrate God's existence and the positive qualities of his nature by appeals to a priori principles or empirical experiences. On the other hand, the *Dialogues* do not claim to demonstrate that God does not exist or that God can be known with absolute finality not to have particular attributes. Rather, what emerges is a skepticism with respect to all claims for genuine knowledge in these areas.

The *Dialogues* consist of discussions between three figures: (1) Demea, a religiously orthodox man, believes that God's existence is self-evident, but he affirms the primacy of faith in understanding God's nature and opposes the view that men can comprehend and demonstrate God's attributes through reason. If men could do the latter, God's sovereignty and majesty would be compromised. (2) Philo, a skeptic, agrees that reason is severely limited in knowing the nature of God, but he extends his view by denying the validity of man's claims to know conclusively that God exists. (3) Cleanthes, an advocate of natural theology, thinks that God's existence and nature can be known conclusively by reasoning from experience and the natural order. Hume did not specifically identify himself with any particular figure in the *Dialogues,* but it is generally thought that Philo represents his position.

At the beginning of the *Dialogues,* Philo and Cleanthes debate the limitations of man's senses and reason in providing us with genuine knowledge. Philo points out that the senses can mislead us and that reason produces conflicting conclusions in many instances. The fact that this is true in the empirical experiences of everyday life ought to make us wary of trusting the validity of any of our claims to have genuine knowledge, but especially those which deal with things that transcend our direct experiences (for example, the attributes of God). Cleanthes counters with the point that although such skepticism may be an interesting theoretical position to hold, men do not, in fact, live in terms of it. Directing his comment to Philo, Cleanthes says, "Your own conduct, in every circumstance, refutes your principles; and shows the firmest reliance on all the received maxims of science, morals, prudence, and behaviour."[5] Moreover, Cleanthes asserts, theological reflection and demonstrations are neither more abstruse and difficult nor essentially different in kind or in certainty from the reasoning and conclusions of science and mathematics. Practically speaking, no rational man seriously doubts the validity of the findings of science and mathematics, and it is only a mark of irrational prejudice when skepticism holds with respect to the claim that we can and do have genuine and conclusive knowledge concerning the existence and nature of God.

Some interesting points emerge at this juncture of the *Dialogues.* Demea intervenes to suggest that Cleanthes has really overreacted to Philo's remarks. No one is questioning the fact that we can know that God exists. The issue is only over the possibility of grasping God's nature through reason without reducing God to a simple extension of human qualities. Philo concurs. It is unquestionable and self-evident that God exists: "Nothing exists without a cause; and the original cause of this universe (whatever it be) we call GOD; and piously ascribe to him every species of perfection."[6] What we must avoid, however, is the claim to comprehend through reason the full content of God's perfection. Such claims are sure to lapse into anthropomorphic distortions. At this point, Philo seems to think that an argument based on causal principles can constitute a proof for the existence of a God who creates the universe. This fact would appear to be inconsistent with the view that Philo truly represents Hume's opinions, but later in the *Dialogues* we will see that Philo submits the causal argument to criticism, thus suggesting that his early agreement with Demea is far from complete.

Cleanthes, however, is unwilling to let things rest as Demea and Philo have left them. Not only can the existence of God be demonstrated by an appeal to experience and the natural world, but also such an appeal enables us to obtain genuine knowledge concerning God's nature. To prove his point, Cleanthes presents a version of the argument from design. If a person looks at the world, he will see that it is one great machine, which can be broken down into an infinite number of smaller machines. These parts are adjusted to each other so as to function harmoniously. These harmonious relationships include an adaptation of means to ends. That is, there is a manifestation of purpose and planning in the universe. Moreover, this "curious adapting of means to ends, throughout all nature, resembles exactly, though it much exceeds, the productions of human contrivance; of human design, thought, wisdom, and intelligence."[7] Since the effects (that is, natural objects and human artifacts) resemble each other so closely, we infer by analogy not only that the natural objects are like the human artifacts in having a cause, but also that the causes must closely resemble each other. In this way, we prove both the existence of God and the fact that he has a mind and a will not unlike ours.

Philo proceeds to analyze the significance of this argument. His intention is to show that Cleanthes' approach leaves one, at best, with an ambiguous outcome which can hardly be taken as sufficient in itself to provide an adequate grounding for a positive religious orientation. Philo develops his critique by concentrating on two related features of Cleanthes' argument: (1) its use of analogical reasoning and (2) its use of the cause and effect relationship. The validity of Cleanthes' argument, which is based on an analogy, depends on the closeness of similarity between the effects under examination. Here both the parts and the whole of nature are taken to be analogous to human products or works of art, thus requiring a divine artisan not unlike a human creator. However, Philo argues that Cleanthes' analogical reasoning rests on a weak foundation.

Philo's first move is to point out that the resemblance between the effects being compared is not as elaborate as Cleanthes supposes. Not only is it clear that the natural world differs in many respects from a machine or a human product such as a house or a work of art, but experience tells us that "[t]hought, design, intelligence, such as we discover in men and other animals, is no more than one of the springs and principles of the universe, as well as heat or cold, attraction or repulsion, and a hundred others, which fall under daily observation."[8] It is not certain that these other principles of order require active intelligence as their source, and it is not impossible that intelligence can itself be the product of some of these other principles. To argue that all order reveals the existence of intelligence at its base is to make the move of attributing the qualities of a small part of the universe to the whole. Moves of this kind are always subject to question.

Furthermore, since our idea of cause and effect relationships actually rests on the experience of constant conjunction, the fact that the resemblance between the universe and the products of human intelligence is so slight severely undercuts the possibility of making conclusive judgments concerning the cause or causes of the universe. If we are dealing with a particular member of a class of things, we may be able to make some sound judgments concerning its cause or causes. For example, from the existence of a particular house, I can infer the existence of a builder on the basis of the experience I have had of other houses whose builders I know. But this situation does not hold with respect to our universe. Not only is it considerably different from the products of human intelligence, but it is not a member of any group of things that we know. Thus, since we have no experience of the production of other universes and no direct access to the causes that may have produced this universe, we are left in a position of ambiguity with respect to our knowledge of the source of our universe.

Cleanthes is not yet convinced, however. He stresses the naturalness of our belief in an intelligent creator of the universe. In addition, he clings to the view that we can know causes from effects, even in the case of the universe, and that the universe reveals its cause to be the traditional God, who, out of his power and goodness, creates a world of purpose, beauty, and harmony.

Now, Demea enters the attack, indicating still other dangers in arguing from effects to causes. For example, if we obtain knowledge about God through analogy with human existence, how are we to cope with the fact that the human mind is finite and often subject to confusion, change, and emotional influence? If we say that the effects reveal the cause, then we may end up saying that the cause is also subject to confusion, change, and emotional influence, which is clearly contrary to traditional teaching about God. On the other hand, if we deny that God is this way, then in what sense does the effect reveal the cause, and what are we to say about the origin of possible defects in human existence?

Philo continues the attack by arguing that the claims that Cleanthes makes are vacuous because so many alternative accounts are equally possible and probable. The effects (that is, the parts and the whole of the universe) are sufficiently ambiguous to call into question any claims to move from them to clear knowledge of God's nature. If Cleanthes' claims are maintained in the face of this ambiguity, they reveal themselves not only to be anthropomorphic, but also to be selectively anthropomorphic in a way that is ungrounded. To illustrate this, Philo points out that we cannot affirm anything very clearly about God's perfection from this universe. We lack a standard of universe construction that is sufficient to measure the perfection of this universe. We cannot, in addition, be sure that this universe was created by only one God. Perhaps a plurality of deities, none of them perfect, was involved. Or it may be the case that transcendent deities are not involved at all. The world might be the product of a growth process such as we see illustrated frequently in nature when seeds grow into organized plants without an outside designer introducing their order. Or it may even be that the world is simply the result of a fortuitous arrangement of atomic particles. In short, Philo's conclusion is this: We lack sufficient data to corroborate any particular theory about the origin, structure, and order of the universe as a whole. No particular system of religious belief can be demonstrated on the basis of appeals to experience and the natural order.

Demea, as well as Cleanthes, is troubled by these suggestions, for Philo now seems to question the existence of a sovereign, creating God. Demea believes that the existence of such a God is self-evident, even though he holds that one cannot rationally comprehend God's nature. Starting from the principle that all that exists has a reason or a cause grounding its existence, Demea asserts that there must be a first cause that exists necessarily. Even if the sequence of causes occurring in the world is infinite, something will be needed to account for the existence of the series of causes in the world. The only being that is capable of accounting for the existence of such a series, whether finite or infinite, is an ultimate necessary being, whose reason for existing is internal to himself and who cannot be conceived not to exist without contradiction. This being is God.

Cleanthes, rather than Philo, takes exception to this line of thought. Cleanthes objects that matters of fact cannot be demonstrated a priori. Anything that we can conceive as existent, we can also conceive as nonexistent without contradiction. Where it is possible to conceive of alternatives without contradiction, final demonstration is impossible. Thus, an a priori proof of God's existence such as that attempted by Demea is not binding on the intellect. To put the conclusion another way: "The words, therefore, *necessary existence,* have no meaning; or, which is the same thing, none that is consistent."[9] In addition, Philo points out that even if Demea's a priori proof could be legitimately used, it does not necessarily give us a transcendent creator. The ultimate necessary being and source of change and movement could just as well be matter itself.

Philo's next important suggestion is that a priori proofs always leave men feeling uneasy and that it is unlikely that such demonstrations have ever had much power in the religious life of men. Demea picks up this latter point and agrees that man's religious life does not develop primarily from proofs and demonstrations but as a response to the experiences of finitude, destruction, and suffering that characterize human life. It is man's need of help and security that turns him to God.

Philo seems sympathetic to this point of view, but the main fact that strikes him is that the features of human existence which Demea has noted conflict with the emphasis traditional theology and religion place on the perfection of God (that is, primarily his absolute goodness and power). It is difficult to see that the positing of such qualities is rationally grounded. We have no a priori grasp of God's nature, and the empirical facts do not necessarily imply God's absolute perfection, since they indicate that, at best, existence is a mixture of good and evil. If we could get a clear comprehension of God's nature and all existence, we might see the perfection of his total plan with respect to this universe. But we lack the power to comprehend the totality. Thus, for example, Philo would not find it acceptable to say that we have good grounds for believing that this life, in which evil occurs, is merely a small, but perhaps necessary, interlude in a broader existence in which pure goodness triumphs. In addition, it is not possible for us to take the position that evil is really illusory and that everything is actually good. Evil stands as a brute fact in this life, and it is a serious obstacle to the soundness of the claim that God's perfection is absolute.

Philo summarizes his position with respect to the moral qualities of the possible first cause or causes of the universe. There are four main options. The first cause or causes could be (1) absolutely good, (2) absolutely evil, (3) both good and evil, or (4) really indifferent to good and evil. Since our world is a mixture of good and evil, the first two options are unlikely. Moreover, the steadiness and regularity of things mitigates against the third. No conflict of interests or powers is indicated in the ultimate foundations of existence, since the mixture of good and evil in existence does not alter very much one way or the other. In addition, indifference of the first cause or causes to good and evil seems more likely than a mere stand-off or balance between conflicting interests or powers in the first cause or causes. For Philo, then, the fourth option seems to be the most likely.

By this time, Demea sees that Philo is a genuine religious skeptic, not his ally. Demea and Philo do hold much in common in their approach to claims about knowledge of God, but Demea sees that Philo is not a man of religious faith. Revelation and religious commitment, which are valid and crucially important in Demea's thinking, do not have a positive place in Philo's orientation.

Demea leaves the scene, but Cleanthes and Philo stay on for further discussion. Philo dominates the final exchange, but he is more mellow than before. He admits that he likes to play the part of the skeptic, but that he thinks Cleanthes is right in stressing the idea of design in the universe and the naturalness of thinking in terms of an intelligent designer as its source. Moreover, Philo is prepared to admit that Cleanthes is right in asserting that there are some likenesses between the works of nature and the productions of human creativity. He is not, however, ready to agree with Cleanthes that the likenesses are sufficient for drawing any precise analogies between human and divine intelligence. Nor are the likenesses sufficient to ground our claims to having a clear comprehension of the nature of the cause or causes of order in the world. This is particularly the case where claims concerning the moral qualities and interests of the cause or causes are involved. The most that natural theology will allow us to say on these matters is *"that the cause or causes of order in the universe probably bear some remote analogy to human intelligence...."*[10] Thus, even if religion has some positive utilitarian value for society, which Philo doubts because he believes that the sources and practical effects of religion are largely fear and terror, it cannot really be said to have a firm rational grounding.

Assuming that Philo speaks for Hume, the *Dialogues Concerning Natural Religion* reveal Hume's belief that constructive philosophical theorizing about reality as a whole (that is, metaphysics) and natural theology are largely doomed. There are two main reasons for this conclusion. First, a priori demonstrations of matters of fact are impossible. Second, the facts to be accounted for are so vast and ambiguous that many explanations are possible and no particular one will be capable of being sufficiently corroborated so as to convince all rational men that it should be accepted. This assertion suggests that many traditional claims about God's existence and nature are in jeopardy, especially if one's intention is to show that these claims can be rationally demonstrated or verified overwhelmingly by appeals to empirical data. Where, then, does this position leave us? Should the metaphysician and the philosophical theologian be silent and seek other work? Or is it possible that Hume's critique can have a beneficial effect in clarifying what they can and should do? In concluding our discussion of Hume, let us think about these issues.

Some Problems and Useful Insights in Hume's Thought

Hume's theories seem antimetaphysical and antitheological to a great degree. How is it possible that his thought might help to lay the foundations for a fresh approach in these areas? One way to begin answering this question is to point out that Hume's analysis of natural theology goes far toward convincing us of the improbability of obtaining final, conclusive demonstrations about matters of fact. Strictly speaking, Hume cannot even claim final proof of his principle: "Whatever *is* may *not be*. No negation of a fact can involve a contradiction."[11] To do so would violate his own belief that final demonstration is not possible where matters of fact are concerned. Hume's critique, then, emphasizes the notes of possibility and pluralism in the development of theories. Many theories offer accounts of the phenomena under investigation, but metaphysics and theology seem unable to produce absolute agreement on any single account.

Such a result can be viewed in at least two ways. One might take the position that undermining the likelihood of absolute agreement on a single account leads to the death of metaphysics and theology. But that is the case only if we assume that these disciplines must involve such agreement. Hume's critique gives us another option. He helps us to see that metaphysics and theology are pluralistic disciplines. Men can give more than one description or account of existence. The task of the metaphysician and the philosophical theologian is to explore these possibilities, and then to do what they can to determine which accounts may be the best. In our inquiries, we may always be left with a multiplicity of accounts, but it is precisely this openness and possibility that may give impetus to creative efforts. No one is bound to accept any particular view as finally binding. This perspective does not entail, on the other hand, that no agreement will obtain, but it does mean that if one feels hemmed in by the views that are current, one may try to work out a theory of his own that is more adequate.

But now another question appears: Granted that a plurality of metaphysical and theological theories is possible, how should we deal with Hume's view that it is virtually impossible to differentiate between them with respect to their validity? Hume takes the position that we lack an a priori grasp of being, which might be one way to ground our selections. Moreover, he thinks that the empirical data with which we must work are so ambiguous as to make it extremely unlikely, if not impossible, for us to obtain sufficient evidence to show that some theories are more probable than others. Hume may be right, *but it is not incumbent upon everyone simply to take his word for it.* After all, the most that Hume can give us is a promissory note about our grasp of being or the possibility of verification for our theories. His own theory does not allow him to do more.

Far from being a destructive critic of metaphysics and theology, Hume provides a constructive analysis that opens up fresh possibilities while making us aware of the need to ground our theories in the facts of experience. Hume offers an opportunity and a challenge: Develop your own theory if you want, but seek to make it as believable as possible by tying it closely to experience. This is precisely what Hume himself attempted to do. It would be strange indeed if we take our legacy from him to be the final demonstration that constructive efforts should cease.

VII

KANT AND THE
CRITIQUE OF REASON

Kant's Life and the Influence of Leibniz and Hume

Few philosophers have been more influential than Immanuel
Kant. Yet, of all the men considered in this book, his biography is
the least impressive. Kant was born in 1724 in the Prussian town
of Königsberg. His family was deeply religious, but Kant did not
become an official of any church. Instead, after studying classics,
physics, and philosophy at the University of Königsberg, financial
needs led him to take jobs as a private tutor. Such work allowed
him time for additional study in science and philosophy, but,
unlike Leibniz and Hume, Kant found no time or opportunity for
extensive travels or political adventures. In 1755, Kant received an
advanced degree and began to teach at the University of Königsberg.
He remained there for the rest of his life lecturing on philosophy,
and he was highly admired as a teacher. He died in 1804.

Kant's writings made him a figure of lasting importance. His
main works are *Critique of Pure Reason* (first edition, 1781; second
edition, 1787), *Prolegomena to Any Future Metaphysics* (1783),
Foundations of the Metaphysics of Morals (1785), *Critique of Practical Reason* (1788), *Critique of Judgment* (1790), and *Religion
Within the Limits of Reason Alone* (1793). In these works Kant
developed a philosophy that was not only a response to basic problems of his day, but that also came to be a major touchstone for
philosophical developments in the nineteenth and twentieth
centuries.

117

Philosophers get their new insights by reflecting on what previous thinkers have done. Kant is no exception to this general rule, and Leibniz and Hume were dominant influences on his thought. Kant's philosophical training was largely Leibnizian. His early outlook revolved around the view that experience and reality itself conform to fundamental rational principles (for example, those of noncontradiction and sufficient reason). These principles are knowable a priori, and it is the task of philosophy to discover them. Moreover, by reasoning about experience in conjunction with these principles and by showing the connections between them and our conclusions, the human mind can know with certainty the basic structure of all reality.

Kant never gave up these Leibnizian ideas completely. However, Hume's intrusion on the philosophical scene led Kant to modify his early understanding of their validity and significance. Part of Hume's broad attack on rationalistic metaphysics and theology was to question our right to assume the principle that anything that begins to exist must have a cause that determines its existence. Hume argued that such a principle was not self-evident, demonstrable a priori, or conclusively verifiable by appeals to empirical experience. Only by assuming the principle could it be "proved."

Hume's attack cuts to the core of Leibnizian philosophy. The full intelligibility of reality and the power of human reason are called into question at the same time. Hume's world may defy the principle of sufficient reason, and in this world the human intellect lacks the power to show that all of its basic principles are adequately grounded. Our rational capacities help us to get along practically, but finality and completeness of knowledge elude them.

Clearly there are basic disagreements between these philosophies. From his sensitivity to the problems and positive insights on both sides, Kant drew out a novel view that was powerful in its effect. He regarded Hume's criticisms as seriously undermining the assumptions of Leibniz and his followers, but he refused to accept all of Hume's conclusions.

In particular, Kant was troubled by the skepticism of Hume's outcome. Not only did Hume question the possibility of metaphysical knowledge, but moreover, by denying (1) that we can have certainty about whether the physical world has a causal structure and (2) that necessary truths tell us anything about matters of fact, Hume implied that even the best scientific claims might not qualify as genuine knowledge. To admit that we could not legitimately claim to have conclusive knowledge on every interesting metaphysical issue was ultimately acceptable to Kant, but to exclude the claims of physics from the class of genuine knowledge was going too far. Saying that physics qualifies as genuine knowledge, however, does not make it so, and therefore Kant's move was to seek a new grounding for man's claims for knowledge. By carrying further Hume's idea of a critique of experience and reason, new and certain foundations for our investigations in science and philosophy might be found. An exploration of Kant's efforts in this direction is a necessary condition for seeing his position on the existence and nature of God.

Kant's Theory of Knowledge and the Traditional Proofs of God's Existence

The basic issue between Hume and Kant can be defined in the following way. Kant believed that there are *synthetic a priori* judgments and tried to show how they are possible, while Hume thought that there are no judgments of this kind. Hume had argued that all of our meaningful judgments are concerned either with relations of ideas or with matters of fact. Judgments concerned with the former are true a priori (that is, they hold universally, necessarily, and their truth does not depend on empirical testing). However, these judgments are true a priori only because the predicate is already contained at least implicitly in the subject of the judgment (as in the claim that all triangles have three angles). To use Kant's term, such judgments are *analytic*. According to Hume, these judgments do not, strictly speaking, give us new information, and they tell us nothing about matters of fact. They are, however, necessarily true because of the meaning of their terms. On the other hand, meaningful judgments about matters of fact (such as, "Many roses are red") are understood by Hume to be neither necessary and universal nor true by virtue of the meaning of the terms involved. To use Kant's term, such judgments are *synthetic a posteriori*. Here the subject does not contain the predicate, and the truth status of the judgment depends on empirical testing.

Hume would say that all judgments are either analytic a priori or synthetic a posteriori, but Kant argues that some judgments fall into neither of these groups. Some judgments are synthetic a priori. They are of special interest to science and philosophy because they convey new information (that is, the judgment's predicate is not already contained in its subject); yet their truth is necessary, universal, and not dependent on empirical testing. Although the existence of these judgments in metaphysics is uncertain, Kant claims that we can find numerous examples of them in the mathematical and physical sciences. The geometrical claim, "The straight line between two points is the shortest" is one instance.[1] Another is the physical principle, "In all communication of motion, action and reaction must always be equal."[2]

Assuming that he has genuine instances of synthetic a priori judgments, Kant takes his task to be two-fold: (1) to see how such judgments are possible in mathematics and physics and (2) to discover whether such judgments are possible in metaphysics. The accomplishment of these tasks will go far toward clarifying and securing the foundations of our claims for knowledge.

Kant deals with the former issue first, and he regards his approach to this task as constituting a "Copernican revolution" in the theory of knowledge. That is, instead of taking the position that human experience and knowledge must conform to the objects that we encounter, Kant suggests that we ought to regard objects in experience as conforming to our capacities for perception and knowledge. Instead of thinking of the human mind primarily as an instrument that duplicates an external world, we concentrate on what we bring to experience and knowledge in the way of order and form. Ultimately, Kant believes that this hypothesis is the only one that is capable of making intelligible the possibility of synthetic a priori judgments. All other theories are forced to account for the universality and necessity of these synthetic judgments in terms of inductive generalizations based on empirical experiences. Kant, however, denies that an inductive foundation is sufficient to ground the necessity and universality of the synthetic a priori judgments that we make.

Before we examine Kant's ideas concerning the form and structure that we bring to experience, we must note that although his move is bold, it makes one major concession to Hume. If human knowledge and synthetic a priori knowledge in particular always involve a constructive contribution from the mind, then the world that appears in our experience and knowledge cannot automatically be equated with the world in itself. Thus, Kant distinguishes between a *noumenal* and a *phenomenal* reality. The latter is reality as it appears to us, while the former is reality as it exists apart from the form and order introduced by us.

Two further points need to be noted in this context. First, Kant's "Copernican revolution" and his distinction between noumenal and phenomenal reality mean that adequately grounded human knowledge will be restricted to the realm of phenomena or appearances and the conditions necessary to account for our experience in it. In fact, as we shall see, when we try to extend our understanding beyond these boundaries, we only succeed in producing confusions and difficulties. Second, Kant firmly believes that there is a noumenal reality. Some critics interpreted Kant's theory as a pure idealism (that is, as a view that holds that the realm of mind is synonymous with that of reality). Kant rejects this interpretation. Something real and independent appears to us. Mind does not create a world out of itself, but only orders and shapes what we encounter in the noumenal realm so as to form the world of our experience.

Kant says, "But though all our knowledge begins with experience, it does not follow that it all arises out of experience."[3] What, then, do we bring to experience that helps to form our knowledge and that makes synthetic a priori judgments possible? Essentially, two factors are involved. First, there are two *forms of intuition* (namely space and time) which shape all our perceptual life. No object is imaginable without spatiality being implied. Moreover, all of our perceptions, whether of objects external to us or of our own feelings and thought, follow each other temporally. Space and time are not things that are merely discovered empirically. They are the very forms into which all perceptual experiences are cast. They do not determine the precise content of perceptual experience. This content depends largely on the things that we encounter. But the forms of intuition do constitute the structural framework in terms of which things appear. Space and time, then are *empirically real,* but, Kant says, they are *transcendentally ideal.* That is, things that appear in our empirical experiences are never devoid of both spatial and temporal qualities, but we have no assurance that space and time exist except as conditions which we bring to experience. Therefore, insofar as we think of space and time apart from empirical experiences, we call them transcendentally ideal. Using this term prevents us from making the unwarranted claim that space and time are either independently real or qualities of things in themselves.

Kant says, "Without sensibility no object would be given to us, without understanding no object would be thought. Thoughts without content are empty, intuitions without concepts are blind."[4] This means that although knowledge has its roots in perceptual experiences, it also entails the application of the human understanding or reason to the sensory content. It is in the function of the understanding that Kant finds the second factor that grounds both synthetic a priori judgments and our claims for knowledge in general. Knowledge entails the organization of sense experience so that judgments can be made. Kant argues that this organization requires bringing sensory content into relation with an active intellectual power. By examining the characteristic logical forms that are present in the judgments we make, Kant concludes that the reality of these logical forms requires the existence of twelve basic *categories of the understanding*. Through these categories, sensory content is organized, and judgments are possible.

It is beyond the scope of this book to present a full account of Kant's argument concerning the existence and nature of these categories, but two examples will give us some understanding of the direction of his thought. First, if we look at a categorical judgment (for instance, Socrates was a great philosopher), we see that it involves a subject or substance and a property or attribute that characterizes the subject or substance. Many of the claims we make have this form. Kant argues that our use of this form points to the fact that the understanding is structured so as to organize experience in terms of a substance-attribute relationship. This relationship is found in experience only because the understanding functions in this way. Without the presence of this organizing principle or category, our experience and knowledge would be very different, to say the least. As with his analysis of the forms of intuition, Kant goes on to assert that we cannot be sure that this category, or any other category, applies to things in themselves. The categories function in the realm of phenomena, but claims for knowledge which depend on the categories of the understanding are unwarranted if they refer to things in themselves.

A similar analysis holds for the category of cause and effect, the existence of which is implied by judgments that have the logical form "If ... then ...." The significance of these hypothetical judgments depends on the reality of causal relationships between things. Moreover, many of the basic concepts of our language (for example, to make, to create, to produce, and the like) imply the relationship of cause and effect. Thus, Kant argues that this relationship is also fundamental in our organization of experience and in our knowledge. It is not a relationship that is merely discovered through empirical experiences, but it stands as a foundational organizing principle that makes our experience and knowledge possible. As with the substance-attribute relationship, however, we are not entitled in Kant's view to assume that cause and effect relationships hold among things in themselves. The categories of the understanding organize empirical data, and apart from such data they are merely empty forms.

We are now in a position to see how synthetic a priori judgments are possible. When, for example, we make the synthetic a priori judgment "Every alteration must have a cause," we see that the ability to make this judgment depends on the structure of our capacities for knowledge. All synthetic a priori judgments reflect and exist because of the organizing powers of our rational faculties.

Hume could find no adequate rational grounding for our use of the relationship of cause and effect. Our use of the relationship was ultimately a puzzling habit. Kant accepts the idea that the mind does function habitually in terms of the cause-effect relationship, but he argues that this is due to an intelligible and knowable structure of the human understanding, which is a necessary condition for our experience and knowledge of our world. Kant agrees with Hume that we extend ourselves too far if we presume to think that the relationship of cause and effect holds in the noumenal realm, but within the realm of phenomena causal inferences are firmly and legitimately established. Kant follows Hume only part way. Although Kant's treatment of the categories of the understanding leaves him convinced that metaphysical claims concerning things in themselves are not synthetic a priori, at least physics, rightly understood as a science of phenomena, is preserved.

Kant thinks that human understanding legislates to experience but that our rational capacities are not sufficiently powerful to give us demonstrable conclusions about things in themselves and about specific metaphysical issues such as the immortality of the soul, the origin and extent of the universe, and the existence and nature of God. Although he believes that it is natural for reason to ask questions about these matters, since it craves completeness and finality of knowledge, the plain fact for Kant is that our capacities to think and imagine far exceed our capacities for knowledge. All men may raise metaphysical questions, but insofar as these questions carry us beyond the appearances of things in empirical experience and the conditions necessary to account for these appearances, no genuine knowledge to answer them will be forthcoming. Reason instills us with a desire to know. This impetus is of great value so long as we seek knowledge of phenomena, but once extended beyond that sphere, serious difficulties arise.

Kant's theory of knowledge leads him to regard the traditional arguments for God's existence as inconclusive. He considers three of them, the first being the ontological argument, which he takes to be at the foundation of the other two. Kant understands the ontological argument to assert that a necessary connection holds between God's real existence and the idea of God as the being who is absolutely perfect. From this idea of God, God's existence must follow, for if he does not exist, the referent of our idea will lack some perfection. Hence, we will have to say that, contrary to the facts of the matter, our idea is not of the absolutely perfect being. Or, to put it another way, an absolutely perfect being who fails to exist is a contradiction in terms. Therefore, since we have a genuine idea of an absolutely perfect being and since a contradictory state of affairs is impossible, God must exist.

Kant's objection to the ontological argument rests on his fundamental principle that "[w]hatever . . . and however much, our concept of an object may contain, we must go outside it, if we are to ascribe existence to the object."[5] Existence is not a predicate or an attribute that can be legitimately deduced from the idea of a thing. From the conception of a triangle we can assert that the triangle must have three angles, but our conception does not allow us to assert that any triangle exists in reality. By the same token, if we think of God or an absolutely perfect being, we can assert that this being must be omnipotent, but it does not follow from the conception alone that such a being must exist. If we claim existence to follow from our conception of a thing, this will be only because we have already smuggled existence into our idea of the thing. In this case, however, our claim is hardly justified, since our entire procedure begs the question. Thus, Kant regards all statements of the form "X exists" as synthetic a posteriori. That is, the human capacity for knowledge requires that such statements must be established on empirical grounds and that there is no existential judgment that cannot be denied without contradiction. Kant's theory of knowledge allows no exceptions to this rule, so the claim that we deal with a unique concept in the case of God carries no weight with him.

The cosmological argument is the second that Kant considers. As Kant understands it, this argument moves from two basic premises: (1) if anything exists, a necessary ground of being must exist and (2) I exist, to the conclusion that there is a necessary ground of being (that is, God). This argument involves an improper application of the cause and effect relationship, for it seeks to extend that relation beyond the sphere of phenomena. Moreover, by its appeal to an ultimate necessary ground, the argument entails completion of the series of phenomena. Reason's natural tendency is to seek such a completion, but the assertion of its existence goes beyond the scope of the understanding and is unwarranted.

One further point is important. Even if we allow the existence of the necessary being referred to by the proof, our concept of this being is indeterminate. We cannot know its properties by an appeal to empirical experience, since the necessary being is outside the phenomenal sphere. Thus, the only way we can determine whether the necessary being in question is, in fact, God (that is, the most perfect being) is to reflect on concepts alone. But this reflection ultimately pushes us back to the ontological argument, which is supposed to demonstrate the existence of the most perfect being. We are left with curious results. If the ontological argument were valid, the cosmological argument would be superfluous. But since the ontological argument is inconclusive, the cosmological argument can hardly be regarded as a conclusive proof of the existence of God.

The final argument that Kant analyzes is the physico-theological argument, or the argument from design. He is more sympathetic to this argument, but he finds it full of difficulties nonetheless. It moves from our experiences of order in the universe. This order is itself contingent and, hence, requires some explanation beyond itself. The argument asserts that this explanation requires the existence of an ultimate intelligent cause of the order we experience. Kant interprets this argument to rest on an analogy with human creativity and its products. It has problems on this score alone, but the major objection that Kant brings against the argument is this: "The utmost . . . that the argument can prove is an *architect* of the world who is always very much hampered by the adaptability of the material in which he works, not a *creator* of the world to whose idea everything is subject."[6] To become a full demonstration of the existence of God, the argument from design would have to appeal to the cosmological argument and ultimately to the ontological argument. For reasons we have seen already, this dependence is sufficient to make the argument from design inconclusive as a demonstration of God's existence.

By helping us to think of the world as the work of a rational and purposeful creator, the idea of God serves an important regulative function in human existence, but this in no way compromises Kant's view that the traditional argument for God's existence are inconclusive. Neither the existence nor the nonexistence of God can be finally proved. To claim that either can be done involves extending the categories of the understanding beyond their scope.

In the light of Hume's criticism, Kant tries to reestablish the foundations of human knowledge. His analysis of experience leads him to claim that knowledge is secure provided we understand that it does not extend beyond the realm of phenomena and the conditions necessary to account for our experiences in it. The knowledge claims of rationalistic metaphysics and theology must go, however. Where things in themselves and God are concerned, we lack the possibility of obtaining demonstrable conclusions. Strictly speaking, without this possibility there can be no knowledge.

Kant acknowledges that he has restricted rationalistic metaphysics and theology from the sphere of knowledge, but this is not the final word he speaks on the issues they involve. Human existence is broader than this sphere and Kant's claim is that by imposing his restrictions he has left room for faith. The intention behind this claim is not to encourage people to believe anything they want once they are beyond the boundaries of knowledge. Rather, Kant's desire is to leave room for beliefs that are well-grounded but not finally demonstrable. Belief in the existence of God is one of the factors that Kant has in mind. The human intellect can analyze our existence as moral agents so as to move us toward a grounded faith in God that gives our lives unity and significance. Faith and knowlege are not identical spheres in Kant's view, but they can complement each other. Moreover, they need never be in conflict, for our knowledge does not extend to things in themselves, and it is with this realm that faith is primarily concerned. Now let us see in more detail how God comes to have a more positive part in the Kantian framework. This investigation will also allow us to examine Kant's insights concerning freedom and the problem of evil.

Morality, Freedom, and God

Although our knowledge is restricted to the realm of phenomena and the conditions necessary to account for our experience there, it does not follow that there is no genuine moral knowledge. In addition to our ability to know what *is* the case with respect to phenomena and their conditions, Kant also believes that men can have genuine knowledge concerning what *ought to be* the case in their lives.

To show this, Kant capitalizes on what he takes to be a basic fact: Human existence is structured so that we find ourselves presented with a sense of moral obligation or duty. Men do not automatically agree on the nature of this obligation, but the experience that one ultimately ought or ought not to do some things because they are one's duty is a fundamental fact of our lives as moral agents. Kant sets himself the task of investigating the foundations of this experience, which he regards as the heart of morality. Since the qualities of the experience that interest him most are those of being universal and ultimately unconditioned by outside factors, he thinks that our sense of moral obligation or duty must have an a priori foundation in reason itself. Appeals to empirical experiences cannot provide an intelligible foundation for these qualities, for they only tell us what is the case, not what ought to be the case. On the other hand, without a critique of the powers of reason, both rationalistic attempts to claim that particular duties are self-evident or demonstrable and appeals to religious authority to ground norms of conduct are likely to be misleading. Thus, Kant's problem in dealing with the moral aspects of existence is essentially the same as that with respect to scientific knowledge. We must see what grounds our experiences and makes them valid, but at the same time the only way to do this is to be critical of the powers of reason.

The emphasis that Kant places on *duty* in morality and the relation of duty to reason is clarified by unpacking his famous claim that, "Nothing in the world—indeed nothing even beyond the world—can possibly be conceived which could be called good without qualification except a *good will.*"[7] If a man will reflect, he will see that many things that we call good are not so without qualification. Material wealth or mental brilliance, for example, can be misused and hence evil. But a good will (that is, one that strives persistently to achieve good) can stand as good without qualification.

Now what constitutes the goodness of the human will in Kant's view? Kant's answer is that one's will is good insofar as it acts for the sake of duty. That is, the goodness of a man's will depends not on its success in achieving some proposed end but on its orientation in willing. Because men are finite, they may not always succeed in accomplishing what ought to be done or in willing as they ought, but a human will that is good without qualification is one that always acts for the sake of duty. The emphasis on duty is clarified when Kant points out that there is a difference between acting for the sake of duty and acting merely in accord with duty. In the latter instance, one may be motivated by considerations of self-interest or utility and still do what duty alone would dictate. In such a case, however, the moral goodness of the action and the will is compromised. Moral goodness really depends on the presence of the motive to act solely for duty's sake.

One additional point about Kant's conception of duty is essential. Kant says, "Duty is the necessity of an action executed from respect for law."[8] In this statement, the reference is not to any particular law, but to law in general. If we consider the idea of law in general, the fundamental feature that strikes us is that of universality. Law makes no exceptions with respect to the things that fall under it. Kant believes that men are unique creatures because they are capable of acting self-consciously in terms of law, which means not taking themselves as exceptions. This capacity is at the heart of acting from the motive of duty. To act from the motive of duty, Kant asserts, implies a reverence for the concept of law as such. Thus, the moral goodness of human actions depends on their being done out of reverence for law.

For Kant, the outcome of this analysis is clear: ". . . I should never act in such a way that I could not also will that my maxim should be a universal law."[9] That is, I will not be acting from the motive of duty if the maxim (for example, it is all right for me to lie when I am in trouble) which governs my action in a situation cannot be universalized (made applicable for all men) without negating its own effectiveness. In the example cited, if everyone lied when in trouble, the likelihood of anyone being believed would be severely undercut. However, it is precisely the hope of being believed and, hence, being spared from undesirable consequences that stands behind the original maxim. In short, I cannot act on the original maxim without taking myself as an exception. But to do that is to act immorally (that is, without reverence for law), and hence, from some motive other than that of duty alone.

The principle that I ought never to act in such a way that I could not make my maxim a universal law is only one of the ways that Kant formulates his famous *categorical imperative.* For example, he also puts the imperative in a positive form: "Act only according to that maxim by which you can at the same time will that it should become a universal law."[10] By calling this principle a *categorical* imperative, Kant contrasts it with *hypothetical* imperatives. A hypothetical imperative declares that an action is required only if one has some other end in mind for which the action in question is a necessary condition. A categorical imperative, however, is unconditionally binding. It is an end in itself, and it is binding on us by virtue of our nature as rational beings. Moreover, by calling the principle an *imperative,* Kant underscores the fact that men do not always act in accord with reason and that they do not possess a holy will (that is, one that would never be inclined to do anything except to will the good). The principle comes from reason alone acting in its practical function, but the principle comes in the form of a demand. Men can and do fail to act in terms of the demand, which is the essence of evil for Kant, but this in no way alters our obligation to act in conformity with it.

Kant claims that his analysis ultimately results in knowledge of the fundamental principle of morality (the categorical imperative), which has an a priori status and provides the test for judging the moral quality of our actions. His account places a premium on the idea that reason legislates the moral law to men without outside intervention. For Kant, this implies that men are free both in this legislative function and in their actions of obedience or disobedience to the moral imperative. This implication, however, leaves Kant with a problem. His earlier analyses led him to conclude that in the phenomenal realm everything is structured deterministically in terms of cause and effect relationships. In this view, the autonomy and freedom needed to make morality intelligible would seem to be lacking. While Kant never admits freedom into the phenomenal realm, he does find a way to argue that belief in its ultimate reality is justified. At the same time, he also finds a way to bring immortality and God back into view, not with the claim that men can have final knowledge of their existence and nature, but with the view that belief in their reality can be warranted on good practical grounds.

Kant argues that if our moral life under the categorical imperative is to be intelligible, three postulates are required. They cannot be demonstrated conclusively, but they are assumptions demanded by reason in order to make sense of the facts before us. The first is that freedom is real. Kant's argument in support of this postulate is that to act morally (that is, for the sake of duty) entails thinking in terms of freedom. To say that I ought to do something implies both that I can do it and also that I am free to obey or to disobey. Moreover, to affirm that practical reason is the autonomous source of the moral law is also to affirm the reality of freedom. In short, if freedom is unreal, then morality is unintelligible. But morality is as much a significant part of real experience as physics and mathematics. Therefore, some place for freedom must be found. Kant finds this place in the noumenal realm. Freedom is ruled out of the phenomenal realm of existence, but there is nothing contradictory about the idea of freedom, and thus he postulates that in the realm of things in themselves freedom can be assumed to hold. We are precluded from demonstrating the existence of this freedom, but the postulate of freedom's reality is well warranted nonetheless.

To see how Kant argues for the second and third postulates of practical reason, we must understand his belief that the goal of conformity between the will and the moral law is to achieve the highest good that is possible. For Kant, this highest good consists

of a perfect match between (1) virtue (that is, the perfect conformity of the will and the moral law), which is what makes one
worthy of happiness, and (2) happiness itself. With respect to the
attainment of virtue, Kant points out that "complete fitness of the
will to the moral law is holiness, which is a perfection of which no
rational being in the world of sense is at any time capable." [11]
Nevertheless, the demand of the moral imperative stands. Although
the human will cannot simply be holy, it is still required to move
toward holiness. Kant argues that the demand placed upon us requires us to make endless progress from lower to higher states of
perfection. But this progress is, in turn, possible only if we postulate our endless existence as rational beings. Thus, the reality of
personal immortality emerges as an assumption that is necessary to
make the moral life intelligible. Immortality is neither something
experienced directly in the present phenomenal realm, nor is it
something that can be conclusively demonstrated, but reason
demands its postulation in order to make sense of the facts of
existence.

Finally, a third postulate, the existence of an intelligent, moral,
and creating God, is required if the relations between virtue and
happiness implied by the moral law are to be realized. If the highest good is a perfect match between virtue and happiness, the
implication is that happiness should exist in proper proportion to
virtue. Rational beings in the world, however, are not sufficient in
themselves to guarantee that this relation necessarily exists. In fact,
the only sufficient guarantee of this relationship is a creator of the
universe who orders it in terms of these moral relations and who
knows his creation exhaustively so as to apportion happiness and
punishment justly. Kant's moral theory entails the view that we
ought to strive for the highest good, and that we can make genuine
progress toward it, if not achieve it completely. But without the
postulate of God's existence, the intelligibility of these obligations
is threatened. God's existence and nature have not been conclusively demonstrated, but belief in his reality is warranted because it is
required to make full sense of the undeniable facts of the moral
life.

God comes to play an important role in Kant's philosophy even
though his existence cannot be conclusively demonstrated. Without
God to guarantee a proper proportionality between virtue and
happiness the world would likely be a far less rational and moral
place than Kant thinks it is. Nevertheless, it is surprising that he
finds it so easy to postulate God's existence on these terms without saying more than he does about the fact that we seem to

inhabit a world where virtue and happiness all too often are not in proper proportion. In short, the problem of evil lurks behind Kant's analysis. Therefore, let us conclude our study of his philosophy by thinking about this issue: Does Kant give us a conception of God that will fit adequately with contemporary experience?

Some Problems and Useful Insights in Kant's Thought

Where God is concerned, Kant's philosophy is more critical than constructive. That is, his primary concern is to decide how, if at all, it is possible for us to speak legitimately of God rather than to describe in detail what God might be like. Directing his energies to the former issue, he concludes that it is possible to speak of God as a regulative epistemological ideal and as a postulate for the moral life. We can neither demonstrate God's existence with finality nor have a direct grasp of his nature, but the idea of God is useful to us in the sense of providing a stimulus for rational inquiry. Moreover, the existence of an intelligent and moral creator needs to be postulated to make our moral experience fully intelligible.

Kant's theory makes it possible to say a little about God's nature, but the drift of his philosophy fails to encourage constructive efforts in this area. Kant sees his philosophical task as that of laying secure foundations for our claims for knowledge. The primary order of business is to examine reason, not God. Thus, when Kant finds it necessary to speak about God's nature, as he does in describing the postulates of the moral life, he falls back on traditional theological doctrine. The God that he postulates is essentially the God of Leibniz and his predecessors. Kant accepts the traditional understanding of God as an omnipotent, omniscient being who transcends time. He also emphasizes the moral goodness and justness of God. The God who grounds the moral life is a holy will, assuring the proper proportionality between virtue and happiness in existence.

In some of his writings (for example, *Religion Within the Limits of Reason Alone*), Kant deals with the problem of evil in terms of the relation between man's freedom and his failure to conform to the moral law in every case. Kant does not, however, do much to join the issue between his view of the moral justice of God and the fact that virtue and happiness frequently do not coincide in this life. That this problem is not resolved is a major reason why his theological perspective is inadequate for our present needs.

The understanding of God that Kant does have leads him to take this position: God's existence assures us that in the long run,

which includes our existence as immortal, virtue and happiness fit
together in perfect proportion. If this does not seem to be the case
now, it is only because we lack a full understanding of existence
and the divine plan. Leibniz is very much alive in Kant's theology,
but the contemporary mood is too rebellious to accept this solution to this aspect of the problem of evil. Today a believable theological theory will require more insight and detail than Kant provides concerning God's nature and relation to the world. In particular, our experiences of evil will force philosophical theologians to
deal more adequately with basic questions about the nature of
God's goodness and his purposes in creating, and a fuller account
will need to be given of the lack of proportion between virtue and
happiness in this life.

Contemporary men are unlikely to find Kant's theological views
completely adequate as they stand. In fact, some may say that,
given the facts of existence and his treatment of the problem of
evil, it is more intelligible not to postulate God's existence at all.
But if there is a refusal to accept Kant's views totally, his philosophy does have insights useful for our appraisal of two major
options that are open to us. One of these options is to eliminate
God from our theories and our lives. Kant, however, points out
that a world without God is very likely to be one in which hope,
if not intelligibility, is ultimately missing too. The world may ultimately be a hopeless absurdity, but Kant's suggestion is that the
structure of our lives as rational beings will tend to push us away
from such a view. If we succumb, therefore, to a belief in the
absurdity of existence, there is a sense in which we are fundamentally untrue to ourselves.

This idea leads to a second main alternative, namely, the
attempt to construct a believable theory about God that can meet
the facts of existence and perhaps at the same time help to produce meaning and hope in human lives. Kant's theory presents a
difficulty at this point, however, because it does not really encourage fresh constructive efforts in philosophical theology. His rationalism includes the view that philosophy must be primarily concerned
with seeking final demonstrations and necessary truths. Discourse
about God does not fit into this scheme very well, and therefore
Kant's philosophy lacks speculative boldness in this area. Nevertheless, his work reveals a crucial insight: Kant's own philosophy is a
daring and novel construction. If he was free to develop a fresh
perspective, so are we. We are bound by the recommendations and
arguments of previous thinkers only if we choose to be. If we
work with a critical eye to the past, but without being needlessly

intimidated by it, there may be a bright future for philosophical theology, and consequently a chance for men to find a deeper and more satisfying understanding of life's structure and significance than they may presently possess.

VIII

KIERKEGAARD
AND THE
STAGES OF EXISTENCE

The critique of rationalistic metaphysics and theology introduced by Hume and Kant becomes a full-scale rebellion in the works of Kierkegaard, Nietzsche, and James, the three philosophers we will consider in the final chapters of this book. These philosophers emphasize the fact that man is a being who searches for meaning, but they also stress the idea that human reason is finite and fallible. Thus, they do not place first priority on the final demonstration of metaphysical truths or on the quest for the necessary foundations of synthetic a priori judgments. Rather their insight is this: Existence has a structure, but this structure is radically contingent and it involves open-endedness, ambiguity, and freedom in ways that earlier philosophies have missed. The human task is not primarily to discover and demonstrate that existence has a necessary pattern and significance, but it is rather to create order and meaning in an ambiguous situation through our freedom to choose, think, and act. Let us see how these themes are developed and what problems and insights they contain for contemporary thought about God. We begin with Kierkegaard.

Kierkegaard's Life and Writings

Søren Kierkegaard's short life (1813-1855) began and ended in the Danish city of Copenhagen. He was brought up in a strict

Christian home which was dominated by his father, a wealthy but melancholy man who was tormented by feelings of guilt. As a young man, Kierkegaard was unsure about his goals and the vocation that he ought to pursue. Although he followed his father's wishes and entered the University of Copenhagen in 1830 to study theology, an increasing rebelliousness against his upbringing distracted him from serious pursuit of this initial plan. His lack of motivation for theological studies was accompanied by an interest in literature and philosophy and by enthusiastic participation in the liberal social life of his intellectual friends.

For several years, Kierkegaard lived without a clear sense of direction except that of rejecting his past. This life style, however, produced no lasting satisfaction but only a growing mood of futility and despair. Gripped at last by the recognition of this fact, Kierkegaard worked to remove himself from his predicament. Reconciliation with his father and a new moral orientation was followed in 1838 by what Kierkegaard himself regarded as a religious conversion. In 1840, he took his degree in theology at the University and became engaged to Regina Olsen.

Kierkegaard's life seemed to stabilize, but he broke his engagement after about a year. Not all of the reasons behind this action are clear, but one major factor was Kierkegaard's conviction that he had a religious task to fulfill and that marriage was not compatible with it. His religious experiences and theological studies led him to believe that Christianity needed to be reintroduced into Christendom. That is, although most of his countrymen called themselves Christians, Kierkegaard believed that they lacked an adequate grasp of the significance of Christian faith and its relation to the structure of human existence. Kierkegaard knew that he had talent as a writer, and he felt called to put his talent to use in clarifying the meaning of the Christian faith.

His decision to write involved a novel plan. Between 1843 and 1846, Kierkegaard wrote many books and essays, but they were of two fundamentally different kinds. On the one hand, there was a series of pseudonymous writings (for example, *Either/Or* [1843], *Fear and Trembling* [1843], *Philosophical Fragments* [1844], and the *Concluding Unscientific Postscript* [1846]). In these pseudonymous writings, Kierkegaard portrays three basic life styles: (1) the aesthetic, (2) the ethical, and (3) the religious, which in its highest development is manifested in the life of Christian faith. Kierkegaard's pseudonymous works are subtly dialectical as well as descriptive. They are intended not only to point out what is involved in each perspective on existence and how each stage differs from the others, but also to suggest that the first two tend to result in a lack of authenticity and significance in human life. Kierkegaard has a name for the technique of his pseudonymous writings: *indirect communication.* The overarching goal is to clarify the structure of human existence and to help people choose a genuinely Christian style of life, but the approach is to try to relate to people on their present level of existence. Instead of merely proclaiming the Christian faith directly, Kierkegaard seeks to help people recognize themselves and the structure of existence and, by so doing, he hopes to move them toward the highest stage of existence, namely, the religious.

Despite the disguise, the true identity of the author of the pseudonymous works was no secret in Copenhagen. However, to clarify where he himself stood and to provide some guidance about the direction of the pseudonymous literature without at the same time destroying its indirectness, Kierkegaard published a series of "edifying discourses" (for example, "Every Good and Perfect Gift Is From Above," "Love Shall Cover a Multitude of Sins," "The Expectation of Faith," "The Expectation of an Eternal Happiness") to which he attached his own name. These writings, which have a sermonic quality, develop Christian themes in a more straightforward manner. They are intended to deepen the religious understanding of those who are in the religious stage of existence or are being moved in that direction by the indirect communication of the pseudonymous writings.

Kierkegaard's plan was too subtle for the citizens of Copenhagen. His works were not widely read, and few persons who did read them grasped the connections he hoped they would see. Kierkegaard had planned to end his writing project with the completion of the *Concluding Unscientific Postscript.* However, some attacks against him in a literary journal, coupled with the fact that his works were largely ignored or poorly understood, convinced him that the times were not well suited for indirect communication. Thus, Kierkegaard took up his pen once more. In 1848, he composed *The Point of View for My Work as an Author,* which provided a full explanation of the relations between his earlier works. This account was not published until after Kierkegaard's death, but the fact that he wrote it at all indicates a shift in his outlook. Kierkegaard's output of pseudonymous works did not cease entirely, but the writing of his later years was primarily concerned with direct statements about the content and significance of the Christian faith and with a critique of "Christian culture" and the Danish State Church in particular.

Like many important philosophers and theologians, Kierkegaard exerted much more influence on the generations that followed him than he did on his own. His concern for the individual, who must face the question "What does it mean to exist?" and who must ultimately choose an answer for himself, developed into a novel philosophical and theological view which stands at the foundations of much twentieth century thought. We can best grasp the unique insights of Kierkegaard by concentrating on his analysis of the aesthetic, ethical, and religious stages of existence as they are described in pseudonymous works such as *Either/Or, Fear and Trembling, Philosophical Fragments,* and the *Concluding Unscientific Postscript.*

Three Stages of Existence

The aesthetic stage is the first that Kierkegaard describes. *Either/Or* portrays this life style in several different ways, but its basic qualities are brought out in one selection entitled "The Rotation Method." The aesthete who is supposedly the author of this piece claims: "Boredom is the root of all evil."[1] He recommends that the chief goals of existence should be to escape boredom and to fill one's life with novel and interesting experiences. No attempt to escape from boredom, however, will be successful unless it is carefully planned. A successful aesthetic life demands self-control. Haphazard pleasure-seeking is sure to lead to frustration. Thus, the aesthete suggests a "rotation method" as a plan of action to assure triumph over boredom. This method does not depend on radical changes of location and scene. A method based on changes of the latter kind is likely to be self-defeating, since, for example, one may not always have the means necessary to change his physical location. A more subtle method of rotation is required: "My method does not consist in change of field, but resembles the true rotation method in changing the crop and the mode of cultivation."[2]

Instead of depending on a physical change of location, the aesthete's idea is that one strives for flexibility and novelty in seeing and experiencing things within the particular place he occupies. In addition, the practice of this method of rotation requires that one must be careful not to get too tied down, either to people or experiences. One should avoid carrying friendship or pleasure so far that a dependence on people or things is established. If such dependence occurs, the freedom one needs to seek the novel and interesting may be threatened.

Romance can be wonderful, but marriage is considered especially undesirable because of its limitations on freedom. For the aesthete, then, "The essential thing is never to stick fast . . . ."[3] One must learn to practice the art of forgetting. The successful aesthete will learn to let go of people and things, but not in a way that eliminates the enjoyment that can come from pleasant memories.

Not all of Kierkegaard's aesthetes are so sophisticated, but the writer of "The Rotation Method" captures the essential qualities of the aesthetic stage of existence. An aesthetic life style is characterized by a quest for the interesting and for novelty. The immediate moment takes precedence over long-range commitments. Freedom is understood primarily as the absence of dependence and commitment. If it is not preserved, boredom, the worst of all human conditions, is sure to occur.

Kierkegaard does not deny that there is a place in human existence for novelty and that which is interesting. However, without a radical transformation, the aesthetic stage, which is the most widespread of the three, has serious defects and can ultimately destroy a person. Over the long run, the aesthetic life fragments the self. The aesthete is more dependent than he realizes, for the escape from boredom depends largely on the external circumstances and on the moods and whims that he happens to feel. What if a new situation or opportunity does not present itself, or what if the new situation turns out to be less exciting or interesting than an earlier one? Boredom is likely to triumph after all. In fact, it may manifest itself not merely as boredom with a thing, a place, or another person, but in the more devastating sense of *boredom with oneself.* After a time, the aesthetic approach to life may itself become boring and an aesthete is likely to find that he is sick of himself. Melancholy and then despair set in. The flavor of life goes stale. One finds his life to be without a center, without meaning that lasts and sustains.

There is a resistance factor in human existence. Inner stability and the achievement of lasting meaning are incompatible with the dispersal of the self that is required for pursuit of an aesthetic life style. To avoid or to extricate oneself from the ultimate self-destruction that can emerge from an aesthetic life, a fundamentally different orientation is needed. At the very least, what is required is a turning within to cultivate a sense of resolute commitment to a goal or ideal that transcends the capriciousness of the aesthetic life.

The ethical stage, the second of the three that Kierkegaard delineates, concentrates on the resolute commitment that is needed to escape the dangers of the aesthetic stage. The ethical life style is personified by Judge William, who is another of the characters in *Either/Or*. Judge William gives counsel concerning the ethical life by using the marriage relationship as an example. Contrary to an aesthetic evaluation of marriage, the Judge finds that this relationship provides a lasting sense of meaning and self-identity. Through commitment to another person and to the fulfillment of the duties that marriage entails, continuity and stability emerge. Whereas the aesthete must constantly be on the move to avoid boring repetition, Judge William lives so that the repetition of everyday activities and responsibilities in marriage become a source of deepened commitment and satisfaction. The Judge points this out when he says, "How monotonous, and yet how rich in change! Such is the home life of marriage . . . ."[4] In fact, it is within this context of duty and commitment that the aesthete's goals of enjoyment, pleasure, and a lack of boredom are truly achieved.

Kierkegaard's Judge is no sentimental fool. He sees that there is truth in the aesthete's contention that marriage may have disastrous consequences. There is no guarantee that meaning and joy will deepen through time simply because one has entered into the marriage relationship. Everything depends on what one does with marriage. Perpetual striving to deepen one's commitment to his partner is required. Choosing a commitment and remaining true to the choice are the crucial factors.

The Judge, like Kierkegaard himself, sees life as constituted by radical disjunctions, by either/or situations. Judge William thinks it is clear that one cannot spread himself thin in a quest for aesthetic delights and expect to cultivate and retain internal stability, without which one will find himself moving toward the abyss of meaninglessness. Moreover, Judge William thinks that specific choices mean less to the aesthetic man than they do to the ethical man. An aesthete may plan his choices to some degree, but he does not anguish over them as the ethical man does. It is not absolutely crucial for the aesthete to go one way rather than another, and he lets the external circumstances largely determine his course of action. The difference, the Judge thinks, is that the ethical man is trying to win himself. Each choice, therefore, is a matter of seriousness, for the integrity and unity of the self are on the line. For the aesthete, on the other hand, the task is only to seek and find the interesting, and that can be done in many different ways. Thus, contrasting the ethical and the aesthetic stages on the understanding of choice, Judge William says, "He who would define his life task ethically has ordinarily not so considerable a selection to choose from; on the other hand, the act of choice has far more importance for him."[5]

Kierkegaard takes the ethical stage of existence to be an improvement over the aesthetic. The former can contain the good elements of the latter, but to enter the ethical stage one must come to grips with himself in a way that is not required by the aesthetic life. Self-consciousness and awareness of the structure of freedom and the importance of commitment are heightened in the ethical life. Nevertheless, this stage is neither the highest nor the most authentic form of existence, for it does not deepen inwardness and self-awareness sufficiently.

Although the ethical man may see the weaknesses of the aesthetic form of existence, he thinks that meaning is adequately secured by steadfastness of will and moral determination. There is a note of self-sufficiency in the ethical stage of existence, and it is precisely this quality that constitutes its defect. The ethical man feels obliged to fulfill an ideal, but Kierkegaard suggests that every ethical man has some experience of having failed to do his duty, of having left undone the things that he ought to have done. If it is rightly understood, the ethical stage clearly demands more than any man gives. Guilt is unavoidable, and the ethical stage has no way to remove it from the individual. Thus, if the inescapable boredom of the aesthetic life can drive one to despair, the inescapable guilt of the ethical stage can do the same and the result is likely to be the experience that life seems hollow and that fulfillment is negated.

The experience of guilt can heighten the self-awareness and inwardness of the ethical man. He may come to reflect on the despair that guilt can produce and on the possibility of release from both guilt and despair. Although the ethical life alone provides no release of this kind, Kierkegaard believes that such a possibility is realized in the religious stage of existence. The transition from the ethical to the religious stage, however, is not automatic. The experiences of the aesthetic life may prepare one for a movement to the ethical stage and the ethical stage may prepare one for the religious, but there is no assurance that upward movements will occur. The three stages are sufficiently different from each other that a fundamental reorientation of one's will, a definite choice and commitment are required to accomplish a transition.

What is the nature of the religious stage of existence? Its essence is the affirmation of one's allegiance to and dependence on God, the transcendent but personal source of existence. More specifically, and in its highest form, the religious stage of existence shapes one's life in terms of the faith that God has acted through Jesus Christ to redeem man from sin (that is, from his estrangement from God) and to endow one with peace, meaning, and eternal life. Kierkegaard's writings not only attempt to set forth the content of the Christian message with clarity, but they also strive to show the dynamics of faith and the difficulties and risks that must be faced to live the religious life. With respect to the difficulties and risks of the religious life, Kierkegaard believes that Christianity has too often been interpreted so as to make it easy for people to accept it. Kierkegaard regards such trends as falsifications of Christianity, and he protests against them. The Christian faith is not something that can be conclusively verified, demonstrated, or rationalized so as to assure everyone that it is highly probable, if not absolutely certain. Instead, Christianity offers hope and meaning to individuals through the paradox of the Incarnation, and the appropriation of this hope and meaning ultimately depends on a movement of faith that goes beyond the boundaries of reason.

We can clarify Kierkegaard's understanding of the radical nature of the Christian faith by drawing on three of his pseudonymous works. First, in *Fear and Trembling,* Kierkegaard uses the Old Testament figure of Abraham to illustrate that the orientation of the religious life style is much different from that of the aesthetic or the ethical. When Abraham obeys God's command to prepare to sacrifice his son Isaac, he is moved neither by a desire for enjoyment and novelty nor by abstract, rationalistic concepts of duty or universal moral law. Instead, his response is to a personal and transcendent God, who may direct men in ways that cut against the criteria of aesthetic existence and the norms of conventional morality or rationalistic ethics. To be a man of faith like Abraham is to be qualitatively different from aesthetic or ethical men. The difference may not always be visible to an observer. But it is there nonetheless, and it is constituted primarily by the awareness that one is a unique creature of God and that one's ultimate allegiance is to him and not to pleasure, novelty for its own sake, public opinion, the State, or a rationalistic concept of ethics.

Kierkegaard's analyses of (1) the paradoxical quality of the Christian message and (2) the nature of the faith that is required to appropriate its content are highlighted in the *Philosophical Fragments* and the *Concluding Unscientific Postscript.* Writing under the name of Johannes Climacus, Kierkegaard begins the former work by drawing a contrast between two ways of learning the truth. One way to learn the truth is exemplified by the approach of Socrates. He claims to be a teacher who draws out what is essentially already within the learner. The category of *recollection* is central here. The learner has more understanding than he thinks he does. The teacher's task is to make him aware, to help him recall that which, in a sense, he already knows. In this case, the teacher aids his student, but the teacher's role can ultimately be pushed into the background, for the teacher is only the occasion for making the learner cognizant of the truth that is already within him.

Another way of learning the truth is more radical. Suppose that the learner is not already in possession of the truth in some sense but is rather fundamentally and hopelessly in error. When this is the case, a different kind of teacher and a different relation between the teacher and the learner will be required if the latter is to grasp the truth. In the state of error that Kierkegaard imagines, the teacher will have to provide the learner both with the truth and with the personal condition for moving away from error and comprehending the truth. Kierkegaard suggests that such a teacher would have to be more than human. No human teacher could perform this task of transforming the learner into a possessor of truth.

Kierkegaard's account of the state of radical error is an indirect description of man in sin, and the teacher referred to is Jesus Christ. Christ provides the condition for recognition of sin, which is necessary for moving beyond sin and for grasping the truth. Then Christ brings us the truth, namely, that through faith in his atoning love one is a redeemed child of God participating in God's triumph over sin, death, and evil. In the Christian understanding, the relation between the sinner and his teacher-savior is different from that between Socrates and his pupil. In the former instance, the relation with the teacher is not merely an occasion for learning the truth, but a condition for doing so that is absolutely necessary. "Such a Teacher the learner will never be able to forget."[6] He has essentially recreated the learner, produced a change within him that is "like the change from non-being to being."[7]

One further point about this relationship is important. The teacher-savior, who is really God himself, seeks to recreate the learner, but not in a way that annihilates him. That is, God acts from his love for the learner, and therefore God does not coerce or totally overwhelm him but rather strives for the goal of eliciting a free and loving response. Thus, God comes in the form of a servant instead of in a state of regal splendor. At the same time, however, there are risks involved in appearing as a servant. A servant may be missed, ignored, or even abused. In fact, as Kierkegaard understands it, God's love led to God's suffering, for the teacher was received by many in precisely these ways.

Kierkegaard's contrast of two ways of learning the truth enables him to outline indirectly the main points of Christian doctrine. He goes on, however, to elaborate his idea that the personal appropriation of the Christian message requires a movement of faith that goes beyond the boundaries of reason. Christianity rests on the Incarnation, on the claim that the eternal and transcendent God has come into temporal existence in the man Jesus. Kierkegaard asserts that this claim constitutes an *absolute paradox*. There is no reconciling (1) the idea that God is eternal and transcendent (that is, absolutely other than man) with (2) the idea that God has come into temporal existence in human form. The doctrine of the Incarnation asserts that God is both absolutely other than man and not absolutely other than man. It also entails that the eternal, which simply *is, comes into existence* in time. In Kierkegaard's view, no amount of explanation removes the radical incompatibility between these claims. Yet, the Christian faith keeps them together.

Kierkegaard allows no rational demonstrations of the truth of Christianity. It is not even possible to obtain conclusive arguments for the existence of God. Reason helps us to see the structure of existence from within. It enables us to interpret that which we encounter. But it does not enable us to assume a detached spectatorial position from which absolute certainty and final proofs of existence can be obtained. Reason may seek such completeness, but in fact it comes up short, reaching a point where ultimate resistance is encountered. Left with incompleteness, we find that shadows of doubt are widespread and that our understanding seems never to be totally free of ambiguity and uncertainty.

Kierkegaard's emphasis on the incompatibility between reason and Christian claims plays an important part in his understanding of faith. He does not believe that human reason establishes the final criteria that determine what has been, is, or can be real. Reason's inability to comprehend does not eliminate the possibility that God came into temporal existence in Jesus of Nazareth. What does follow, however, is that if the Christian claims are to be understood as true they must be appropriated through faith. As Kierkegaard understands it, however, this faith is neither a form of knowledge (that is, it is not merely the gathering of information or the demonstration of eternal truths) nor purely the result of a human choice. Faith is a condition of existence that ultimately requires God's action in a man. It is a gift that God bestows. It is not, however, forced on anyone. God does not compromise the freedom of the individual. Without the individual's openness, seeking for God, and passionate interest in the significance of Christ,

Christian faith cannot be born. But God may bring it to life wherever there is such openness, seeking, and passion.

This analysis allows Kierkegaard to say that the men who knew Jesus personally had no essential advantage over those who are many years removed from his historical existence. Only through the creation of faith could Jesus's contemporaries recognize that he was more than a good man. The divinity of Jesus was not apparent to all who saw him. Recognition of it was not a matter of gathering empirical data. Some men who sought God and who were open to Jesus came to see the latter through the eyes of faith, although their openness and seeking were not sufficient in themselves to produce faith. Thus, if the action of God in Jesus's contemporaries was needed to make them men of faith, being a contemporary of Jesus is neither a necessary nor a sufficient condition for faith. Where faith is concerned, the contemporary of Jesus had no essential advantage over the "disciple at second hand." In fact, it may be the latter who has the advantage, for he confronts centuries of testimony that the man Jesus is also God.

If the *Philosophical Fragments* clarifies the fundamental claims of Christianity, the *Concluding Unscientific Postscript* elaborates Kierkegaard's conviction that the life of religious faith is the most authentic form of existence. For Kierkegaard, existence confronts a man as an open-ended process. Existence cannot be fully comprehended by any man or system of philosophy. Kierkegaard puts it this way:

Reality itself is a system—for God; but it cannot be a system for any existing spirit. System and finality correspond to one another, but existence is precisely the opposite of finality.[8]

Where system and finality are lacking, uncertainty, ambiguity, and risk emerge as basic qualities. Since objective certainty is unavailable, Kierkegaard holds that the task of the existing individual is to face this situation honestly. One's task is to become a subject in the fullest possible way. That means that one must come to grips with the fact that he is a free and self-conscious being who seeks meaning and understanding in a world that appears unfinished and always opaque to some degree.

How does this task of becoming a subject fit with the claims of the Christian faith? Kierkegaard's answer is that the Christian claims provide the occasion for one to realize his subjectivity to the highest degree. First, by speaking about sin, guilt, death, and God, the Christian faith raises questions about the ultimate significance of life. The Christian claims provide the occasion for serious reflection on one's existence. Moreover, in the midst of a man's quest for meaning and understanding, these claims offer what Kierkegaard calls "an eternal happiness." That is, they offer hope and meaning by asserting that life is eternal and there is victory over sin, guilt, and death.

There is a catch, however. The eternal happiness is proclaimed in the form of "an objective uncertainty." The Christian claims are grounded in the absolute paradox of the Incarnation. Thus, they can only be appropriated through faith. But, for Kierkegaard, it is precisely when one lives in faith that he is truly an existing individual. A man who lives in faith recognizes that he is a finite creature in a precarious world. At the same time he acknowledges that he is a being who seeks meaning and who hopes for fulfillment and understanding. In faith, both the awareness of the precariousness of existence and the qualities of hope and desire for meaning are extended to a maximum. Faith, the passionate trust in an objective uncertainty (that is, in the reality and significance of the Incarnation), increases subjectivity to the highest degree.

Kierkegaard says that "subjectivity is the truth."[9] This provocative comment is neither a denial of the importance of the publically verifiable propositions of mathematics and science nor a way of recommending an extreme form of epistemological relativism. Kierkegaard's meaning is rather that in an existence that is risk-filled and open-ended the honest and hopeful facing of one's predicament constitutes the highest truth that is available to an existing individual. By becoming a genuine, authentic subject, which is what Christian faith requires and encourages, one experiences truth in the fullest way possible in this life. One knows truth by being true.

Kierkegaard believes that genuine subjectivity is manifested most fully in the stage of existence characterized by Christian faith. This existential condition rests on an objective uncertainty, but from the perspective of one concerned with becoming an authentic subject, the life of Christian faith is the truth. Kierkegaard hopes that his analysis will help to move men toward true Christian commitment, but he emphasizes that no progress toward this level of existence can be made unless a person chooses to strive in this direction. Moreover, while the risk factor in our present existence is such that one can never rest secure at any point, this is especially true where Christian faith is concerned. This faith never comes without a struggle, and it can easily be eroded or lost if one does not work to cultivate and deepen it.

Kierkegaard sees that existence can be patterned in different ways. It is possible to move from one life style to another, but the form of a person's life and the movements that he makes within a single life style or from one style to another depend largely on his choices. Understanding how existence can be patterned may help one to choose well, but choice always remains an essential factor. Kierkegaard tries to clarify the basic options that are open to us and to show that their relationship is ultimately that of *either/or* rather than *both/and*. This is not to say that aesthetic factors are missing from the ethical orientation of existence or that aesthetic and ethical factors are missing from the religious life. But Kierkegaard is convinced that there are basic qualitative differences in the stages, and that if one stage contains elements from another, these elements have also been modified in their new context. Thus, the genuine Christian, whose life comes closest to full subjectivity, may experience qualities of aesthetic delight and moral obligation, but these experiences are shaped against the horizon of his relation to God and not against the backdrop of the aesthete's fear of boredom and pursuit of novelty for its own sake or the ethical man's abstract concept of duty.

Some Problems and Useful Insights in Kierkegaard's Thought

Many of the themes Kierkegaard emphasizes in his analysis of human existence are also stressed in our contemporary outlook. The contemporary mood agrees with Kierkegaard's assessment that we are thrown into existence with a finite capacity for understanding and that the open-endedness of life leaves us free and requires us to choose to make existence determinate. Life is a perpetual striving in a context of risk and uncertainty, and meaning is to be found more in the authenticity of our actions than in the achievement of complete rational comprehension. Kierkegaard sees men as living in a world of freedom where suffering, failure, and evil are mixed up together with hope, promise, and periodic tastes of fulfillment. Thus, Kierkegaard's world is in many ways the world that we find ourselves inhabiting now.

Kierkegaard understood his task to be largely that of reintroducing Christianity into Christendom. For him, this meant mounting an attack against the "reasonableness" of Christianity, the notion of "Christian culture," and all other interpretations that would lead people to think that they were essentially religious and Christian by virtue of being born in nineteenth-century Europe and participating in a State Church. Kierkegaard's move was to show

the radical quality of the Christian faith, to illustrate both its conflict with reason and its grounding in the inwardness of subjectivity, which Kierkegaard claimed was seriously lacking in the mass
society of his day.

Thus, Kierkegaard's emphasis is on the paradoxical quality of the
Christian faith, but we need to ask this question: Is his approach
adequate for our present situation? Kierkegaard's analysis suggests
that men can be brought to Christian commitment by becoming
aware of the human predicament and at the same time being
gripped by the hope and meaning offered in the Christian proclamation. Even if the Christian claims rest on an absolute paradox, a
person may be attracted toward them and find himself transformed
as a result.

Kierkegaard's approach is shaped in reaction against the excesses
of speculative and rationalistic metaphysics, but the fact is that he
is not metaphysical enough for our times. If one's assessment is
that most people think they are Christian but that they have an
easy and mistaken conception of what being a Christian entails,
then it may be useful to emphasize paradox in order to illustrate
the difficulty of being a Christian. But our culture today does not
fit this model. We have the experiences of freedom, ambiguity, and
suffering that Kierkegaard describes, but in general our situation is
not that of thinking that we are Christians in Christendom. In
many ways, we do not know what to think of ourselves. We are in
rebellion, in search of an identity, but we are not sure where we
are going or where we will come out. We need a believable, hopeful, and intelligible metaphysical grounding for our existence. Kierkegaard could afford to play with paradox and irrationality because
he regarded his own time as dominated by a stifling rationalism.
Our situation, however, is much more volatile and charged with
irrationality. Thus, our need is for a metaphysical perspective that
can give meaning and hope and yet be intelligible and rational.
Kierkegaard's absolute paradox may meet the first requirement, but
it fails with respect to the second.

Our indictment of Kierkegaard is not intended to eliminate the
possibility that a Christian perspective can be a genuine option for
us now and in the future. This possibility will depend on how the
Christian faith is interpreted and presented. Here we should note
that without the assumption of a traditional and conservative doctrine of God (that is, one that dwells primarily on God's eternality,
absolute transcendence, omniscience, and unchangeableness), it is
not clear that the Christian claims need to be interpreted as resting
on an absolute paradox that is antithetical to reason. This position

does not necessarily imply, on the other hand, that the Christian claims can be objectively demonstrated, but merely suggests that Kierkegaard's understanding of the Incarnation assumes a particular doctrine of God, which, moreover, may not be the only one that is possible. Some views of God may avoid turning the Incarnation into an absolute paradox. Given the facts of contemporary life, these theories are the ones that Christian thinkers need to seek and develop now.

More than one theory about existence is possible and perhaps even adequate for dealing with the basic features of existence that we need to acknowledge. We need to seek, explore, and evaluate the options. In particular, if the philosophical theologian does this with respect to views of God, he may help us to see who we are, what we are doing, and whether we have grounds for hope. The philosophical theologian will do well to take his cue from Kierkegaard's analysis of the freedom, open-endedness, ambiguity, striving, and suffering that characterize human existence. But then one of his most important tasks is to think constructively about what kind of God might create such a world and how we might find value in it. Kierkegaard's abhorrence of the excesses of metaphysical speculation in the past prevents him from doing all that needs to be done on this score. He prefers to rest with the absolute paradox that emerges when he brings his penetrating analysis of human existence into contact with his understanding of the fundamental teachings of the Christian faith.

Kierkegaard's philosophy of religion is, like most philosophies, shaped by his reaction against previous theories. But no reaction against the past can meet all the needs of the future. We can rest content neither with the rationalism of an earlier time nor with Kierkegaard's absolute paradox. We need to be somewhere in between. If we are bold enough to seek more metaphysical and theological intelligibility than Kierkegaard allows, without at the same time making excessive claims for our rational powers, we may find both that we have done all that is humanly possible and that our accomplishment is sufficient to satisfy the desire for meaning and hope in our lives.

IX

NIETZSCHE AND
THE DEATH OF GOD

Nietzsche's Life and Writings

Recently some writers have suggested not only that God is dead but also that we live in a time when a new morality is dawning. This morality emphasizes the radical freedom and responsibility of men, and it rebels against the stifling conventions of the past. Life is authentic only if the individual chooses his own values and makes his own decisions. Men have "come of age." They no longer need to see themselves as dependent on a God who is omnipotent, omniscient, transcendent and supposedly just and loving. In fact, belief in such a God has a harmful effect on the human spirit. God interferes with a sound understanding of individual freedom and responsibility. Far from making existence meaningful and intelligible, God stands as an obstacle to an honest appraisal of our situation. Existence without God may have its tragic elements, but when God is dead our freedom and responsibility cannot be shirked.

The presence of these themes in current discussion is due largely to the influence of the nineteenth-century philosopher Friedrich Nietzsche. Contemporary statements concerning the death of God and the moral stagnation of Western civilization are often up-dated versions of his statements on these subjects. Who, then, was this man and what are the analyses and insights that he offers?

151

Like Kierkegaard, Nietzsche rebelled against a strict Christian up-bringing. Unlike Kierkegaard, however, he never achieved a positive reconciliation with his past. Nietzsche was born in 1844 in the little Prussian town of Röcken. His father, a Lutheran pastor, died when Nietzsche was only five years old. Thus, the boy was raised essentially by women—his mother, sister, grandmother, and two aunts. Nietzsche would no doubt agree with the adage that "a boy needs a father," for his writings came to reveal contempt for women and feminine culture.

Nietzsche's family saw that he received good schooling. Greek and German literature were his early interests, and he also worked to develop skill as a poet and musician. By 1865, Nietzsche was at the University of Leipzig studying philology. Not only had he given up an earlier idea that he might enter the Lutheran ministry, but also he was essentially alienated from the Christian faith. In 1869, after publishing some brilliant philological papers, Nietzsche accepted an offer to teach classical philology at the University of Basel in Switzerland. His teaching career was interrupted by service in the ambulance corps of the German army during the Franco-Prussian War. Illnesses contracted during his military duty left him in a weakened condition, and in 1879 poor health forced him to end his teaching career.

The next decade of Nietzsche's life was marked by a search for medical help to restore his health and by the development of certain philosophical themes that had already started to emerge in his years at Basel. While at Basel, Nietzsche had analyzed Greek civilization and contrasted it with his contemporary German society. He believed that the height of Greek culture had been realized in instances where two main tendencies had been carefully blended. One of these seemed to Nietzsche to be symbolized by Dionysus, the god of wine and revelry. It incorporated an emphasis on instinct, passion, and the primordial forces of nature. Where this tendency dominated, men were characterized by unrestrained desires for conquest, passionate love, and mystical ecstasy. The other tendency was symbolized by Apollo, the god of art and science. Self-control, measured behavior, and serenity were traits that came to the fore when the Apollonian spirit was in command.

In Nietzsche's analysis, early Greek life had been characterized primarily by the Dionysian traits, but after a period of successful blending, the Apollonian qualities became dominant. The fruitful merger between the two tendencies, which had been the greatness of Greece, had not lasted, and the result—namely, the suppression of Dionysian qualities and dominance of the doctrine "Nothing in excess"—was a prelude to the tame mediocrity that would later become the central motif of Western civilization through the rise and spread of Christianity. Thus, Nietzsche's analysis entailed that in contrast to the highest culture of Greece, nineteenth century Europe and Germany in particular were sick and in need of an infusion of passion and a desire to excel that might outstrip the conventional dictates of prudence and Christian morality which had taken over Western civilization.

As we will see later in more detail, Nietzsche views existence as a struggle. Moreover, his understanding of life is influenced by the Darwinian conception that nature encourages the survival of the strong and fit and the elimination of the weak. The sickness of his own society is evidenced, Nietzsche thinks, by the fact that the powers in control are those which advocate leveling everything down to mediocrity so that the strong are held in check and the weak can survive. Nonetheless, there is a chance for men, at least for a few of them, to be something more than the stifling structures of current society permit. If society's sickness can be exposed and if a sketch of genuine excellence in life can be set forth, there is hope that some unique individuals may transcend the low state into which life has lapsed and help to transform the quality of life.

Nietzsche's most significant attempts to perform these tasks are found in the writings he published in the 1880's. These works include *Thus Spake Zarathustra* (published in parts between 1883 and 1885), *Beyond Good and Evil* (1886), and *On the Genealogy of Morals* (1887). By the end of the decade, Nietzsche's literary output had ceased. In January, 1889, while in Turin, he suffered a serious mental breakdown from which he never recovered. He died on August 25, 1900.

Before we take a closer look at Nietzsche's critiques of society and religion, a brief comment about his philosophical style is in order. Nietzsche never produced a series of pseudonymous writings, but, like Kierkegaard, he was an advocate of indirect communication. The themes of his philosophy are sometimes cast in aphorisms. On numerous occasions the development of his ideas appears nonsystematic and disconnected. Furthermore, there often seems to be conflict, even contradiction, between the assertions that Nietzsche makes. He does not try to explain these tensions away or to make everything crystal clear and easy for his reader. Instead, he hopes that the reader will be provoked to think out the appropriate connections for himself. Nietzsche's style of writing is both a strength and a weakness. It does have the power to force one to think for himself. Nevertheless, the tensions and ambiguities in his thought are sometimes so great that it is difficult to avoid the conclusion that Nietzsche himself is not completely clear about the position he wants to hold. When this occurs, it is likely to be in the context of his attempts to sketch his positive ideals rather than in his reactions against the weaknesses of society.

In any case, Nietzsche's philosophical style is a miniature of the world that he experienced. This world has some patterns and structures that can be delineated, but it is not a rational system which is connected at every turn by the principle of sufficient reason and in which final demonstrations are possible. Nietzsche tries to describe the structural features of existence as he sees them, and he offers interpretations of broad trends in the development of morality and religion, but he does so without the systematically ordered deductions of the rationalist.

The Existence of God and Nietzsche's Critique of Morality

On the Genealogy of Morals begins with this sentence: "We are unknown to ourselves, we men of knowledge—and with good reason."[1] Nietzsche is addressing his contemporaries and perhaps ourselves. His theme is that even though men may regard themselves as well-informed, sophisticated, and knowledgeable, they have failed, perhaps because of a lack of courage, to uncover what stands at the foundations of human existence and morality in particular. This is not to say that there have been no attempts to speak to these issues. Philosophers and theologians have discussed them at length, but Nietzsche's assessment is that these accounts reveal more about the decadence of Western civilization than they do about the way things really are.

When men are deluded about themselves, sickness reigns. Nietzsche, however, starts to work on a cure. He will probe the depths of the human spirit to discover honest answers to the following questions: "Under what conditions did man devise these value judgments good and evil? *and what value do they themselves possess?*"[2] Nietzsche will seek to lay bare facts that men have suppressed and hidden from themselves. He will be a therapist who frees men from self-imposed restrictions that stifle excellence. The freedom that results may overwhelm many, and they will retreat to the security that their illusions provide. "Independence is for the very few; it is a privilege of the strong."[3] But for the few who are bold and courageous, the twilight of the idols of conventional morality and religion can be the dawn of new possibilities and hope. Through the efforts of these exceptional individuals, a transformed environment may emerge which is more conducive to the achievement of quality than that provided by nineteenth-century Europe.

How does Nietzsche answer the questions that he poses for himself, and what does his analysis suggest about the existence of God? One way to approach these issues is (1) to clarify his understanding of the origin and nature of the distinction between *good and bad* and *good and evil* and (2) to unpack his claim that our need is to move *beyond good and evil.*

Nietzsche believes that the distinction between good and bad, which is the heart of what he refers to as "master morality," is fundamentally different in origin and function from that between good and evil, which constitutes the core of "slave morality." Interpreting his historical and etymological data, Nietzsche argues that the concept of "good" as it appears in the former distinction arose primarily out of the noble and aristocratic classes of the ancient world. The noble aristocrat used the term in referring to men who shared a level of power, genuineness, beauty, and nobility similar to his own. On the other hand, the term "bad" was used to contrast persons who lacked the qualities designated by the term "good." To say that someone was "bad" was to say that he was weak, inauthentic, common, and lacking in nobility.

The good-bad distinction was more aesthetic than ethical, and for a time, Nietzsche believes, this distinction and those who made it dominated antiquity. Noble and aristocratic men were in control of life, but a basic change occurred, and Nietzsche believes that his own society is still in its shackles. The change was symbolized by the ascendency of the distinction between good and evil.

How did this change occur, and what was its significance? As the masses gradually became self-aware of the qualitative differences between themselves and the exceptional individuals who dominated life, *ressentiment* emerged. This French word is used by Nietzsche to refer to a deep-seated hatred and jealousy that grew out of the new self-awareness of the masses and was directed toward the masters. The nobility of the masters was recognized, and the masses saw their own lack of quality and perhaps even their inability to achieve genuine distinction. But through the power of numbers and psychological intimidation of the masters, men of mediocre quality, motivated by hatred, were able to effect a reversal of power and value.

Psychological intimidation was achieved through the cultivation of a *bad conscience* and *guilt* in the masters. The seeds of these phenomena were not entirely lacking in the masters themselves. At their level of human existence, the boldness, passion, and desire to excel that Nietzsche admires were often accompanied by violence and destruction. These unique men were warriors for the most part. But if they sought to conquer, a desire to secure what had been won also began to emerge. They started to work to establish order, structure, and stability. Thus, they found that a tension existed between their dominant thirst for conquest and struggle and their emerging interest in preserving the spoils of victory. Self-control and restraint were needed in addition to passion and daring, and in recognizing that the latter traits were dominant in him, the primordial aristocrat of Nietzsche's analysis began to have some doubts about himself. He became more intensely aware of mistakes, and perhaps saw that he lacked full self-control. In short, he came to see that perhaps not all of his traits were entirely desirable. These critical judgments produced feelings of regret and guilt and a bad conscience.

Nietzsche regards this growth of self-awareness as both a positive and a negative factor in human history. It was positive because it impressed the naturally superior man with the need for self-control and restraint in addition to boldness and a desire to excel. Passion and discipline needed to go together for high achievement. Nietzsche sees this realization only beginning to dawn in the primordial era that he describes. Thus, it is clear that he does not extol this age for its own sake, but only as a step on the way toward a higher level of existence as yet unrealized.

The bad conscience was a negative factor in the sense that once the masters achieved a level of self-questioning, they also laid themselves bare to the negating criticisms of the slaves' *ressentiment*. In a way, the slaves were subtle psychologists. They sensed that if one feels some guilt and doubt about himself, he could be made to feel more, with the result that his power and confidence would be undermined. Thus, having little to lose, they interpreted the life style of the masters as one of evil, wickedness, and depravity. Moreover, the slaves worked to inculcate a sense of guilt at every appearance of self-assertion and nonconformity as opposed to traits such as selflessness, sympathy, charity, and pity, which the slaves took to be the essence of goodness. In any case, the cultivation of guilt was a method used by the slaves to effect a revolution, and it was largely successful.

Once more it is clear that the primordial masters are not Nietzsche's ultimate ideal. In a sense, the slaves out-smarted their masters by producing internal fragmentation in them. Nevertheless, rather than being a positive and affirmative phenomenon, as was the case with the differentiation between good and bad, Nietzsche believes that the distinction between good and evil, which stood at the foundations of the power reversal, rested essentially on a negation of value. That is, there was a spontaneity and freshness in the good-bad distinction. It was not the result of a deep hatred or a reaction against that which one did not or could not possess. On the other hand, the good-evil distinction made its "positive" values merely by the revenge-motivated negation of the good qualities of the aristocratic life. The "good" of the good-evil distinction emphasized the essential equality of men, selflessness, meekness, humility, sympathy, pity, and other qualities of weakness, and it castigated the noble qualities of self-assertion, daring creativity, passion, and desire for conquest by calling them evil.

The introduction of the concept of evil was a crucial feature in the reversal of value and power that occurred when the slaves came to dominate. Whereas the older designation of someone as bad was primarily an aesthetic distinction which did not necessarily imply that such a person ought not exist, the use of the term "evil" did suggest that the thing, quality, or person referred to ought not to exist at all. For Nietzsche, the prevalence of this concept of evil means that the reversal of value and power had the goal not only of placing qualities of weakness and mediocrity in dominant positions, but also of annihilating other qualities that are essential for excellence in existence. Nietzsche's view is that the low state of his contemporary society indicates that a great deal of progress has been made toward the fulfillment of these ends.

At this point, it is important to note that Nietzsche sees human existence as a process that is characterized by a *will to power*. In fact, "life simply *is* will to power."[4] Individuals vary greatly with respect to their talents and abilities. There are basic qualitative differences between men that leave them unequal and separated from one another. (Nietzsche is no advocate of the democratic ideal of the equality of men. Such a doctrine only contributes to the leveling process that makes the quality of life mediocre.) Nevertheless, each individual or group will do what it can to assert itself; it will strive to achieve and hold a position of dominance. The existence of this tendency means, in turn, that struggle is a basic fact of life. There will be fierce competition for the top positions of power, and if anyone at the top happens to falter, someone else will be eager to take over.

How does this emphasis on the will to power fit with Nietzsche's idea that the reversal characterized by the ascendency of slave morality over master morality replaced nobility with mediocrity? Several things must be noted to clarify the conception. First, Nietzsche denies that the assertion that life is a will to power entails that life is automatically getting better and better. Thus, if he has hope for the future, it is guarded and cast against the horizon of the desperate sickness he finds in his society. In addition, strength of numbers plays an important part in determining the interests that will be dominant in any particular period. Thus, the *ressentiment* of the masses may have sufficient strength to triumph over the genuinely exceptional individuals, and this in fact is precisely what has happened. Qualitatively ' inferior men, brought together by common objects of hate, have generated energy sufficient to transform the world.

Nietzsche does not discount the impressive display of power manifested in this transformation. He deeply regrets its occurrence, but he does not deny that the world has seen a genuine revelation of power in this change. His regret is based on the conviction that the ascendency of the slave morality has an essentially negative quality. It seeks a level of conformity that is antithetical to the development of creative genius, which by its very nature must stand out from the mass of humanity. Men should glory in the emergence of exceptional individuals of this kind, but neither their appearance nor the joyful celebration of their existence is possible as long as the hate and negation generated by the slave morality are in control.

Human existence, however, need not end on this dismal note. If Nietzsche sometimes regards himself as a voice crying in the wilderness, he also thinks that men have a chance to redeem themselves. But redemption depends upon a movement beyond good and evil. Men must recognize that the moral framework which presently restricts them produces only mediocrity and negation of true value. They must be encouraged to reinstate a perspective like that of the good-bad distinction of antiquity. The spirit of nobility, an affirmation of life, struggle and conquest, and a passionate desire to excel need to be held up to men once more, not with the goal of simply duplicating the past, but rather with the objective of bringing these essential qualities back to life in a contemporary setting. In short, a new revolution of values can and must occur. Nietzsche summarizes these themes in the following way: "Must the ancient fire not some day flare up much more terribly, after much longer preparation? More: must one not desire it with all one's might? even will it? even promote it?"[5]

Proclamation of the death of God is one essential ingredient in the reestimation of values that Nietzsche advocates. Let us see why such a proclamation is needed and what it entails. The need for the proclamation rests on Nietzsche's conviction that slave morality and the existence of God, especially as it is understood in Christianity, are inextricably tied together. In fact, nothing has done more than the Christian religion to entrench the slave morality in the minds of men. For example, the Christian emphasis on love, in Nietzsche's eyes, is simply a way of extolling all of the qualities of weakness that we have been noting. Christianity urges that it is man's responsibility to cultivate these attributes, not because of an abstract concept of duty or because they follow from a philosophical apprehension of the good, but rather because it is God's will that we do so. As this conception is developed, it not only binds men in debilitating guilt, but it also leads them to the escapist tendency of seeking for fulfillment and meaning beyond this world. Failure to fulfill the will of God totally (that is, failure to cultivate fully the qualities of weakness) is a universal trait of men. Thus, men are guilty before God, and they are guilty in a way that leads to judgment and damnation unless they humble themselves, beg forgiveness, and strive earnestly to grow in Christian virtue. On the other hand, a life of Christian faith results in the reward of joyous eternal life, a state that is removed from the struggle, conflict, and suffering of this world.

Nietzsche's critique is clear: Christianity and its conception of a transcendent, omnipotent, omniscient, just, and loving God essentially deny and negate all that is valuable in this world. True value and meaning are not to be found here but in another sphere entirely. Institutionalized in Church and State, Christian theology and morality have made prisoners of Western man. Christianity claims that true freedom exists in serving God, but it denies a genuinely creative freedom by asserting that the world and its value structure are complete and fixed by the will of God. It claims to offer men release from guilt and sin, but it does so at the expense of their being reduced to a hopeless and helpless nothingness. Christianity extols a doctrine of love and charity, but this teaching actually rests on feelings of hatred and revenge that are directed toward genuine qualities of nobility. Nietzsche denies neither that the long dominance of the Christian faith is a real manifestation of the will to power nor that certain individuals have revealed unusual qualities of strength in establishing Christianity's authority, but he is convinced that the result has been to place an inferior breed of men in control of life.

What remedy does Nietzsche propose for the correction of this situation? His answer is that it must be made clear that God is dead. If this understanding can be achieved, the underpinning of Christian morality will be eliminated, thus making it less difficult for men to move beyond good and evil. Now, what does Nietzsche mean when he says that God is dead? Nietzsche's tendency is to think of the question of God's existence more as a psychological problem than as a metaphysical one. That is, operating with his conviction that the link between slave morality and belief in God is not mere coincidence, Nietzsche thinks that the latter factor is simply an additional tool used by the slave mentality to distort the facts of existence and to bring down men of noble character. Thus, the issue is not so much to prove or disprove the existence of God, but rather to show men that belief in God creates sickness, and to convince them that the highest achievement in human life depends on the elimination of this belief. Nietzsche, then, largely assumes the conclusion that God does not exist and moves from this assumption to concentrate on the psychotherapeutic task of freeing men from the idea that they are dependent on God.

Several other points need to be noted to fill in Nietzsche's conception of the death of God. We can uncover them by discussing a section from *The Gay Science* (1882). In the section in question Nietzsche speaks of a madman who runs into a marketplace crying, "I seek God! I seek God!"[6] This action provokes laughter in many of the men in the marketplace, who, Nietzsche tells us, do not believe in God. In jest, they ask the madman whether God is lost, hiding, or traveling on a voyage. But with a penetrating glance, the madman confronts his tormenters with this announcement: "God is dead. God remains dead. And we have killed him."[7]

It is significant that Nietzsche's story involves men who do not believe in God and the claim that men have killed God. Nietzsche's idea is that although nineteenth-century Europe is still dominated by Christian concepts, their strength is not as great as it once was. Men still profess to be Christians and to have faith in God, but, as Kierkegaard saw a few decades earlier, these actions are in many instances habitual responses that lack depth and authenticity. Although nineteenth-century Europe may reek of mediocrity, it is nevertheless a fact that its developments in science and technology have eroded the idea of man's dependence on God and replaced that conception with a new trust in man's power and the possibility of progress through human efforts alone. Moreover, philosophical critiques of theological arguments and the ever present conflict between the presence of evil and suffering and the traditional assertions about God's omnipotence and goodness have taken their toll. Thus, a combination of factors has turned man's attention toward himself and his world and away from God. Practically speaking, this change of outlook constitutes the death of God for Western man.

Nietzsche's view, then, is that nineteenth-century men are living in a world that is largely devoid of God, but the men who hear the madman's announcement stare at him in astonishment nevertheless. These men, who are really Nietzsche's contemporaries, do not give God a place of central importance. They have put God to death, but they lack a real awareness of this fact and its significance. The madman puts it this way:

Lightning and thunder require time, the light of the stars requires time, deeds require time even after they are done, before they can be seen and heard. This deed is still more distant from them than the most distant stars—*and yet they have done it themselves.*[8]

The madman believes that he has come before his time. Men have killed God, but they are not yet ready to confront fully this fact and its significance.

With respect to the significance of the death of God, the madman provides some fundamental insights. He asks, "What did we do when we unchained this earth from its sun?"[9] In a series of rhetorical questions, he suggests that the death of God leaves us disoriented and in darkness.

Is there any up or down left? Are we not straying as through an infinite nothing? Do we not feel the breath of empty space? Has it not become colder? Is not night and more night coming on all the while? Must not lanterns be lit in the morning.[10]

Nietzsche's view, however, is not that this dizzying instability should be the occasion for despair and sorrow. On the contrary, the death of God is an occasion for a cheerful affirmation of life, for it signifies a release, the possibility of a new awareness of freedom and responsibility, and fresh opportunities for creative action.

Nietzsche acknowledges that the situation is full of uncertainties. It is unclear how men will react when they are brought face to face with the fact that God is dead. There is no guarantee that they will take advantage of the new freedom and opportunities for

162 NIETZSCHE

creativity that are available in a world where God is absent. Nevertheless, Nietzsche retains a guarded optimism:

At last the horizon appears free again to us, even granted that it is not bright; at last our ships may venture out again, venture out to face any danger; all the daring of the lover of knowledge is permitted again; the sea, *our* sea, lies open again; perhaps there has never yet been such an "open sea." [11]

Having explored Nietzsche's claims concerning the death of God, let us turn to this question: What is the ideal that Nietzsche holds for men in a world without God? The glimpses Nietzsche gives of this ideal are not always free of ambiguity, but at least the following factors are central to his conception. The individual who meets Nietzsche's ideal of excellence, who distinguishes himself from the anonymity of mass society, will first of all be one who is totally honest about the world he inhabits. Released from a stifling belief in the existence of God, he will see that men live in a world of process and freedom that is devoid of overarching rational purpose. He will live with this insight: "In everything one thing is impossible: rationality." [12] This does not mean, of course, that there is no human purpose or that thought is impossible. What is entailed, however, is the need to face the fact that these phenomena exist against a horizon composed of the ultimate indifference, resistance, and unintelligibility of existence.

In the face of this coldness, Nietzsche's ideal individual neither despairs nor sorrows. Instead, he affirms life. He is even cheerful as he confronts the opacity of being. The reason for his good humor is that he recognizes himself as one who is left free to bring into existence whatever order and meaning he can create. He sees that his life is genuinely his own, and that he is bound to the conventions of society only if he chooses to be. Nietzsche has no illusions that everyone will find joyous affirmation possible when confronted with such a world. He expects that most of us will regard this view of existence as tragic and unbearable, and if the claims of traditional theology can no longer give us solace, we will find other ways to rationalize our existence.

Nietzsche's hope, however, is that at least some exceptional individuals will have the courage to live in this world of freedom and the desire to develop and use their creative talents to the utmost. Through their efforts, others may be encouraged, and the sickness of the human spirit may be transcended. In any case, wherever the full use of creative talent is found, it will require discipline and self-control. Nietzsche sometimes suggests that the exceptional individuals will be ascetics. They will place stiff demands on themselves and strive vigorously toward their objectives, even to the point of suffering and dying for the sake of the goals they wish to achieve.

Now consider this question: What will or should an exceptional individual choose to do? For Nietzsche, the answer can only be that the content of choices depends ultimately on the individual alone. The exceptional individual is totally honest about this fact. He recognizes that even if one thinks that he is forced or required to do one thing rather than another, freedom to choose enters into the appraisal of the situation. Strictly speaking, then, no one does or can decide for another what he will or should do. The difference between the exceptional individual and the common man of mass society is that the former accepts this fact with joy, while the latter finds such freedom dreadful and tries to flee from it.

Nietzsche is greatly concerned about *how* a man chooses. His primary interest is to show that, no matter what is chosen, a choice should be made with the realization that it is one's own responsibility. A person does not ultimately make a choice because of an abstract conception of duty or because it is understood to be God's will. Rather, the authentic, exceptional individual makes his choices with the awareness that his own will is their final grounding. A plurality of options is open to such an individual, but he picks some options over others because, after honest deliberation and self-appraisal, they strike *him* as the best for his situation.

Although Nietzsche is perhaps more concerned about how choices are made than about their specific content, the latter factor is still of great importance in the deliberations of the exceptional individual. Nietzsche's ideal of honesty entails that one needs to choose with his eyes open as far as the consequences of action are concerned. The ideal is not to choose carelessly and then to find oneself regretting what has been done. Rather, the goal is to choose thoughtfully so that feelings of regret never occur. One ought to choose so that if he were confronted by an identical situation an infinite number of times, he could honestly say that he would do nothing differently.

On some occasions, Nietzsche uses the artist as an example to summarize his ideal. The artist seeks to create something that is valuable to him and perhaps to others. If his creativity is to be genuine, the artist must conceive of himself as free, as ultimately unrestricted by the norms and conventions of others except insofar as he chooses to be influenced by them. But if the artist finally sets his own standards, this does not mean that he lacks discipline and critical self-appraisal. On the contrary, to draw out the best that is within him, to blend his talents and his materials into a work of art, discipline and self-analysis of the highest order are required. Moreover, suffering is to be expected, for one always battles in the face of the fact that no guarantees of success are forthcoming. Finally, the opportunity to strive in these circumstances is taken up with joy and with an affirmation of existence, in spite of the fact that life is swallowed up at last in a sea of nothingness.

Nietzsche's philosophy stands in direct conflict with that of Kierkegaard. While the latter argues that the highest quality of human existence comes with faith in God, the former's basic conviction is that belief in God's existence has only a debilitating and corrupting influence on the human spirit. Let us conclude this chapter by thinking critically about Nietzsche's fundamental claim.

Some Problems and Useful Insights in Nietzsche's Thought

In many ways, Nietzsche and Kierkegaard are in agreement about the fundamental structures of human existence. Both men reject the idea that existence confronts us as a complete rational system. Instead, order and patterns of meaning emerge largely as the result of human choices. Nietzsche may stress the ideas of conflict and struggle more than Kierkegaard, but both men have a keen appreciation for the uncertainties and risks that men must face and for the suffering they may experience. Moreover, they share the insight that existence involves a basic element of loneliness. Although men exist communally, situations and decisions must often be confronted in solitude. This solitude is intensified for Nietzsche by the conviction that God is dead. Kierkegaard's world contains God, but loneliness is still a major factor, for God is apprehended only through a risk-filled life full of either/or situations that the individual must resolve for himself. Through their development of the themes of freedom, the open-endedness of existence, uncertainty, suffering, and solitude, Nietzsche and Kierkegaard anticipate our present feelings about existence.

On the other hand, rather than accepting Kierkegaard's analysis that the claims of traditional Christian doctrine provide men with hope and that the mode in which they are apprehended (that is, faith) constitutes the highest development of subjectivity, Nietzsche regards religious faith as a dishonest escape from the brute facts of life. Not only does Christianity preserve qualities of weakness in men and eliminate those of genuine strength, but also Nietzsche simply rejects the view that the structure of the existence we live through is compatible with the Christian doctrine of a God who is omnipotent, omniscient, loving, and just. The problem of evil lurks under the surface of Nietzsche's account. His world is one of conflict and suffering. In this world life is a struggle against the ultimately impenetrable factors of existence. Such a world does not fit with the theology that classical Christianity offers. Thus, it is dishonest to leap out of this world through faith in an absolute paradox; rather, the honest thing is to accept one's situation with the realization that except for the accomplishments that men can provide for themselves there is no hope. The affirmation of existence, the striving to live creatively and joyfully in the face of these facts, constitutes the finest hour of our presence in this world.

Our analysis of Kierkegaard suggested that his option of faith in an absolute paradox is not the only one open for men. Nietzsche offers us another; namely, cheerful affirmation of life against a horizon of ultimate nonrationality and opacity. But if we reject Kierkegaard's absolute paradox, are we pushed inevitably toward acceptance of Nietzsche's assessment of existence? The answer, which incorporates one of his strongest emphases, is that we accept Nietzsche's assessment only if we choose to do so, and our choice will be made in a context that always allows a plurality of possible options, provided we work to make them clear.

To illustrate the latter point we need only point out that Nietzsche's proclamation of the death of God is really a rejection of a single view of God. The target of his attack is the God of classical theology. Although Nietzsche's assessment of existence is sometimes a one-sided polemic rather than a soundly documented, conclusive analysis, it does raise serious questions about the adequacy of the classical conception. But Nietzsche does not show that every view of God is incompatible with the fundamental structure of our existence and incapable of providing meaning and hope that do not smack of escapism. Thus, although some conceptions of God are no longer fully viable for our times, it may be premature to accept Nietzsche's proclamation of the death of God as a final statement of fact.

As far as human consciousness is concerned, the life or death of God depends largely on our skill as philosophical theologians. Both by what it underscores and what it ignores, Nietzsche's analysis of human existence can help the philosophical theologian to see what is needed in constructive thought about God. To bring God to life for us we need a theological view that allows our experiences of freedom and responsibility and the open-endedness of a world in process to stand without compromise. In all likelihood, understanding these concepts as compatible will require a conception that emphasizes God's detachment from existence as well as his involvement in it, that stresses the incompleteness of God's experience as well as the completeness of his grasp of possibilities, and that places a priority on God's interest in freedom. In addition, this view of God will have to deal with our experiences of evil and suffering without merely reducing all of them to disguised forms of good. It will have to recognize that men find themselves responsible for their actions, but at the same time thrown into a world of wildness that is not entirely of their own making. The difficulty of existence and the suffering that it involves will have to be accounted for. Here Nietzsche himself may give us an insight that we need. The value of struggle to pursue and achieve excellence in the face of extreme difficulties may play a major part in God's plan. The trick will be to see whether such suggestions can be developed into a view of God that not only squares with the facts of our existence but also adds hope and meaning to life.

With respect to the latter point, one of the weaknesses of Nietzsche's analysis of existence is this: He tends to think that all religious hopes for victory over evil and death and all philosophical suggestions that the world is ultimately intelligible and rational are forms of escapism and inauthenticity. Nietzsche's conclusion on this matter would be worth more if he would show that the only viable option for interpreting existence is one that sees life against a horizon of meaninglessness and nonrationality. Nietzsche assumes that this is the case, but an assumption is not sufficient to rule out other possibilities.

Moreover, Nietzsche's reductionistic tendencies where hope is concerned may ignore the fact that to be a self-conscious, rational man, who seeks and even creates meaning and value, naturally involves the hope that existence is intelligible and that death, destruction, senseless repetition, and negation of value are not the final words. Nietzsche's analysis moves in the direction of killing such hope, but in so doing he does violence to man's nature. Nietzsche offers us the ideal of the tragic hero, a man who affirms existence in the face of absurdity. There is a certain nobility in this view, but it is likely that even a tragic hero will affirm more in the way of intelligibility and rationality than Nietzsche's view allows, provided he can be shown that such options are really possible. An ultimately tragic note will sound for us when we stop trying to develop and explore ways to make life intelligible, for when we do so we will have rejected a basic component of our uniqueness; namely, our capacity to think, to hope, and to seek understanding. We may never achieve completeness and certainty, but if we fail now to take up the difficult tasks of constructive metaphysics and theology, we may find not only that God is dead for us, but also that the human spirit itself is perishing.

X

JAMES AND HUMAN HOPE

Today students in the United States often know more about European philosophers than they do about those in their own tradition. The need to correct this situation is one important reason for ending our study with an American philospher, and with William James in particular. Although every American philosopher and theologian owes a great debt to his European predecessors, it is also true that in our country's relatively short existence we have produced our share of distinguished men in these areas. For our purposes, James stands out. He not only has an understanding of existence that makes him our contemporary, but he also has some important insights that can help us now as we seek intelligibility and meaning for our lives in this world of freedom and ambiguity. To be more specific, James is deeply impressed by the positive significance of man's religious life, and he makes suggestions that may aid us in revitalizing our awareness of God. Let us explore his philosophy, looking for ideas that can help us.

James's Life and Philosophical Development

On January 11, 1842, William James was born in New York City. His father, an independently wealthy man, wrote on theological subjects. The family, including William's younger brother Henry, Jr., who became a famous novelist, traveled extensively both in America and Europe. Thus, if the continuity of William's early

169

education was sometimes interrupted, he had the advantage of wide and varied experiences, and he was able to learn French and German. For a time James was seriously interested in art, but science prevailed, and in 1864 he entered the Harvard Medical School. He took his M.D. degree in 1869.

Poor health curtailed his activities after graduation, but in 1872 he became an instructor in physiology at Harvard. The stimulation and pluralism of this academic community proved to be the right setting for him, and most of his teaching career was spent there. James's interests were wide-ranging. In addition to his concern about the structure of the body, he was fascinated by questions about the structure of human thought and emotion and the sheer variety of man's experiences. He was also troubled by problems concerning the debate between freedom and determinism, the possibility of necessary truths, and the reality of God. The academic setting allowed all of these interests to flourish.

As the years passed, the psychological and philosophical concerns came to dominate James's energy. By 1875, he was teaching courses in psychology, and before the decade was over he started to offer courses in philosophy at Harvard. James also began to write in these areas. Essays on the freedom-determinism debate, the nature of rationality, and the compatibility between science and religion appeared in the 1880's. In addition, after twelve years of work, James's two-volume *The Principles of Psychology* appeared in 1890. In this book, which is still of great importance, James tried to delineate the foundations, boundaries, and findings of the relatively new science of empirical psychology. James found, however, that the task of securing the foundations of the new science was especially difficult, for philosophical assumptions were involved at every turn. He saw that a sound psychology requires a firm philosophical base, and he worked to clarify issues in both areas. Thus, his book discusses such traditional philosophical problems as the relation between the mind and the body, the reality of freedom, and the nature of judgments.

After the publication of *The Principles of Psychology*, James devoted himself even more to philosophical pursuits. This is not to say, however, that he severed himself from his earlier physiological and psychological interests. In fact, his philosophical work in the years around the turn of the century can be viewed as drawing out some of the central ramifications of his earlier emphasis on one idea: that human consciousness is an active, selective, purposeful force through which man shapes a malleable and ambiguous environment into meaningful patterns. Working from this founda-

tion, the writings of the last fifteen years of James's life concentrate on (1) the importance of choice in the fixing of our beliefs, (2) the appraisal of man's religious life, (3) the nature of meaning and truth, and (4) the development of a pluralistic metaphysics (that is, a view that stresses the autonomy and independence of individual things in the universe as well as their relations and dependence on each other). The most important works in which these ideas are developed include *The Will to Believe* (1897), *The Varieties of Religious Experience* (1902), *Pragmatism* (1907), *A Pluralistic Universe* (1909), and *Essays in Radical Empiricism* (published posthumously in 1912).

When James died on August 26, 1910, he was well known on both sides of the Atlantic, both for his contributions to psychology and for his often controversial philosophical views. Interest in his work declined during the middle decades of this century, but now he is being rediscovered. Contemporary philosophers see that James's psychology and philosophy contain and in some cases anticipate many of the themes found in the existential philosophies of Kierkegaard, Nietzsche, Heidegger, Merleau-Ponty, and Sartre, which have exerted such a great influence on us. Moreover, theological work in this country is beginning to take new cognizance of James's insights concerning the presence of pluralism and process in experience and the importance of providing a basis for hope.

Consciousness and Freedom

To clarify the insights that James provides, we must begin with his theory of consciousness, which is most fully developed in *The Principles of Psychology*. James believes that psychology and philosophy are closely related in the following way: Both need to emphasize the description of human experiences as well as the goal of finding causal explanations. He puts this principle into practice and uncovers five basic characteristics about our consciousness and thought:

1. Thought is personal. Experiences are owned; they belong to someone.
2. Thoughts and experiences are in constant change. No two experiences are ever identical. *"No state once gone can recur and be identical with what it was before."*[1] James does not deny that we experience the same objects over again, but only that our experience of an object has different qualities on different occasions. Moreover, even though change is always taking place, he

believes that nothing is ever totally wiped out in experience. Every experience leaves its mark, although not in a way that eliminates autonomy and freedom in the present moments of conscious awareness.

3. There is continuity as well as change in thought and experience. Conscious awareness is not chopped up into bits as Hume's theory of experience implies. Rather, consciousness flows like a stream. In addition, within this flow one basic structural feature stands out. Some object, person, or concept is focused on, but always against a broader, richer background or horizon. The focal point is "fringed" by a field of perceptions, feelings, time, and space, all of which play their parts in constituting the meaning of the central object and our experience. As our attention moves, different objects come to be at the center, but the figure-ground structure remains essential.

4. Thought is cognitive, and it deals with something other than itself. This is James's way of asserting that we inhabit and know a world that is not entirely of our own making. The factors of resistance in existence that we have noted before are fully acknowledged in James's account.

5. Consciousness is selective; it concentrates on some things and ignores others.

Of these five characteristics, the last is the most important for us. From the most primordial sense experiences to the most sophisticated processes of inference and levels of self-awareness, James believes that human experience is shaped by the active, selective powers of consciousness. Consciousness is not a passive receptor of a fixed world. It is rather an organizing force that creates and brings specific patterns of meaning to light. Consciousness inhabits a rich and ambiguous field from the outset, but the particular world that we inhabit is largely due to the interests that we bring with us, some of which are instinctual, and to the choices that we make.

This emphasis on the selectivity of consciousness suggests that freedom plays an important part in James's understanding of man. He believes that we inhabit a world of freedom. Meaning and value are largely determined by our choices, and the significance and quality of human life are primarily our responsibility. The roots of freedom are in the selective powers of consciousness. For James, the assertion that we are free means that in present moments of conscious awareness we always have some power to control our concentration of attention on persons, feelings, ideas, or objects in

the world. James denies that what we attend to in the present and in the future is exhaustively determined by what has already taken place. In addition, he holds that our acts of attending and thinking are choices that naturally result in actions in the world. Our efforts may not always be sufficient to accomplish what we want, but through an original capacity to concentrate attention, which can grow and develop, human life and the world as a whole became permeated with novel purposes, values, and actions, which are the results of our freedom.

These views conflicted with the deterministic theories held by some of James's contemporaries. These theories dealt with human conduct in terms of cause and effect relationships in which the past exhaustively fixes the present and the future. James defends freedom against this determinism in an interesting way. First, he argues that it is impossible to demonstrate conclusively either that human action involves freedom or that it is totally determined, because once an act has occurred, there is no possibility of exactly duplicating the circumstances to see whether the act could be altered. But if final demonstrations are ruled out, it is still possible to have a well-grounded belief in the reality of freedom.

Our existence is characterized by feelings that the future is genuinely open-ended, that we do shape its course in the present moment, and that our actions are not adequately explained as fixed resultants of causes in the past. Furthermore, these undeniable feelings of freedom are fundamental to our experiences of moral striving and our convictions that life's quality can be improved. James believes, therefore, that the meaning and intelligibility of our lives depend largely on the existence of freedom, and he holds that this fact gives us sufficient practical grounds for believing in freedom and rejecting deterministic theories.

Thus, James believes that we live in a world that is malleable, capable of being structured into a variety of patterns and styles. Moreover, our own lives are indeterminate and incomplete. We come to know who we are and where we are only through our freedom to think and act. As this specification occurs, it can be said that each person comes to live in his own world. But at the same time each life is only one perspective on a broader world of natural and social relationships which provide the ultimate horizons against which our lives develop.

Now consider some important ramifications of James's views on consciousness and freedom. The first involves his understanding of the nature of philosophy. Philosophy cannot attain the ideal of a spectatorial science that will give a complete and exhaustive

account of all being. A philosopher is in and of the world, and he is influenced by his own desires and feelings. These desires and feelings may be suspended only partially. Nevertheless, philosophical theories can shed some light on our situation. To do so, James suggests, the theories should fulfill three requirements: (1) meet the logical demand of consistency, (2) deal adequately with the facts of existence so as to provide some guidance about what we may expect in the future, and (3) make a direct appeal to our capabilities for moral striving and our hopes for meaning.[2]

The third factor distinguishes James's view from many others. Logical consistency is certainly a minimal requirement for a sound philosophical theory, and philosophers also claim to account for facts and give us guidance, although there may be disagreement as to what the facts and proper expectations are. But in the case of human hopes, especially when these move into religious and moral areas, not everyone would agree that providing a place for these hopes should form any part of the criteria for the adequacy of a philosophy. In fact, it would often be claimed that just these factors ought to be rigorously bracketed out.

James believes, however, that when one develops a philosophical theory, the whole man contributes. Man's intellect, will, and desires function together, and no theory is free from the influence of these factors. Total objectivity and complete knowledge escape us, but these limits on knowledge make room for hope and faith. An openness emerges with respect to man's possibilities for understanding himself and his world. Every theory should be taken as a hypothesis to be tested at all levels of experience. If some are reductive and narrow with respect to the claims and hopes of morality and religion, a man may modify such theories or seek to develop others that do justice to those claims and hopes. On the other hand, if it is claimed that this perspective is too subjective and individualistic, James can argue that moral and religious claims and hopes that fail to meet minimal standards of logical consistency and publicly acknowledged facts are simply foolish. Thus, James argues for a logical and empirical grounding for moral and religious beliefs, but he also thinks that it is possible and important to obtain philosophical theories that keep the best of these alive.

James agrees with Kierkegaard and Nietzsche: Existence does not lend itself to complete comprehension by a finite intellect. On the other hand, he disagrees with them on other points. He rejects Nietzsche's view that authentic existence entails affirming life against a backdrop of absurdity and nonrationality. In this sense, he is more sympathetic to Kierkegaard's appreciation of man's need

for hope. At the same time, however, James rejects the Kierke-gaardian suggestion that the hope we need is possible only through appropriation of an absolute paradox which transcends rational comprehension. James recognizes that man's quest for meaning may force him to make a move of faith that goes beyond the realm of conclusive, publicly verified facts, but he denies that these moves must be toward an absolute paradox that is devoid of solid ground-ing in human reason.

The position that James holds is illustrated in his essay "The Will to Believe." In this essay, he argues that there are times when we are confronted by situations in which we must make a decision without having all of the evidence we might like to possess. Life does not always allow us the luxury of waiting until we have con-clusive data confirming the correct course of action. James's goal is to delineate some of the basic characteristics of such situations and to defend the view that the rational course of action in these cir-cumstances is not to flee from reality by claiming the necessity of having to wait for more objective evidence before deciding what to do. Rather, James urges men to face such circumstances squarely, to meet them with full awareness of the risks and uncertainties that they involve, and then to·choose the course of action that is most likely to add significance and fulfillment to their lives.

What are the conditions that constitute situations of this kind? First, James thinks that a man must be confronted by alternatives for belief or action that constitute a *genuine option.* In such an option, the public and objective evidence that is available does not clearly designate one of the alternatives as correct. Three additional qualifications are also required to form a genuine option. First, the alternatives in question must be living possibilities for the individual concerned, not unrelated to his concrete desires and interests. In addition, a decision with respect to the alternatives must be forced and not avoidable. The alternatives appear in the form of a radical disjunction: either/or. One cannot get out of the situation by merely deciding not to choose, or by arguing that the presence of other opportunities removes one from the confrontation with the option in question. To make these moves is, in fact, to affirm one of the alternatives and to deny the other. Finally, the decision to be made must be momentous. The situation is unique, and the decision made in it cannot be reversed.

Unless we are in circumstances that have these characteristics, James believes that we are better off to seek additional data before we make a choice, but some crucial issues about our existence do fit this model. What James calls the "religious hypothesis" provides an example. If religion is taken generically, James finds that it makes the following claims. First, it asserts that "the best things are the more eternal things, the overlapping things, the things in the universe that throw the last stone, so to speak, and say the final word."³ Second, religion affirms "that we are better off even now if we believe her first affirmation to be true."⁴ The latter point implies that the foundational factors with which religion is concerned may be sympathetic to our desires for meaning and fulfillment. This implication is evidenced by the fact that many religions interpret existence as grounded in a power or God that has personal form.

For many men, James believes, these claims constitute an option that is living, forced, and momentous. The claims may lack conclusive public verification, but they say something of vital interest about the significance and nature of my total existence. Moreover, they require a decision from me and in a way that is momentous, for they assert that a failure to decide in their favor results in a loss of meaning in the present. The possibility of merely suspending decision is ruled out. The suspension of decision has essentially the same effect as a genuine decision not to accept the claims. In either case one loses the value that is to be obtained if the claims are true. James's analysis, then, asserts that the general claims of religion confront one as an either/or situation. Either one assumes a risk for the sake of the possibility of adding lasting meaning to one's life, or one decides not to take the risk. In the latter case, one may succeed in avoiding error, but, at the same time, the refusal to commit oneself eliminates a condition that is necessary for apprehending any truth that the claims may have. James's insight is this: We must sometimes move beyond the evidence that we have in order to find out whether a claim is true. We have to put ourselves in the proper position to test the claims fully. The point that James stresses is that when one is confronted by genuine options such as those that occur in religion, one is certainly entitled to commit himself positively toward the claims of religion without being branded irrational, provided, of course, that he acts with a clear awareness of what he is doing.

An Appraisal of Religion and Some Suggestions about God

James's philosophy does more than argue that one is entitled to choose in favor of religious claims under certain circumstances. By arguing that religious commitments, on the whole, have been and are good for human well-being and by offering some provocative suggestions concerning our conception of God, James urges men to cultivate religious faith.

The Varieties of Religious Experience contains James's major attempts to assess the value of religion in man's life. Like Nietzsche, he evaluates religion in terms of its contributions to human excellence, but the conclusions that James draws are very different from those of his German contemporary. The difference is due largely to the fact that James's ideal is more democratic than Nietzsche's. James certainly extols the worth of exceptional individuals, but he places a clearer and stronger emphasis on the importance and integrity of every man's life, the need for men to work together to bring out the best that is in them, and the desirability of establishing an environment where personal freedom and social unity complement each other. At one point in *The Varieties of Religious Experience,* this ideal is described in the following way:

It is meanwhile quite possible to conceive an imaginary society in which there should be no aggressiveness, but only sympathy and fairness,—any small community of true friends now realizes such a society. Abstractly considered, such a society on a large scale would be the millenium, for every good thing might be realized there with no expense of friction.[5]

Taking this society as normative, James's question is this: Is religion a help or a hindrance in the achievement of this ideal? James acknowledges that religion has sometimes been linked with fanaticism, hatred, war, and other forms of destructive action, but he suggests that the crucial test is to judge the value of religion in terms of the significance and worth of the most positive features of life that it has been able to cultivate. This outlook leads him to concentrate on the phenomenon of *saintliness.*

Every major religion has its saintly men, and such lives represent the highest achievment of man's religious life. James describes a saint as one whose faith in a divine power that goes far beyond the finitude of human selfhood produces a willingness to suffer and sacrifice for the well-being of others. Sometimes the saint's plans and actions in this regard may be naively conceived and unfortunate in their results, but James is convinced that the central attributes of the saintly life are essential if we are to make progress toward human excellence.

To illustrate this analysis, when James considers the acts of charity and sympathy that the saint may perform, he notes that they can be pushed to an excess. When this occurs these acts may lead to a permissiveness that lends support to selfish and intolerant forces which repress human freedom and growth. On the other hand, if genuine moral progress is to take place, charity and sympathy are qualities that we must possess and develop. Moreover, James thinks that in their highest manifestations saintly acts of charity and sympathy do not result in a dangerous permissiveness because they are done with reflection on and dedication to achieving an ideal communal order in which freedom, opportunity, unity, and cooperation are maximized for all. This objective implies that, in addition to works of charity and sympathy, the saint's life may reveal instances of resistance, rebellion, and militancy when faced by situations and activities that are clearly contrary to ideal interests. In its highest form, the saintly life is a mixture of tenderness and toughness, and different qualities will dominate depending on what is required in specific circumstances to bring human life closer to the ideal. Essential contributions to the realization of an ideal social order flow from the saintly life. Thus, although religion sometimes reveals a darker side, James asserts that we should acknowledge its importance and value because it produces moral qualities that are desperately needed.

James's validation of religion goes still further, for he also argues that religion, particularly because of its conception of God, can provide the metaphysical grounding that is vitally needed if our full moral sensitivity and energy are to be awakened and sustained. This idea is illustrated by James's conviction that faith in God can be a vital factor in the development and support of the *strenuous mood.* This life style is characterized by an intense desire to find overarching meaning, a sense of an urgent moral imperative to relieve the suffering of men even if personal hardship ensues, and a motivation to strive energetically and courageously toward developing and using one's talents to the utmost. James thinks that the strenuous mood, which is clearly exemplified in the saintly life, is a vital component in human excellence.

How does belief in God's existence help to awaken the strenuous mood in men, and do some conceptions of God do this better than others? To answer this question, consider James's analysis of some alternatives concerning the existence and nature of God. First, there is the possibility of the nonexistence of God. Nietzsche opted for a world devoid of God because he found God an obstacle to authentic existence. James disagrees with this view. A world without God is likely to be a world that lacks overarching purpose and moral intelligibility. Such a perspective on existence is unlikely to awaken and sustain authentic existence (that is, the strenuous mood) because the ultimate backdrop of existence is an indifference and nonrationality that will make questionable the significance of our striving and intentions to suffer and sacrifice for the well-being of others. In a world devoid of God, an aesthetic existence, or what James calls the *don't-care mood* is the probable result. At one point, James puts it this way:

> Many of us ... would openly laugh at the very idea of the strenuous mood being awakened in us by those claims of remote posterity which constitute the last appeal of the religion of humanity. We do not love those men of the future keenly enough; and we love them perhaps the less the more we hear of their evolutionized perfection, their high average longevity and education, their freedom from war and crime, their relative immunity from pain and zymotic disease, and all their other negative superiorities. This is all too finite, we say; we see too well the vacuum beyond. It lacks the note of infinitude and mystery, and may all be dealt with in the don't-care mood. No need of agonizing ourselves or making others agonize for these good creatures just at present.[6]

James asserts that belief in God is helpful in setting free the strenuous mood because (1) such belief can put claims on men with regard to their responsibility for their fellows and their world, and (2) it can provide that human finitude, evil, and death do not have the final words in our lives and that our best values and efforts may find support beyond ourselves. James's analysis of a second position, however, indicates that he is not totally divorced from Nietzsche's announcement of the death of God. Nietzsche's proclamation rests largely on the conviction that the traditional doctrines of God's omnipotence and omniscience make a mockery of human existence by denying man's radical freedom and responsibility. If, for example, God's knowledge of existence is complete from eternity, we are left with a theological determinism which robs our lives of significance and makes the evil we experience essentially unavoidable. James is sympathetic to Nietzsche at this point. A view that regards God as knowing the world as though its development were complete does conflict with our experiences of freedom, and it also stifles the effort and moral responsibility that are vital to meaningful existence. Thus, James has serious doubts about the desirability of retaining any view of God which suggests that the world is complete and finished.

But the vital difference between James and Nietzsche emerges once more, for James does not recommend that we eliminate all concepts of God. Instead, James suggests that we should modify our thinking about God so that our conception of him fits our experiences and needs more adequately. Although James only makes a start in suggesting how this might be done, his ideas are provocative. In one place, he says that we might think of God as "finite, either in power or in knowledge, or in both at once."[7] He does not develop this suggestion very far, but at least three ideas are implied in his analysis, each of which is important in his understanding of a theological view that can spark the strenuous mood and fit with our present knowledge and experience. These ideas are: (1) that the outcome of the world's process is not known beforehand in every detail by God; (2) that although God's existence is everlasting, he is himself in a process of development, rather than being static, complete, and nontemporal; and (3) that a basic value for both God and man may be a creative use of freedom in the face of difficulties.

Pragmatism and Man's Quest for Meaning

James is most famous for his development of pragmatism, which in many ways is a natural extension of his earlier ideas, especially insofar as its ramifications for religion are concerned. His pragmatism involves both an empirical method for clarifying the meaning of concepts and theories and a theory about the nature of truth. With respect to the clarification of meaning, pragmatism rests on this principle: Meaning is revealed by examining a concept or theory with respect to the practical consequences in future experience that the object of the concept or theory leads us to anticipate. A complete account of such consequences would constitute a full analysis of the meaning of the concept or theory in question.

This approach to meaning provides a good starting point for handling disputes. For example, if we are faced by two claims that seem to be in conflict, but no practical differences can be delineated concerning the results that will hold if they are true, then the dispute can be dismissed as purely verbal. However, if substantive differences are present, the pragmatic approach will reveal them. In addition, it will help us to find out the truth or falsity of the claims by urging us to see whether the consequences we are led to expect really do occur.

In *Pragmatism,* James illustrates his approach to meaning in clarifying the major differences between a scientific materialism and a view (James calls it *theism*) that asserts the existence of a purposeful, creating God. If we look from the present back toward the past, James believes that no difference between the two views can be specified. Either perspective is capable of accounting for what has happened thus far. But when materialism and theism are contrasted with respect to what they promise and the expectations they produce in us, crucial differences in the two views begin to appear. The materialism that James has in mind leads us to expect the ultimate negation of human ideals and achievements. Such a world is finally devoid of hope, and life in this world will have a hollowness because the future is basically closed. On the other hand, a theistic perspective allows room for hope. It suggests that finitude, death, and evil are not the final words. Theism posits the hope that "an ideal order . . . shall be permanently preserved."[8] It asserts that because of God's presence "tragedy is only provisional and partial, and shipwreck and dissolution [are] not the absolutely final things."[9]

It is not enough for us, however, simply to specify differences in meaning or to discover that some disputes are merely verbal. We also need to know the truth and falsity of our claims. James believes that an examination of the concept of truth itself can help us in our quest. After a pragmatic analysis of the meaning of the concept of truth, James concludes that truth is a property of those ideas or beliefs which produce expectations concerning our future experiences that do, in fact, get fulfilled. Thus, truth is synonymous with verification; an idea is true to the degree and only to the degree that it is empirically corroborated. This definition, in turn, suggests that truth has a temporal quality. James believes that ideas or beliefs *become* true as the expectations they produce are fulfilled. Truth is not eternally fixed and static in our world of change, freedom, and novelty. Rather, truth itself is in a process of growth and development.

James's denial of the completely static nature of truth leads him to equate it with concepts such as usefulness, expediency, and workability. The true is what works, or what is expedient or useful. Some critics found such moves dangerously ambiguous, for it seemed that James ignored the possibility that some ideas or beliefs could be useful or expedient without being true. In James's account, truth seemed to be reduced to subjective opinion.

James was aware that such objections might arise, and he tried to qualify his ideas to meet them. Some of these qualifications are illustrated in the following passage from *Pragmatism.*

"The true," to put it very briefly, is only the expedient in the way of our thinking, just as "the right" is only the expedient in the way of our behaving. Expedient in almost any fashion; and

expedient in the long run and on the whole of course; for what
meets expediently all the experience in sight won't necessarily meet
all farther experiences equally satisfactorily. Experience, as we
know, has ways of *boiling over*, and making us correct our present
formulas. [10]

The claim that the truth of beliefs or theories involves their
being expedient over "the long run" and "on the whole" is James's
way of stressing the need for testing them repeatedly and for
obtaining consistency and coherence among all the beliefs and
theories that we find to be true. Although James recognizes and
defends the importance of the fact that each person's experience is
uniquely his own, the qualifications that he notes have a basically
communal orientation. He denies the validity of narrowly subjective
interpretations of expediency and usefulness when these terms function in conjunction with the concept of truth. It may be that no
one is forced to evaluate his beliefs critically, but if a person fails
to do so, there is little chance that repeated experience will
support his truth claims.

These views have some important ramifications for questions
concerning the truth of religious beliefs and theological theories.
James's study of religion convinced him that the primary evidence
for the existence of God lies in the lived experience of individuals,
not in rationalistic proofs. The religious experiences of men are real
data that must be confronted openly and clarified. In so doing,
claims and theories about the existence and nature of God and his
relation to the world may emerge. When they do, we must ascer-
tain several things about them: (1) Are these propositions coherent,
consistent, and meaningful from a pragmatic point of view? (2) Do
they do justice to the experiences that spawned them? (3) Are
they compatible with other affirmations that we want to make
about our existence? (4) Do they illuminate our existence with
respect to our desires for hope and meaning? If there is evidence
that such claims or theories are grounded in these ways, James
thinks they can legitimately be said to "work," and there will be
good grounds for believing that they are true. But such an appraisal
cannot always be completely performed by a detached spectator,
for the fourth condition above may often require the risk of
commitment to find out whether illumination, hope, and meaning
grow when one appropriates the claims and theories in question.

Ambiguity and risk are never totally removed in James's world.
His pragmatism reflects this fact, but at the same time it encourages us to seek clarity, illumination, and meaning. It urges us to

move from our experiences to the formulation and testing of hypotheses concerning the overarching structures of existence. In this enterprise, James does not merely tolerate religion and theological investigations. He regards them as vital components in the highest achievements of human understanding.

Some Problems and Useful Insights in James's Thought

James's description of human existence emphasizes the features of process, choice, risk, uncertainty, and our search for meaning. These factors not only play important parts in the views of Nietzsche and Kierkegaard, but they are also fundamental to our experience now. On the other hand, James underscores these themes without interpreting our lives as existing against an ultimate horizon of absurdity or as finding their fulfillment only in an absolute paradox. James is sensitive to life's ambiguities and to the finitude of the human intellect, but he refuses to accept all the conclusions of either Nietzsche or Kierkegaard. Instead he opts for a view of existence that allows for a greater extension of meaning and purpose in existence than Nietzsche permits. At the same time, James suggests that this view involves relations between God and the world that can be comprehended by reason, although the inward commitment of faith may be fundamental for testing such claims in experience.

The philosophy which James develops tells us that an important option remains open. If certainty and completeness of understanding concerning our existence escape us, we can still move between the extremes of appropriating meaning which is grounded in an irreducible paradox or of asserting that our lives are ultimately swallowed up in an absurdity which negates meaning and value. Instead, by describing and reflecting on our existence with the goal of looking for its intelligibility and the grounds for hope that it provides, we may both acknowledge the puzzling qualities of life and find more in the way of meaning and rationality than Nietzsche or Kierkegaard would lead us to expect.

James does not, however, fill in the details of a metaphysical and theological view that will fit this middle path. He offers interesting suggestions on which we can build, but in their present form his insights do not give us all the clarity and content that we need. For example, James was deeply troubled about the relation between our experiences of freedom and evil and the existence and nature of God. James saw that the traditional emphases on the completeness of God's knowledge, goodness, and power set up conflicts with the open-endedness and incompleteness of existence that are implied by our awareness of freedom and responsibility and by our sense of moral striving to transform evil into good. Thus, James suggests that we might do well to conceive of God's nature as involving notes of temporality and incompleteness. By doing so, we can preserve our experience of freedom and responsibility and the significance of moral struggle while at the same time leaving open the possibility that meaning and value are not finally negated by evil and death.

Here is a provocative suggestion, but James does not follow through to develop the theory and to show in detail how it works to help us. James's weakness is that he does not sustain his constructive metaphysical and theological efforts long enough. This limitation is due in part to the fact that, like the other nineteenth-century figures we have studied, James reacted against the rationalistic excesses of some of his contemporaries and predecessors. His criticisms of previous theories move toward the formation of a positive metaphysical and theological view of his own, but James's interest is directed more toward opening wide possibilities for intelligibility, meaning, and hope rather than in working out the details of particular options.

James accomplished the task of opening such possibilities. Moreover, he also helps us to see that honesty with ourselves impels us to search for intelligibility and clarity at every turn. Announcements of the absurdity of existence are premature until this search has been undertaken. If James has cleared away some major obstacles to the achievement of meaning and hope in existence, our task may be to become constructive thinkers who can develop the details of metaphysical and theological hypotheses that are consistent, adequate for coping with the basic facts of our lives, and capable of speaking to our desires for fulfillment and a sound grounding for hope. It is not an easy thing for a man to make sense of his existence. Even if we try our best as metaphysicians and theologians, we may fail. But if we do not take up the challenge to strive persistently and to do our best in this regard, experiences of life's absurdity and the negation of meaning and value may swallow us up simply because we have given up too soon.

EPILOGUE

In the preceding chapters, we have explored the thought of nine major figures in the history of philosophy and theology, concentrating on problems concerning the existence and nature of God and some possible relations between God and our experiences of freedom and evil. If we step back from the details of our account, what are the most important points that stand out as we face the future? My feeling is that there are at least three. First, the history of philosophy and theology shows that more than one view about God and human existence can be developed. Although each of the men we have encountered learned something positive from his predecessors, he also found that he was forced to disagree with them at some points. When he tried to develop his own views, he found that a new pattern of thought could emerge. Like these men, we can and should learn something from our past, but we are not bound to accept previous theories as final and exhaustive. Some theories try to place restrictions on us, but there is no necessity for us to be needlessly intimidated by them. We are free to use our talents and energies to develop metaphysical and theological views that make sense to us and that fit our needs.

The second point is closely related to the first. Although some men have argued that we live in a time when God is dead, we should see that this announcement is essentially a reaction against a specific view of God and that this conception of God is not the only one possible. It may be well to modify this conception, but it is neither necessary nor desirable for us to eliminate concepts of God completely. It is not necessary for us to do so because some concepts of God may be free of the inadequacies of the classical concepts that are presently under attack. It is not desirable for us to eliminate all concepts of God because if we do so we will likely eliminate options for life patterns that can bring meaning and hope into existence. Philosophy and theology should be critical disciplines, but this statement is not incompatible with saying that they also have an important task to perform in keeping options open where positive hypotheses about God are concerned.

185

Third, if one chooses to work on the important task of developing options about the relation between God and the world that will speak both to our experiences of freedom and evil and to our desires for hope and meaning, the following questions will be among the most crucial that will have to be faced: (1) Why might God choose to relate to a world that has such vast potential for destruction, negation, and suffering? (2) What does it mean to say that God is good? (3) What place does freedom occupy as a value for both God and men? (4) What does human freedom imply about the nature of God? (5) What may be the scope of God's power and knowledge? These questions are by no means new, but they seem to press on us with great urgency now, and our answers to them will need to move beyond many of the responses that have dominated the past. Life may become more intelligible and meaningful if we are bold enough to think about God critically and creatively. The only way to find out is to try. In this case, the risk ought to be worth taking, for the reward for success is great.

NOTES

Chapter II

1. Augustine frequently used the dialogue style in his writings. Here is one more link between him and the Platonic tradition.
2. As we shall see, the dialogue centers around the idea that evil is due to a misuse of human freedom. Augustine would even attempt to account for the evil that results from natural events such as earthquakes and floods by attributing it to human wrong-doing. The argument in some instances would be that the event is God's just punishment for man's sin. In this case, however, the evil that men see is only apparent, for just punishment is actually a good.
3. Augustine, *On Free Choice of the Will*, trans. Anna S. Benjamin and L. H. Hackstaff (Indianapolis: Bobbs-Merrill Company, 1964), p. 3.
4. *On Free Choice of the Will*, p. 34.
5. *On Free Choice of the Will*, p. 88.
6. *On Free Choice of the Will*, p. 95.

Chapter III

1. Anselm, *Proslogium* in *Proslogium; Monologium; An Appendix in Behalf of the Fool by Gaunilon; and Cur Deus Homo*, trans. Sidney Norton Deane (LaSalle, Illinois: Open Court Publishing Company, 1958), p. 7. All *Proslogium* references are to this edition.
2. Anselm, *Monologium* in *Proslogium; Monologium; An Appendix in Behalf of the Fool by Gaunilon; and Cur Deus Homo*, trans. Sidney Norton Deane (LaSalle, Illinois: Open Court Publishing Company, 1958), p. 69.
3. *Proslogium*, p. 1.
4. *Proslogium*, p. 7.
5. *Proslogium*, p. 8.
6. *Proslogium*, p. 8.
7. *Proslogium*, p. 22.
8. *Proslogium*, p. 24.
9. Anselm, *On Freedom of Choice* in *Truth, Freedom, and Evil: Three Philosophical Dialogues*, ed. and trans. Jasper Hopkins and Herbert Richardson (New York: Harper Torchbooks, 1967), p. 142.

10. *On Freedom of Choice,* p. 122.
11. *On Freedom of Choice,* p. 126.
12. Anselm, *The Fall of Satan* in *Truth, Freedom and Evil: Three Philosophical Dialogues,* ed. and trans. Jasper Hopkins and Herbert Richardson (New York: Harper Torchbooks, 1967), p. 183.
13. *The Fall of Satan,* p. 184.
14. *The Fall of Satan,* p. 185.

Chapter IV

1. Thomas Aquinas, *Summa Contra Gentiles,* trans. Anton C. Pegis (Garden City, New York: Image Books, 1955), Bk. I, Ch. 11, para. 6. Hereafter abbreviated *SCG.*
2. Thomas Aquinas, *Summa Theologica,* ed. Pegis, in *Basic Writings of Saint Thomas Aquinas,* 2 vols. (New York: Random House, 1945), Pt. I, Ques. 2, Art. 3. Hereafter abbreviated *ST.*
3. *ST,* Pt. I, Ques. 2, Art. 3.
4. *ST,* Pt. I, Ques. 2, Art. 3.
5. *ST,* Pt. I, Ques. 2, Art. 3.
6. *SCG,* Bk. I, Ch. 13, para. 35.
7. *ST,* Pt. I, Ques. 25, Art. 6, Reply Obj. 3.

Chapter V

1. Gottfried Wilhelm Leibniz, *Theodicy,* ed. Diogenes Allen and trans. E. M. Huggard (Indianapolis: Bobbs-Merrill Company, 1966), p. 10.
2. *Theodicy,* p. 10.
3. *Theodicy,* p. 18.
4. *Theodicy,* p. 36.
5. *Theodicy,* p. 35.
6. *Theodicy,* p. 35.
7. *Theodicy,* p. 41.
8. *Theodicy,* p. 37.
9. *Theodicy,* p. 40.
10. *Theodicy,* p. 41.
11. *Theodicy,* p. 49.

Chapter VI

1. David Hume, *An Inquiry Concerning Human Understanding,* ed. Charles W. Hendel (Indianapolis: Bobbs-Merrill Company, 1955), p. 40. Hereafter abbreviated *Inquiry.*
2. *Inquiry,* p. 171.
3. *Inquiry,* p. 27.
4. *Inquiry,* p. 41.
5. David Hume, *Dialogues Concerning Natural Religion,* ed. Norman Kemp Smith (Indianapolis: Bobbs-Merrill Company, 1947), p. 137.
6. *Dialogues,* p. 142.
7. *Dialogues,* p. 143.

8. *Dialogues*, p. 147.
9. *Dialogues*, p. 190.
10. *Dialogues*, p. 227.
11. *Inquiry*, p. 171.

Chapter VII

1. Immanuel Kant, *Critique of Pure Reason*, trans. Norman Kemp Smith (London: Macmillan & Co., Ltd., 1963), B16 [B refers to Kant's second edition], p. 53.
2. *Critique of Pure Reason*, B17, p. 54.
3. *Critique of Pure Reason*, B1, p. 41.
4. *Critique of Pure Reason*, A51 [A refers to Kant's first edition] or B75, p. 93.
5. *Critique of Pure Reason*, A601 or B629, p. 506.
6. *Critique of Pure Reason*, A627 or B655, p. 522.
7. Immanuel Kant, *Foundations of the Metaphysics of Morals*, trans. Lewis White Beck (Indianapolis: Bobbs-Merrill Company, 1959), p. 9.
8. *Foundations*, p. 16.
9. *Foundations*, p. 18.
10. *Foundations*, p. 39.
11. Immanuel Kant, *Critique of Practical Reason*, trans. Lewis White Beck (Indianapolis: Bobbs-Merrill Company, 1956), p. 126.

Chapter VIII

1. Søren Kierkegaard, *Either/Or* (Garden City: Doubleday & Co., Inc., 1959), I, 281. Volume I was translated by David F. Swenson and Lillian Marvin Swenson with revisions of the translation by Howard A. Johnson. Volume II was translated by Walter Lowrie with revisions of the translation by Howard A. Johnson. All references are to the Anchor Books edition.
2. *Either/Or*, I, 288.
3. *Either/Or*, I, 292.
4. *Either/Or*, II, 147.
5. *Either/Or*, II, 171.
6. Søren Kierkegaard, *Philosophical Fragments*, trans. by David F. Swenson with revisions of the translation by Howard V. Hong (Princeton: Princeton University Press, 1967), p. 21.
7. *Philosophical Fragments*, p. 23.
8. Søren Kierkegaard, *Concluding Unscientific Postscript*, trans. David F. Swenson and Walter Lowrie (Princeton: Princeton University Press, 1960), p. 107.
9. *Concluding Unscientific Postscript*, p. 183.

Chapter IX

1. Friedrich Nietzsche, *On the Genealogy of Morals*, trans. Walter Kaufmann and R. J. Hollingdale (New York: Vintage Books, 1967), p. 15. Hereafter abbreviated *Genealogy*.

2. *Genealogy*, p. 17.

3. Friedrich Nietzsche, *Beyond Good and Evil*, trans. Walter Kaufmann (New York: Vintage Books, 1966), p. 41.

4. *Beyond Good and Evil*, p. 203.

5. *Genealogy*, p. 54.

6. *The Gay Science* in *The Portable Nietzsche*, ed. and trans. Walter Kaufmann (New York: The Viking Press, 1960), p. 95.

7. *The Gay Science*, p. 95.

8. *The Gay Science*, p. 96.

9. *The Gay Science*, p. 95.

10. *The Gay Science*, p. 95.

11. From a section added to *The Gay Science* in 1887 and reprinted in *The Portable Nietzsche*, p. 448.

12. Friedrich Nietzsche, *Thus Spoke Zarathustra*, trans. Walter Kaufmann (New York: The Viking Press, 1966), p. 166.

Chapter X

1. William James, *The Principles of Psychology* (New York: Dover Publications, 1950), I, 230.

2. See William James, "The Sentiment of Rationality," *The Will to Believe and Other Essays in Popular Philosophy* (New York: Dover Publications, 1956), p. 110.

3. William James, "The Will to Believe," *The Will to Believe and Other Essays in Popular Philosophy*, p. 25.

4. "The Will to Believe," p. 26.

5. William James, *The Varieties of Religious Experience*, 2nd ed. (New York: Longmans, Green, and Company, 1902), p. 375.

6. William James, "The Moral Philosopher and the Moral Life," *The Will to Believe and Other Essays in Popular Philosophy*, p. 212.

7. William James, *A Pluralistic Universe* (New York: Longmans, Green, and Company, 1909), p. 311.

8. William James, *Pragmatism* (Cleveland: Meridian Books, 1963), p. 77.

9. *Pragmatism*, p. 77.

10. *Pragmatism*, p. 145.

DISCUSSION
QUESTIONS

Chapter I

1. Does it make sense to say that we live in a time of religious crisis? If so, in what respects? If not, why?
2. Is man by nature a religious being? Why or why not?
3. In what ways, if any, do religion and philosophy depend on each other?
4. In what ways, if any, do our experiences of freedom and evil raise the problem of God's reality and require us to reflect on God's nature?

Chapter II

1. Does Augustine present an adequate account of the relations between faith and reason? Why or why not?
2. How do you appraise Augustine's suggestion that man's experience of finitude and contingency pushes us toward affirmation of God's existence?
3. What do you take to be the major strengths and/or weaknesses in Augustine's account of the relations between God, freedom, and evil?

Chapter III

1. What is the significance of Anselm's ontological argument for God's existence?
2. In what ways does Anselm move beyond Augustine in discussing freedom and evil?
3. To what extent does Anselm offer an adequate interpretation of the relations between God, freedom, and evil?

Chapter IV

1. How does the perspective of Thomas differ from those of Augustine and Anselm? What is the significance of these differences?
2. What is the significance of the arguments for God's existence which Thomas provides?

191

3. Is Thomas on solid ground in affirming that God's omniscience is compatible with human freedom?

4. To what extent does Thomas offer an adequate account of the relations between God and evil?

Chapter V

1. What is the significance of the "principle of sufficient reason" in Leibniz's philosphy? Is the principle valid?

2. How do you assess Leibniz's view that God has created the best of all possible worlds?

3. How do you assess Leibniz's conception of human freedom?

4. Is Leibniz successful in maintaining that there is a distinction between God's *permitting* evil and God's *willing* evil? If so, explain how. If not, what changes in our understanding of God's nature would be required to allow such a distinction?

Chapter VI

1. What effects does Hume's skepticism have on human claims to know the existence and nature of God?

2. What are the most valuable insights that are provided by Hume's discussion of the problem of evil?

3. Does Hume's philosophy ultimately undermine or support religious perspectives on existence?

Chapter VII

1. What significance, if any, does Kant's response to Hume's skepticism have for our understanding of religion?

2. How do you assess Kant's efforts to show that our experience of moral obligation pushes us toward awareness of God?

3. To what extent does Kant offer an adequate account of the presence of evil in human life and the relation of evil to God?

Chapter VIII

1. Does Kierkegaard's philosophy differ radically from those of the other men we have studied? If not, why? If so, how?

2. How do you assess Kierkegaard's descriptions of the various "stages" of human existence?

3. Does Kierkegaard offer an adequate account of the relations between faith and reason?

4. What is the significance of Kierkegaard's concept of the "absolute paradox"? Does this concept help to make our experiences of freedom and evil intelligible?

Chapter IX

1. How do you assess Nietzsche's analysis of the role of religion in human history?

2. What does Nietzsche mean when he says that God is dead, and how do man's experiences of freedom and evil relate to that claim?

3. If God is dead or unreal, to what extent is it possible for human life to be meaningful?

Chapter X

1. Can James's philosophy be legitimately regarded as steering a successful middle path between the perspectives of Kierkegaard and Nietzsche?

2. How does James's account of human freedom figure into his understanding and evaluation of religion?

3. Why does James suggest that God may be *finite?* How do you respond to this suggestion?

4. To what extent might God be conceived as *temporal* and *changing,* and how would our views on this issue influence our understanding of freedom and evil?

Epilogue

1. Is it important for us to keep thinking about problems concerning the existence and nature of God?

2. How would you begin to answer questions such as the following?

    a. Why might God choose to relate to a world such as ours, which has such vast potential for destruction, negation, and suffering?

    b. What does it mean to say that God is good?

    c. What place does freedom occupy as a value for both God and man?

    d. What does human freedom imply about the nature of God?

    e. What may be the scope of God's power and knowledge?

3. What do you see the future of religion to be?

ADDITIONAL READINGS

Anselm. *Proslogium; Monologium; An Appendix in Behalf of the Fool by Gaunilon;* and *Cur Deus Homo.* Trans. Sidney Norton Deane. LaSalle, Illinois: Open Court Publishing Company, 1958.
———. *Truth, Freedom, and Evil: Three Philosophical Dialogues.* Ed. and trans. Jasper Hopkins and Herbert Richardson. New York: Harper Torchbooks, 1967.
Aquinas, Thomas. *Summa Contra Gentiles,* Book I. Trans. Anton C. Pegis. Garden City: Image Books, 1955.
———. *Summa Theologica.* In *Basic Writings of Saint Thomas Aquinas,* 2 vols. Ed. Anton C. Pegis. New York: Random House, 1945.
Augustine. *On Free Choice of the Will.* Trans. Anna S. Benjamin and L. H. Hackstaff. Indianapolis: Bobbs-Merrill Company, 1964.
Hume, David. *An Inquiry Concerning Human Understanding.* Indianapolis: Bobbs-Merrill Company, 1955.
———. *Dialogues Concerning Natural Religion.* Indianapolis: Bobbs-Merrill Company, 1947.
James, William. *A Pluralistic Universe.* New York: Longmans, Green, and Company, 1909.
———. *Pragmatism.* Cleveland: The World Publishing Company, 1963.
———. *The Principles of Psychology,* 2 vols. New York: Dover Publications, 1950.
———. *The Varieties of Religious Experience,* 2nd ed. New York: Longmans, Green, and Company, 1902.
———. *The Will to Believe and Other Essays in Popular Philosophy.* New York: Dover Publications, 1956.
Kant, Immanuel. *Critique of Practical Reason.* Trans. Lewis White Beck. Indianapolis: Bobbs-Merrill Company, 1956.
———. *Critique of Pure Reason.* Trans. Norman Kemp Smith. London: Macmillan and Company, Ltd., 1963.
———. *Foundations of the Metaphysics of Morals.* Trans. Lewis White Beck. Indianapolis: Bobbs-Merrill Company, 1959.
Kaufmann, Walter, ed. and trans. *The Portable Nietzsche.* New York: The Viking Press, 1960.

195

Kierkegaard, Søren. *Concluding Unscientific Postscript.* Trans. David F. Swenson and Walter Lowrie. Princeton: Princeton University Press, 1960.

———. *Either/Or,* 2 vols. Vol. I trans. David F. Swenson and Lillian Marvin Swenson with revisions by Howard A. Johnson; Vol. II trans. Walter Lowrie with revisions by Howard A. Johnson. Garden City: Doubleday and Company, Inc., 1959.

———. *Fear and Trembling.* Trans. Walter Lowrie. Garden City: Doubleday and Company, Inc., 1954.

———. *Philosophical Fragments.* Trans. David F. Swenson with revisions by Howard V. Hong. Princeton: Princeton University Press, 1967.

Leibniz, Gottfried Wilhelm. *Monadology.* Trans. George R. Montgomery, in *Basic Writings.* LaSalle, Illinois: Open Court Publishing Company, 1962.

———. *Theodicy.* Trans. E. M. Huggard and ed. Diogenes Allen. Indianapolis: Bobbs-Merrill Company, 1966.

Nietzsche, Friedrich. *Beyond Good and Evil.* Trans. Walter Kaufmann. New York: Vintage Books, 1966.

———. *On the Genealogy of Morals.* Trans. Walter Kaufmann and R. J. Hollingdale. New York: Vintage Books, 1967.

———. *Thus Spoke Zarathustra.* Trans. Walter Kaufmann. New York: The Viking Press, 1966.

INDEX

197

Imperative:
 categorical, 128-130
 hypothetical, 128
 moral, 178
Impressions, 102-103
Incarnation, 142, 144, 146, 149
Incompleteness, 33-34, 53, 55, 93, 95,
 144, 166, 173, 184
Indeterminateness, 10, 33-34, 173
Indirect communication, 137, 153
Infinite regress, 64-66, 75, 84
Infinitesimal calculus, 78
Inquiry, 7, 100, 131
Intelligibility, 14, 22, 42, 132, 166,
 169, 173, 178, 184
Intuition, forms of, 121
Inwardness, 141, 148
Italy, 37

James, Henry, Jr., 169
James, William, 15, 135, 169-184,
 190, 193
Jena, 77
Jesus, 38, 142-145
Judeo-Christian tradition, 7, 10
Judge William, 140
Judgments, 6, 39, 119, 122, 170
 analytic, 119-120
 of value, 39-40, 42, 67, 94
 synthetic a posteriori, 119-120, 124
 synthetic a priori, 119-121, 123,
 135
Justice, 30, 50, 85, 131, 151, 159,
 165, 187

Kant, Immanuel, 5, 15, 117-133, 135,
 189, 192
Kepler, Johann, 77-78
Kierkegaard Søren, 15, 135-149, 152,
 160, 164-165, 171, 174-175,
 183, 189, 192-193
Knowledge, 2, 11, 18, 21, 27, 30-35,
 40, 52-54, 62-64, 67-69, 72-74,
 82, 84-86, 88, 90-91, 95, 99-
 100, 102, 108, 111, 113, 118-
 122, 124-126, 129, 144, 174,
 180, 183, 186, 192-193
Königsberg, 117

Law, 127-131, 142
Leibniz, Gottfried Wilhelm, 15, 76,
 77-96, 117-118, 131, 188, 192

Leipzig, 77, 152
Life:
 affirmation of, 161-162, 164-165
 human, 7, 25, 27, 112, 137, 141,
 151, 169, 171, 186
 styles of, 4, 10, 136-147, 178, 185
 See also Existence, Man
London, 98
Louis XIV, 78
Love, 96, 143, 151, 159, 165
Luther, Martin, 78

Mainz, Elector of, 78
Man, 1, 6-7, 13, 21-23, 25-26, 38, 50,
 61-62, 78, 135, 170, 172
 See also Existence, Life
Manichees, 18-19
Materialism, 180-181
Mathematics, 3, 28, 77-78, 80, 108,
 120, 129, 146
Matter, 61-62
Matters of fact, 99-100, 102, 104, 107,
 114, 118
Meaning, 14, 35, 56, 60, 76, 135, 140,
 142, 146-147, 149, 159, 166,
 171-176, 178, 180, 182-186,
 193
Memory, 103
Merleau-Ponty, Maurice, 171
Metaphysics, 114-115, 118-120, 126,
 135, 148, 167, 171, 184-186
Milan, 18
Mohammedans, 58-59
Monadology (Leibniz), 79-80, 82
monads, 79-80
Monica, 17
Monologium (Anselm), 37, 41-42, 187
Monte Cassino, 57
Mood, 178-180
Moral claims, 28
Moral imperative, 178
Morality, 126-131, 142, 151, 153-155,
 158-160, 174
Motion, 64-65, 120

Naples, 57
Natural theology, 60, 102, 108,
 113-115
Nature, 58, 67, 70-71, 108-109, 111
 uniformity of, 106
Necessity, 24, 30-32, 34, 40, 42, 44-48,
 50, 52-54, 65-68, 73-74, 78-79,

INDEX

81, 83-84, 86, 88-92,
104-106, 112, 118-120, 123-
125, 135, 143
Negation, 5, 100, 141, 158, 166, 184,
186, 193
Neoplatonism, 19-20, 22-23, 29, 35,
55, 58
See also Platonism
Newton, Isaac, 78
New York City, 169
Nietzsche, Friedrich, 15, 135, 151-167,
171, 174, 177-179, 183, 189-
190, 192-193
Nonbeing, 23-24, 29, 32, 43, 48, 52,
54, 66, 112, 143
Noncontradiction, principle of, 82-84,
86, 107, 118
Nontemporality, 74-76, 180
See also Eternality
Normandy, 37
Nothingness, 159, 164
Noumenal reality, 120-123, 126, 129

Olsen, Regina, 136
Omnipotence, 22, 26, 48, 51, 55, 71,
78, 151, 159, 161, 165, 179
Omniscience, 40, 53, 55, 148, 151,
159, 165, 179, 192
On Free Choice of the Will (Augustine),
21-32, 187
On Freedom of Choice (Anselm), 37,
48, 51, 187-188
On the Genealogy of Morals
(Nietzsche), 153-154, 189-190
One, 19
Ontological argument, 40-48, 54, 61-
64, 83, 123-124, 191
Open-endedness, 11, 34, 53, 76, 92,
135, 147, 149, 164-165, 184
Optimism, 11
Options, James's theory of, 175-176
Order, 85, 87, 95, 135

Paradox, 142, 144, 146, 148-149, 165,
175, 183, 192
Paris, 58, 78
Patricius, 17
Pelagians, 25
Perfection, 20, 23, 28-32, 34, 39-40,
42-45, 49, 51, 55, 67-71, 83,
85, 87-88, 90, 92-93, 109,
111-113, 124, 130

Peter the Great, 78
Phenomenal reality, 120-126, 129
Philo, 108-114
Philosophical construction, 2-3, 5, 14,
114-115, 132, 167
Philosophical Fragments (Kierkegaard),
136, 138, 142, 145, 189
Philosophical theology, 9-10, 94,
114-115, 132-133, 149, 165
Philosophy, 1, 3-4, 6-10, 12-15, 22,
39, 60-61, 78, 118-119, 132,
145, 171, 173-174, 185, 191
Physico-theological argument, 125
Plato, 19, 47
Platonism, 58
See also Neoplatonism
Plotinus, 19
Pluralism, 171
Pluralistic Universe, A (James), 171,
190
*Point of View for My Work as an
Author, The* (Kierkegaard), 137
Possibility, 33-34, 36, 43, 51, 74-75,
83, 86, 93, 95, 107, 111, 114-
115, 166, 184
Possible Worlds, 31-32, 34, 71-72, 79,
81-82, 84-94, 192
Postulates, 129-131
Potentiality, 64-65, 68-69
Power, 5-6, 11, 13, 19, 24, 30, 32, 36,
41, 84-86, 110, 112, 180, 183,
186, 193
Pragmatism, 15, 180-182
Pragmatism (James), 171, 180-181, 190
Predication, 70-71, 109-111
Principle of noncontradiction, 82-84,
86, 107, 118
Principles of Psychology, The (James),
170-171, 190
Probability, 36, 82, 95, 111, 115
*Prolegomena to Any Future Meta-
physics* (Kant), 117
Proofs, 56, 118, 123, 129, 135, 144,
154
of God's existence, 7, 27-29, 41-47,
55, 61-68, 75, 80, 82-83, 97,
107, 109-112, 114, 123-125,
131, 144, 149, 160, 182
See also Argument
Proslogium (Anselm), 37-38, 41-42,
45-47, 55, 187
Psychology, 170-172